**Retail
Design
Lab**

EVERYTHING YOU NEED TO KNOW
ABOUT DESIGNING A STORE

THE BIG BOOK OF RETAIL DESIGN

KATELIJN QUARTIER

Lannoo
Campus

The Big Book of Retail Design carries the GPRC label, which stands for 'Guaranteed Peer Reviewed Content'. Publications bearing this label have gone through a peer review procedure that complies with the international scientific standards.

Second edition: October 2023

D/2023/45/ – ISBN 9789401490436 – NUR 800

Cover and interior design: Adept vormgeving
Photograph cover: Liesbeth Driessen

LannooCampus Publishers is a subsidiary of Lannoo Publishers, the book and multimedia division of Lannoo Publishers nv.

LannooCampus Publishers
Vaartkom 41 box 01.02
3000 Leuven
Belgium
www.lannoocampus.com

P.O. Box 23202
1100 DS Amsterdam
The Netherlands

Table of content

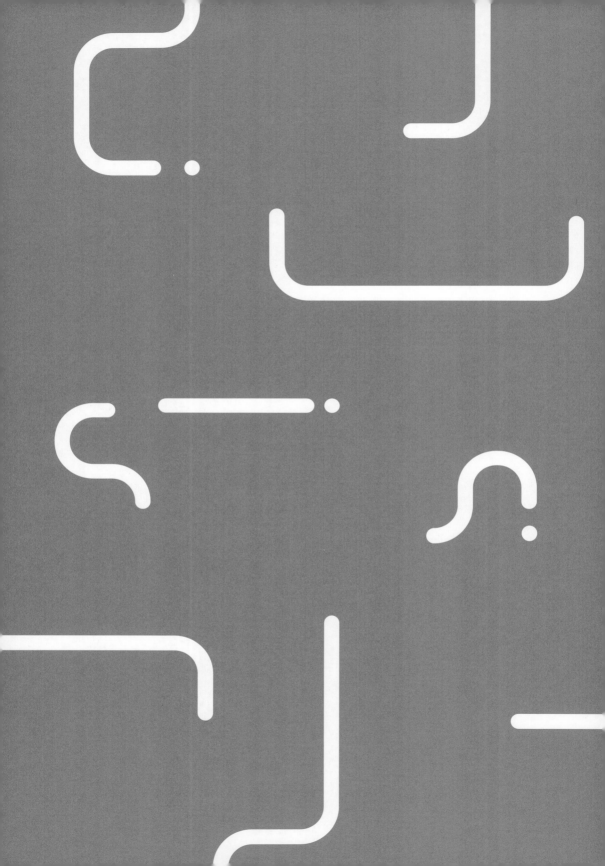

Foreword

Let me first say thank you…

Although it may seem that I wrote this book all by myself, which is true in the literal sense, there is knowledge woven into it from years of work by an entire team. I would like to thank this team for their efforts, their knowledge and fine collaboration. When I refer in this book to PhD students, researchers from the Retail Design Lab, or colleagues from our Faculty of Architecture and Arts and the University of Hasselt, I am referring to this fine team: Carmen Adams, Charlotte Beckers,Stephanie Claes, Lieve Doucé, Nonkululeko Grootboom, Kim Janssens, Elke Knapen, Ann Petermans, Elisa Servais, Koenraad Van Cleempoel &.Jan Vanrie. Of course without the support of Hasselt University and our Faculty there would not even be a team. So thank you.

Although not part of the Retail Design Lab team, I do see them as my 'team' at home: many thanks to my husband Ward and son Bent for their patience and unconditional encouragement and love, and Flo our labrador who provided the necessary companionship.

…and introduce the book…

This book grew out of a feeling to share knowledge, to make as many people as possible wiser in how to design proper stores. Ever since I started teaching at Hasselt University while doing my PhD, this passion to share knowledge has been growing. I was overflowing with passion for retail design, so it felt natural to share it. The first few years I only taught students, but after a few years there was also interest from practitioners. Professionals, including retailers, marketers and designers, needed scientific knowledge that could help them move forward. Not much later, the demand to apply the knowledge, very concretely on a particular case, came. And so our consultancy services were born. We have served both brands big and small and retailers alike. Many consultancy projects, doctorates and research later, we decided to give what we were doing so far a face and a name. Thus the Retail Design Lab was born. Today, we are a small expertise cell at the Faculty of Architecture and Arts of Hasselt University. It is not a company or an independent entity, it is simply a part, or say a brand, of the faculty that bundles all the activities around retail design.

The Retail Design Lab's ambition is to make all available scientific research published in academic journals (not available to the general public) available to practitioners in a relevant and applied way. Surely our main contribution is our platform retaildesignlab.be where a lot of knowledge and tools that came out of these academic insights are available to anyone interested. In addition, we still give training to professionals and provide our services to retailers and designers. I myself also still teach our interior architecture students who can choose a specialization in retail design in their master, as well as master students from the Faculty of Business Economics who are taking the elective course 'customer experience management'. Of course, through research, such as PhDs and projects large and small, we also continue to develop knowledge that then flows back to practice and our students. But we also gather insights the other way around. By working with students, we gain insights and knowledge. These in turn also flow back to the Lab and to practice. We also learn when we work with retailers and designers. So it is a continuous process, a constantly flux of knowledge from different angles coming together. Indeed, also flowing back to the different angles. You can see it as an small eco-system. And now this is shared with you.

...its academic grounding...

So I am constantly in between practice and research. This is also something you will notice in this book. The book is a collection of academic knowledge, insights from practice and a dose of experience. It is therefore not a typical academic book which is full of scientifically based statements and accompanying references. I chose to write a very accessible book that is in line with the ambition of the Retail Design Lab: to bring scientific insights in a way that is relevant to practice. Still, this book is full of scientific insights, only they are interwoven into a story and brought together and told from my specific expertise. And although the book is not purely academically based, I still hope that academics will use the book as well. I have tried with this book to nonetheless make a theoretical contribution to the relatively young (academic) discipline of retail design. The book is written in such a way it can also serve teaching purposes. It is not the typical handbook, but I do use rather typical models and graphs to illustrate the theory. Also sketches are used to illustrate certain statements. They are sketches that serve as examples in which I try to extract the essence of what I want to say. That is why certain parts are colored and others are not. The chosen examples mainly contribute to depicting knowledge rather than inspiring. Therefore, the chosen examples are not the trendiest examples or the latest new stores, but examples that serve the purpose of the story.

...from a Western European perspective...

A large part of the insights in how to design a store are generalizable but we should not forget cultural differences.

One last thing in framing this book I would like to share, is the context in which this book was written. My story stems from a very Western perspective, say Western European perspective. And although people are human beings and thus a very large part of the insights in how to design a store are generalizable to other parts of the world, we should not forget cultural differences. To give an example, in Europe, there is a rich architectural history. We have been building the way we build for relatively a long time. Cities have been steadily developing and building on the past. This makes Europeans generally very respectful of historical architecture and the build environment. This is very different from some Asian countries such as China. Chinese cities are developed very differently. The population explosion has caused large cities to build at a record pace. The former architecture no longer sufficed and was largely replaced by new, high-rise architecture. For the same reason, retail has also grown differently. The leap from markets and street trading has been converted into built-up shops at a record pace, leaving almost no legacy in large cities. Add to this the fact that, despite the diligent building efforts, large cities are still struggling with a shortage of space. For sure, all this contributed to embrace the online story, in which 'space' is unlimited. There are a multitude of other reasons too, but that would lead me too far. My point is that much quicker than Europeans, Chinese people have adopted the online world in their shopping habits, leading to differences in stores and store design. If I make a quick comparison with another large part of the world, America, also here cultural differences play a role. Geographically, America is very different and people rely more on shopping malls, Walmart and Amazon because of the great distances. In Western Europe, everything is 'around the corner'. Something Americans who do not live in cities cannot say. So, America literally has more space than our crowded Europe so stores are bigger, sometimes even huge in my perspective, again leading to differences in store design. Nevertheless, as mentioned, we are humans and a large part of how we behave in a space, how we orient ourselves, and how we make certain choices is comparable worldwide.

...aiming to shed some light in the complex world of retail design

Anyway, with this book I want to give insight into the discipline of retail design, which is much more than designing a nice interior. It is a transdisciplinary design discipline that originated from interior architecture and has grown into so much more. Why so much more? And why is designing a nice interior not enough? Well, the world has become digital at a rapid pace, and while the importance of a physical store is clear, we have to realize that, among other things, that digitalization has made it much more complex to fill out and shape this physical store in a meaningful way. Another reason why it is not getting any easier, and this sounds a bit contradictory, is that we have never known so much about man and earth and even the universe as we do now. But knowing more also means that it becomes more difficult to navigate all this knowledge. Indeed, many more choices can or must be made. The evolution in product design illustrates this quite well. Where once a device contained an on and off button, it has now changed to ten buttons, or a digital screen with legion options. This can be compared to people and their place in this world. With less knowledge, and thus only a few buttons to play, it seems easier than with more knowledge and thus more possibilities. But, if played well, the result is more made to measure. With more knowledge, the desired result can be obtained better and the chance of success can therefore be increased. And this is exactly what I want to do with this book, I want to teach you the buttons you need to get a better result. A customized result, based on scientific insights.

Enjoy reading...

PART

1

From retailing to retail design

The field of retail today only started to make sense to me when I had a look into the past. Indeed, I strongly believe that to understand to-day's ways of working, how people trade and buy, how stores need to function and how they look, one has to understand the past. This goes beyond understanding design. It is about understanding people and the society at large, understanding the evolution of brands, understanding how people have culti-vated space, and how all these things are intertwined.

Did you know that retail design as a profession, or as a discipline, only really has been known since the 1970s? Earlier, it was more an intuitive expression of commercial acumen. It was only then that people realized that designing shops required expertise, and that as a designer you could make a business out of it, with one of my mentors and one of the great retail design gurus, Rodney Fitch, leading the way. I have seen it happening; the more global the world became, the more complex, so the design agencies had to follow to be able to serve global brands. They too became bigger and more complex, meaning that they became more than a group of interior architects. Disciplines such as branding, trend watching, graphic design, product design, packaging design, and later, web design, made their appearance in design agencies with one main purpose in mind: creating one consistent and coherent brand story. If you look at design agencies today, they are a melting pot of different disciplines where even psychologists find a place. This is no coincidence. Almost every societal change can be linked to a change in store typology. Psychologists or sociologists offer great insights into linking such changes to design. So you can link the Industrial Revolution to the heyday of department stores, and the technological revolution to both the rise of multi-channel and the expansion of design expertise at design agencies. Obviously, retailing does not function in isolation; it is deeply embedded in the cultural, economic, geographic and social aspects of its environment. As Rodney Fitch once said, 'Retail is the mirror of society. If you locked the door of a store each decade and left the store as it was, you could learn from that store, many decades later, what the society at that time was about.' In other words, it reflects the transformations and changes, or offers a platform to communicate those transformations. Indeed, where retail is today also reflects the current society, but more about that later.

Also today, understanding how people interact with technology, how the pandemic has changed our ways of shopping and all the knowledge and insights on the human brain that have rapidly developed during the last decade are valuable to designers dealing with these humans. Such insights on the human brain also help to understand the past better. Although it seemed more 'simple' in the past because they knew less, departments stores seemed to understand customers all too well. In the following chapter, I would like to take you back to their heyday and how I, as a designer, look at them. I will also discuss some other evolutions, such as the evolution of self-service, the role of the Industrial Revolution on store development and what retail branding has to do with it. This chapter was created by bringing together various books and papers that described the past often from an art historical or architectural background or from a sociological perspective. My favorite book definitely is Dion Kooijman's 'Machine en Theater' (written in Dutch) which describes the architectural and urban development of retail buildings. I looked at the literature with a retail design lens and extracted the most impactful, in terms of design, evolutions and put them together into a logical narrative.

To make connections between past and present and to illustrate what we have learned from the past, I color coded specific characteristics of the different stores typologies and evolutions discussed.

In a second chapter I will explain how designers and retailers had a say in the development of the discipline of retail design. All to better understand the discipline itself and how it came into being.

Almost every societal change can be linked to a change in store typology. Retailing does not function in isolation; it is deeply embedded in the cultural, economic, geographic and social aspects of its environment.

Chapter 1

WHAT WAS

A. Retail throwback

Halls of temptation

When I read about how department stores used to be, when I look at the drawings in history books, I get a very romantic image of these stores. Reading books like Émile Zola's 'Au Bonheur des Dames' and watching series like 'Mr Selfridge' of course reinforce that image. But even with my nose in more fact-based books, this image does not disappear. I am impressed with the well-oiled machines they must have been, immersing their customers in luxury every visit. Department stores offered a constant supply of products, some of which were even unknown to the general public, each of which had its own place and specific presentation, accompanied by a charming sales clerk. And then there is the other part of the department store, the theatrical. You can still feel this when you visit department stores built in that era, such as the (renovated) Samaritaine, or Galeries Lafayette, both in Paris, or London's Harrods. Although the design of the interiors is entirely different than it was in the 19th century, when entering such majestic buildings you suddenly become part of the experience, the staff engages with you and as you browse the shop, you feel that luxury is at your fingertips. Although the products are the heroes, it is the architecture that gives the grandeur. It is almost unimaginable that in the 19th century so much attention and resources went into the building. Something that today is almost unthinkable (or just unaffordable).

Department stores were definitely the most popular form of retailing in the 19th century. This success did not come overnight though; it was the result of cleverly adopted changes that occurred in society and in industry. Indeed, they were primarily commercial entrepreneurs. Look at Le Bon Marché in Paris – Europe – and Macy's in America, for example. Although both very different in design and management, the store building was considered as an economic unit, with a particular cost per square foot, causing space considerations like layout and departmentalisation to be considered purely from the standpoint of sales per square foot, an idea that lasted until the end of the 20th century. They both pioneered and developed free entry, visual merchandising, direct purchasing, sales, and customer service practices commonly used today. Indeed, they set trends and created the modern retail model that stores follow worldwide today. The route to success for the department store was based on the skills of the retailers that managed them.

From Europe...

In Europe most department store owners were trained as employees in bazaars and *magasins de nouveautés*, the precursors of the department store. They cleverly adapted these skills into their own business that grew into large-scale concerns that stood for variety, novelty and service. The pioneers of the department stores re-invested their profits into their business, similar to the business model of the *magasins de nouveautés*. They tried everything to make shopping as attractive as possible for the higher class customers. This resulted in increasingly beautiful and luxurious department stores with large windows and a central hall with glazed roof offering novelties and a luxurious variety of products. Indeed, department stores were designed from the outside in, attracting people to the store. In Europe, specialists who were involved in the design of the arcades and the *magasins de nouveautés* were hired to design the architecture of the department stores.

 A truly impressive store that I put forward as an archetype for department stores at that time is the first purpose-built department store Le Bon Marché in Paris, as is visible in the image. Before this, department stores grew organically in a city using adjacent buildings. Aristide Boucicaut and his wife Marguerite became partners of Le Bon Marché in 1852, although it was founded in 1838. Being a truly revolutionary couple, they built an entirely new department store designed by Louis-Auguste Boileau and Alexandre Laplanche in 1872, with a floor space of fifty thousand square meters (after an extension designed by Gustave Eiffel) and with 1,788 employees. Yes, 1,788, can you imagine? Just as it does today, increasing competition between stores stimulated innovation in the past. Again Le Bon Marché serves as an example: hybrid functions, such as restaurants, reading rooms with newspapers and journals, and parlours with art exhibitions were added in the department store. Also, concerts and fashion shows were organized to change the department stores into places where social behavior was mixed with commercial activities. Offering such a range of products and services automatically included the stimulation of the senses. Live music, fresh products (from flowers to fruit and vegetables), and a restaurant, together with beautiful product presentations already included the stimulation of our nose, ears, mouth and eyes. Only the liberty to touch all products was not yet included; this is a contribution made by the supermarket, as I will explain later. Indeed, the inside of stately department stores was never to be underestimated. Though contemporary but coherent, creating uniformity in a dozen diverse departments, they were set up to seduce. Department stores were not called 'halls of temptation' for nothing. The richly decorated interiors were similar to the arcades: several galleries around a light court – a glass roof, most often round or oval rather than rectangular – revealed an intriguing glimpse through all the departments. These galleries were transitional spaces that directed the customers' movements and attention to strategically placed displays in a sequential way. The light courts were larger than the ones in the arcades due to technical improvements in glass and iron. The cupolas and the many glass windows flooded the interiors with natural light. Majestic staircases connected each floor. The shop furniture consisted of square counters with sales clerks and a cash register in the middle. These were fantastic places where the products were the heroes.

Department stores as fantastic places where the products were the heroes.

Elaborate presentation techniques, extravagant mock-ups of products showing the way in which products should be used were the main assets of department stores. They used lifelike mannequins, model rooms in the home furnishing departments, a mock-up of a railway coach to present travel accessories etc., giving the customer information about products they did not know anything about. Moreover, the products were lavishly displayed with all sorts of possible accessories, in a way that was sometimes even educational.

...to America...

In America, department stores evolved a bit differently than in Europe. Macy's opened the first department store in 1858. However, it was only in 1904 that a department store specifically designed by Louis Sullivan was constructed in Chicago for Carson Pirie Scott. The wealth of the bulk of the population in the Americas and its strongly developed industry was greater than in Western Europe. This consumer demand contributed to the success of the American department stores. Soon, they were larger in number and turnover than the Parisian ones.

Another type of department store that developed in America at the end of the 19th century: the 'nickel and dime' stores, referring to the uniform prices of the products being five cents (a nickel) or ten cents (a dime). Frank and Charles Woolworth were frontrunners in the nickel and dime businesses and grew their business to one of the largest retail chains in the world in the 20th century: Woolworth. The Woolworth brothers started their first store in 1879; Their empire consisted of more than a thousand stores by 1919, serving many Americans in downtown plazas and shopping malls.

...the timing was right...

With the department stores, larger-scale retailers were born. The difference between European department stores and the American ones rested precisely on this kind of development. European department stores remained large-scale retailers – only having one or just a handful of stores – while the American ones were chain retailers. In America many different types evolved, like the nickle and dime stores, and although Europe also knew such variants they did not last longer than the mid 20th century. They are worth mentioning though, because during the economic crisis of the 1930s, in many cases it was the profit of the uniform price chain stores that enabled the department stores to survive. Afraid of the arrival of Woolworth in Germany at the beginning of the 20th century, German department stores were the first to launch their own 'nickle and dime' stores as subsidiaries. To name a few: Tietz opened EHAPE in 1925; in The Netherlands de

Bijenkorf followed the German trend and launched its Hema in 1926; in France, Nouvelles Galéries started Uniprix in 1928, and Au Printemps launched Prisunic in 1931. These stores gradually departed from the uniform price model and later disappeared. Only Hema is still around and has evolved into a variety store.

Retail is the mirror of society but the advancement of the department stores could only happen in the light of several societal changes. First, the Industrial Revolution, starting at the end of the 18th century in the United Kingdom and gradually spreading throughout Europe and America in the 19th century was key to the development of department stores. It brought new products to the market at a rapid pace and department stores were the place to discover them. It also had an impact on the way we built. Larger sheets of glass could be produced and building with steel became popular. This, of course, was reflected in the architectural style of department stores with, for me personally, the highlight being the period of Art Nouveau. By the turn of the 19th century gaslights were first used in department stores, which gradually led to the closing up of the façades. Paris and London were the first cities that laid gas pipes throughout large parts of the city, making street lighting possible and available to private homes and shops in wealthier neighborhoods. This caused a shift in urban life. The dark 'night' altered to a 'night life', also changing consumer attitudes. Stores were able to stay open longer and street lighting generated 'window shopping'.

Second, the change in fashion during the First World War, from distinct clothing for each social class, gender and political conviction to more uniform and casual wear, played into the hands of the department stores. Indeed, the need to keep mass-produced and ready-made clothes in stock rose and the department stores were the perfect place to keep them.

Prosperity was the third factor to advance the development of luxurious businesses. As standards of living rose, shorter working hours and larger salaries created extra leisure time for a large number of people. Shopping became a leisure activity and a new social custom. So, shops were no longer about satisfying basic needs; they also started to 'create' needs by selling products that the consumer was not even aware of needing. The rise of the department store was a prominent manifestation of the new consumer culture.

...for a rising star

The invention of the escalator was ground-breaking. It allowed the department store to grow, literally and figuratively. Escalators eliminated the drawback which elevators had: in elevators, only a limited number of people can be transported. Alternatively, staircases were not used much, partly due to the dress code of women (try getting up the stairs with several hula hoops around your waist and legs). Escalators however allowed a continuous flow of customers, blurring the distinction between separate floors and, in that way, contributing to customers' in-store experiences. I found it interesting to learn that the first conceptual articulation of an escalator was the 'revolving stairs', described in an 1859 U.S. patent issued to Nathan Ames, as the sketch shows. Though this version was never built, it was designed as a never-ending repetition of steps revolving around three wheels. Jesse W. Reno produced the first working 'moving staircase' in 1892. He sold his patent to the Otis Elevator Company who commercialized it and named it the escalator. It was in 1896 that the Siegel-Cooper department store in New York was the first department store to install an escalator. The Harrods Brompton Road , London, store followed in Europe in 1898. The success and vast expansion of the physical store space of the department store would not have been possible without the escalator, making it one of the most important innovations in retail. This invention democratizes all levels. No wonder Rem Koolhaas has put a sketch of an escalator with dollar signs around it on the cover of his book 'The Harvard Guide to Shopping'. This is a great book, by the way, including several essays of the evolution of stores and cities.

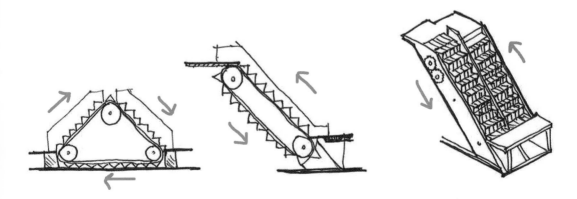

The wheel of retailing

Equally interesting is the reason why the department stores lost their position. There is something called the wheel of retailing, a term coined by Professor Malcom McNair already in 1958. It is a formula that assumes constant renewal in the retail sector – a life cycle in which new types of shops come onto the market, grow and disappear after a certain period of time. It originates from the hypothesis that retailers enter the market with low prices and low status, evolving into stores with high prices and high status until a new player enters the market with low prices and low status, forcing the upgraded store to adapt again to the lower prices, completing the cycle. Although not entirely the same, the department stores did enter the market as the much cheaper arcades and *magasins de nouveautés*. It is only with the Industrial Revolution and the rise in consumerism that the department store could evolve into a store with high prices, high status and high service levels. If Woolworth had entered the European market, department stores would have stumbled into the phase of decline, but by launching these shops themselves, they may have delayed their decline. Indeed, probably not realizing that at the same time they undermined their own authority.

The Second World War was the start of an era of decline. During that War demand surpassed supply and the retail industry struggled to survive. Although recovery after the war was very fast due to overall increased standards of living, the increase in consumer demand did not create equivalent increases in turnover at department stores. A possible explanation is that more money was being spent on holidays, catering and health services. This increased spending on leisure eventually caused the cost-conscious and critical consumers to save on commodities. Consequently, the department stores were forced in to a radical return to 'small profit and quick return' (completing the wheel of retailing). Other reasons were changes in the target group from bourgeois women to a more diverse group of men and women from all age groups and different social classes, resulting in a change in their luxurious image to a more mainstream one; the increasing success of discount stores; and as the modern era of the car grew, city centers became crammed and a lack of parking resulted.

Learnings from history

As the wheel of retailing shows, everything forms a cycle and things reoccur, as have many of the features of the department store. I have highlighted these features in pink throughout the above text. Let's have a look at what we can learn from these.

'Making shopping as attractive as possible', as department stores did so well, is something that retailers should do today. If you want customers to go to a store, this is key. Getting people to a store is already challenging today as there is choice in abundance. Answering the question of how to get people to a store is the reason for writing this whole book. How do we make 'shopping' attractive (again)? Or since shopping is no longer the main target of a store visit, how do we make the customer experience attractive again? There is no one answer; there are several ways, but attractiveness is pretty much the word that sums it all up.

A common way to be attractive is to use *'hybrid retail forms'*, which department stores already were. Offering extra services or combining forces with fellow brands and retailers to extend the product or service range on offer are options to make the customer experience more attractive because the retailer becomes more relevant this way. Put customer service back at the center – how to best serve them. In the past *'social behavior was mixed with commercial activities'*; today, shopping IS a social activity and in many cases a *'leisure activity'*. This offers opportunities to really connect with the customer. What department stores did not have in the past and what helps you connect to the customer on a personal level is technology. Let's go back to my romantic image of the department stores with a layer of technology added. Technology that makes it possible to know the customer better and that makes things easier for customers and staff logistically. Certainly the latter can benefit immensely from this when it allows them to spend more time with the customer. I feel that connecting staff with customers comes close to what retailing should do today.

Departments were attractive as they stood for 'variety, novelty and service'.

The other reason why departments stores were attractive is that they stood for 'variety, novelty and service'. I think that is what customers are still looking for today. Department stores curated the whole experience and the products on offer. Is that not what successful stores are doing today but on a smaller scale? Think of the feeling of a microcosm where service, warmth, exclusivity and uniqueness are back on the map. Where 'products are lavishly displayed', showing inspiring combinations. Retailers today are well aware that they have to invest in more than nice looking stores. That brings me to 'stimulating the senses'. What department stores did in the past can be done today in a much more sophisticated way. A large part of this book will elaborate on this.

One last thing I want to point out is that department stores were king in adapting to what was happening around them. They responded very well to the development of 'street lighting', for example. They were the first to make their shop windows more than just product displays – something they are still known for today. What was a revolution then is common today. They have always put more emphasis on conceptual displays with a lot of story telling in them. Smaller shops have also taken up that idea during the last two decades. Why now? Because of the internet, which we use to orientate our shopping, our window shopping has moved to the small window we have at hand all day. This makes it possible to use actual shop windows to attract people, to get noticed and to tell a retailer's story.

Efficient machines

From Self-Service...

Much younger and with more straightforward development are the supermarkets. Just like department stores, supermarkets are the result of cleverly adopted changes to economical, social, technical and managerial evolutions. Originating from grocery stores they were the first 'stores' selling a variety of food products, changing their product offer from commodities and dry food products to a wider variety of food products including fresh food. In America, shortly after the First World War, progressive grocers started the self-service concept, which caused a shift in store design. It influenced the pattern of shopping in other sectors as well. Self-service decreased the operating costs drastically because fewer working hours and personnel needed to be paid for. One of the proponents was

Clarence Saunders, who started a grocery shop (Piggly Wiggly see sketch) in Memphis around 1917. Until then, it was common practice that the grocer took the product from behind the counter. His sales talk was one of the main selling features. Many commodities, such as oats and sugar, needed to be weighed and packed since they were delivered to the grocer in large sacks. Saunders chose to give the customers the liberty to take the products they wanted from the shelves and then make their purchases. What Saunders did not foresee was that his self-service concept increased theft. To counter this problem, he separated the entrance from the exit. Next, he put the cash register in front of the exit. The shelving islands were placed straight on to the cash desk so the shop attendant had a clear view over the store, as my sketch of Piggly Wiggly indicates. In principle, Saunders' system required only one shop assistant since the weighing of the remaining bulk products was combined with the cash desk. So, high-cost personnel were replaced by relatively low-cost equipment, revolutionizing the relationship between customer and staff. The grocer's sales talk now became a shopping experience enriched with the ability to touch the products (the one sensory cue not fully exploited by the department stores). It also increased impulse purchases, having higher turnover as a result. It is only in the next stage, as a result of the revolution in the packaging industry, that products were delivered perfectly weighed in a closed package, upon which a clear expiration date was mentioned as well as a notion regarding the assurance of hygiene. This innovation was beneficial for the break-through of the self-service concept. Self-service decreased prices significantly,

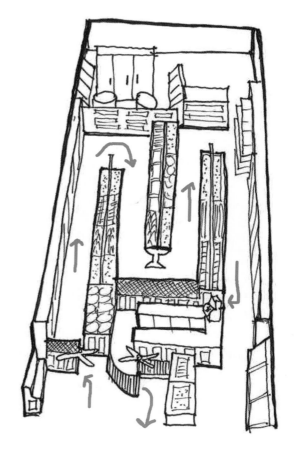

which became the most preferred benefit for customers during the first phase of its implementation. Only later, the freedom to browse and the increase with regards to shopping efficiency was valued. In Western Europe the first step in introducing the self–service concept only happened after the Second World War, around the 1950s. Retailers and consumers were hesitant about it. Simon de Witt was the the first self-service supermarket.

...to self-service furniture...

Department stores adopted the self–service system in response to mass consumption and the demand for increasing staff remuneration. In America this happened just before the First World War and in Western Europe, right after. This adoption required a new type of shop furniture, which changed store interiors completely. Shelving and other types of furniture that support self-service started to replaced the counters. Only jewelry, perfumes, fresh foods and other luxurious products remained staff-serviced. Payment was made at separate cash registers. Customers were now encouraged to browse throughout the store, so the route through the store had to be carefully designed. Some typical plan strategies were developed (see sketch): such as the open plan, offering a continuum of open space; containing escalators with features such as an atrium or an open plan vertical court sometimes crowned with a skylight. Another was the loop plan, which, in a sense, is a combination of the open plan and the centre-core plan. These floorplan strategies are used in all types of stores nowadays.

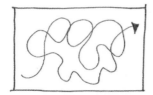
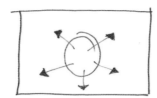
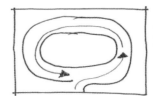

THE BIG BOOK OF RETAIL DESIGN

The development of shopfurniture built specifically for self-service happened by trial and error. Initially everything was presented at one height, which was very restrictive in terms of displaying products. The products were shown standing on end, wedged between glass dividers on the table top of the island counter. No-one considered the idea of displaying products by hanging them or increasing square meters by staking shelves. The first adaption was placing extensions out of the middle of a tabletop so that a kind of cake form arises, as the sketch shows. It took several years before gondola islands as we know them today were used with shelving from top to bottom. Suddenly, stores had to put on a bigger stock because so many extra running meters were added. Customers also had to adjust because they were not used to stooping to the lowest shelf, formerly table height.

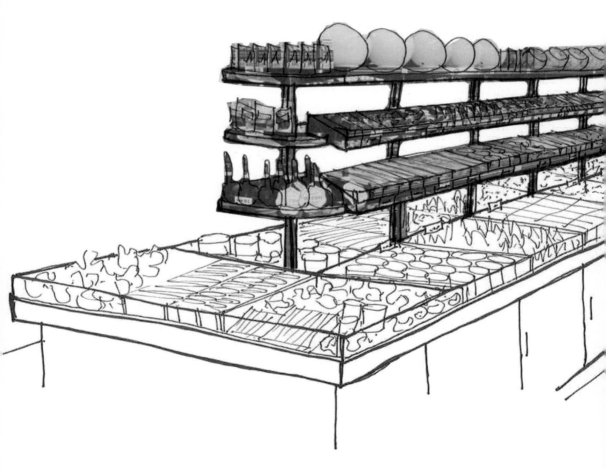

...the start of the rationalization process has begun

The modern supermarket – of the 1930s in America and the 1950s in Europe – was rational and efficient with the elements of the store (i.e. products, shelving and signing) placed as single compounds in a shell (i.e. the building). Supermarkets, then and now, emphasize their interiors, mostly considering the exterior of minor importance. With the adoption of self-service, which shifted the attention from the salesman to the product, the counter disappeared and shopping baskets and trolleys appeared. Next to the entrance a whole battery of cash registers was situated. Also, shopping trolleys and baskets were situated in this area. Management, also housed in this zone, worked in a 'fishbowl' with a view of the cashiers and the shoppers. Next, the customer had to pass a turnstile that emphasized the one-way traffic in the supermarket. The shelving and gondolas were positioned perpendicular to the cash registers to maintain oversight. After entering, a path brought the customer to the back of the store where he can begin his 'journey' back to the entrance/exit zone. Fresh fruit and vegetables were used as pullers (products that draw customers to the store) and were placed to the sides of the store making customers cross the whole store, passing all other dry food products. As a last attempt to lure the customer into buying extra products, impulse sensitive products, such as sweets and snacks, were placed at the front or at the cash registers. The exterior also contained a recognizable feature: the shop window. This window was supposed to highlight the activity in store, making the store the 'model' instead of models placed in the shop window, as was the case in department stores. The modern hypermarket was a radical step ahead in terms of space utilization, productivity, efficiency, and cost management.

Not the most sexy invention, but definitely the one with the biggest impact on store logistics is the Universal Product Code (UPC) – better known as the barcode, being a thumbprint of a product. It made it possible to globally orchestrate the flow of all coded goods. By the end of the 1950s, the growth in size of a supermarket had reached its limits due to difficulties with managing the store and tracing the many products in-store. For instance, an average American supermarket offered 3,000 products in 1946, compared to 10,000 products for a medium supermarket and 40,000 for a large supermarket today. UPC made it possible to increase the size of the supermarket. Although some modifications were made along the way, each UPC barcode consists of a scannable strip of black bars and white spaces above a sequence of 12 numerical digits. It is amazing that something as 'simple' as this is still used worldwide to code products. We cannot really speak of a peak in the development of the supermarket, they have continued to develop, always adapting to the spirit of the times. Wars and financial crises pushed them further into the rationalization process. Indeed, there have been no jolting changes, as we have clearly seen with the department store. Supermarkets have really grown out of functionalism. It is only at the turn of the last century that this has quietly changed. There was more room for experience. Shopping was also no longer something that had to be done quickly in the limited time one had. And it was no longer solely seen as a task for women. Although more attention has been given to enhancing the shopping experience, 'the modern supermarket' as described above is still a blueprint for many discounters.

The modern hypermarket was a radical step ahead in terms of space utilization, productivity, efficiency, and cost management.

Learnings from history

Reflecting on the features I have highlighted in pink throughout the above text, *'touching and taking products'* is taken for granted, as is a certain level of *'self-service'*. This ranges from grocery products and dry foods to a complete self-service supermarket. Only two decades ago it was widely believed that 'the larger the supermarket the better' - thanks to the *'Universal Product Code (UPC)'* this increase in volume was possible. Large supermarkets were popular for their generous product offers and their one-stop-shop character and many of the smaller independent supermarkets and grocery stores disappeared. During the last two decades however, this changed and supermarkets introduced smaller outlets themselves. The trend causing this decentralisation was 'convenience'. In the previous century, convenience used to mean timesaving, now it embodies more. Simplicity, ready-to-eat, ready-to-make, and within easy reach (every moment of the day at every possible location) are current needs of the consumer. This is of course in correlation with the supermarkets wanting to enlarge their market. So, supermarkets also adapt the different formats. According to the retailer location and size, the store's interior changes. It ranges from rationally designed functional spaces of the 1950s dedicated to high- speed shopping, to more social environments, akin to market places. One might look like a warehouse, the other like a department store with each department having its own look and feel. The convenience trend is still developing, with a new pulse due to the pandemic, and has added needs like hassle free shopping, contactless shopping, high speed solutions, etc. Indeed, the latest developments make it possible to shop in supermarkets without even having to speak to or even see a shop attendant. A computer takes in empty bottle returns, the consumer weighs fruit and vegetables themselves, all products are pre-packed and displayed, and self-scan and pay techniques complete the total self-service experience. No matter what form of supermarket we see today, now more then ever, *'the route throughout the store has to be carefully designed'*.

While *'the Universal Product Code (UPC)'* is widely used, lately other codes and systems also made their appearance. Think of the QR code that is now used very conveniently to provide customers with additional information about products and services. Customers can easily scan them with their smartphone and thus gain access to menu cards in restaurants, watch videos about the production process of a product, etc. Also other systems like Amazon's 'just walk out technology' are making their way into retail, pushing the *'rationalization process'* even further. Amazon uses that technology to offer a hassle free shopping experience in their Amazon Go stores. These are small supermarkets (convenience stores) where people just walk in, scan Amazon's app and then just take their desired products from the shelves. Sensors and cameras register everything so all the groceries automatically enter their digital ticket into the app. When the customer leaves the store the checkout process is automatic, including the payment. In Europe, this is slowly taking off, but I predict that it will become more mainstream, especially in high traffic locations such as stations and airports.

In many countries, contemporary supermarkets do not differ much from their forebears, still putting the emphasis *on their interiors, mostly considering the exterior of minor importance*, which is a shame if you ask me. Large ugly 'boxes' are still built – they really hurt my eyes – though perhaps with a little more attention to the façade, including more glass to welcome daylight. There are so many beautiful examples that are attempting to blend into the environment. Examples of buildings designed to blend can be found in countries like Austria and Switzerland, which seem to be more sensitive to designing buildings fit for the environment. My favorite example is MPreis. This supermarket chain respects values such as the natural environment, architecture, quality and tradition while combining generic supermarket characteristics with extraordinary architecture. Usually MPreis aims to blend the supermarket with its environment, sometimes using local architecture, sometimes resulting in discrete buildings. As an example of the latter I really appreciate the MPreis in Matrei (Austria), designed by Machné Architects. As the sketch shows, the architects tried to blend the supermarket with its environment resulting in a discrete building with an inviting entrance.

The green roof is designed as a fifth wall, receiving just as much attention, from an aesthetic point of view, as the four façades. From the adjacent highway only a curve in the landscape is visible. The building overlooks the village through large windows, and offers fantastic views of the beautiful scenery to its customers while shopping. Indeed, relating to the idea that shopping was also '*no longer something that had to be done quickly*'.

The struggle for uniqueness or uniformity

In the past, there was one type of store that constantly struggled with wanting to be unique on the one hand and wanting to grow and be recognizable on the other: the boutique. Flourishing at the same time as the department stores, it was first founded in the 19th century arcades of metropolitan cities. They were soon joined by the prêt-a-porter concerns of haute couture houses in the early 20th century. Boutiques were small, independent outlets with carefully crafted interiors selling specialised merchandise. They were designed in great detail, often referred to as a *gesamtkunstwerk*, a comprehensive work of art that draws on all art forms, from architecture to interior decoration, furniture design, paintings, sculpture, tapestry, and so forth. The boutique was like a microcosm offering its customer something exclusive: advice, service, warmth, and uniqueness. Customers identified with these products, the boutiques they were sold in, and their owners. When the arcades lost their glory and the mass market was established, the boutique-concept was challenged. To survive, they had to relate to mass markets

THE BIG BOOK OF RETAIL DESIGN

without losing the uniqueness that characterised them. Fashion designers Mary Quant and Coco Chanel realised that the ideal relation to the consumer was one that communicated that uniqueness was for everyone. So, in 1929, the single boutique became several boutiques, located in different cities and countries, even in entirely different markets. Still, they retained the aura of uniqueness due to designed outlets particular to the location. Larger concerns were inspired by this. Benetton, for example, was able to operate at the scale of the department store, but its targeted young audience responded to boutique-styled stores. To this end, in the late 1970s, Benetton started using the boutique as a motif. Each store design resembled the boutique-style but was still recognizable worldwide. Soon, other fashion retailers cleverly adopted the traditional characteristics of the boutique, to increase the attractiveness of chain stores, masking the global management behind it.

Benetton started using the boutique as a motif.

And then there was retail branding, too much uniformity

Looking at the evolution of stores in the second half of the last century we can see that with stores expanding nationally and internationally, uniformity and recognizability became a thing. Indeed, creating a recognizable identity with store design is something that emerged from the chains in the 1960s. First, graphics such as logos and fascia were used as the primary identity communicator for a retailer and a store. The design of the logo was critical at that time. Also shopping window display was used as a creative way to express the retailers' identity. During the 1960s there was still a difference between the design of the shop window and the interior of the store. In the store interior, design took a functional role in creating sales-driven environments. Also, many fixtures were sent from manufacturers to promote their products, not taking the store environment into account. Gradually, the development of communicating retailers' identity continued into the design of the store interior. Boutiques, for example, often were inspiring cases to gain insight into how to show a retailer's identity in-store. To create a coherent image, the store facade, the signing, displays, packaging and ticketing were designed with the same graphic elements as the company logo. Via retail branding, a store could become considered as a brand, relating store appearance and identity to their key brand values. Design however also played a functional role, as it needed to display merchandise effectively and create an image of consistency and quality.

Until the beginning of this century, this strategy was pursued to the hilt. Copies of copies of copies of most chains could be found all over the world in any self-respecting shopping city. Designs, or rather copies of designs, were always drawn in at different locations around the world only respecting the form of the building and its layout. I often saw plans appear under my nose from agencies hired by chains to design all the shops, worldwide. Such an agency operates from one location in the world and rolls the original design concept out purely on the ground plan of the location where the store is to be set up, without even having seen pictures or visited the building or the location. Zero respect for local architecture, customs, raw materials, etc. Any typical details or even typical architecture was completely ignored, giving way to a one-size-fits-all solution. That often hurt me, seeing nice architecture or details disappear. Indeed, not only brands need to be held accountable for this; local authorities also play a vital role.

Luckily, brands like Aesop and Camper have resurrected the idea of thinking global but respecting locality. Both brands choose to work with local designers, so each store will look different, yet have the same philosophy, story and values behind it, making it recognizable. This strategy, called glocalization, is adopted by many different brands on many different levels, from products (locally inspired products or locally sourced commodities) to communication (local dialect) and design. Also bigger brands, like Starbucks, who are usuallycopy and paste their design have adopted this localization idea. I remember the attention that went to H&M who, for the first time in their existence, had opened a store in a protected building, in the Portal de l'Àngel, in Barcelona, which used to be the head office of the company Catalana de Gas. A true combination of the 'old' with the 'new'. A respectful, bourgeois, baroque dialogue with a pop, modern, contemporary style. What you see in my sketch is that this building did not have any shop windows. H&M had to be creative to attract people in as they were not allowed to change anything on the facade. Placing lit screens that change color all the time in the corridor was the solution to make people curious and go into the store. Choosing such a historical building was unprecedented for H&M. Since then, more and more cases like this can be found, and nowadays adaptive reuse for commercial purposes has become more mainstream and offers uniqueness and surprise to the customers of such stores.

Of course, we can link this once again to the evolution of society. Not only brands are conquering the world; so are tourists. Due to the increase in travel and especially city trips, people see the same thing everywhere when it comes to shopping. Taking the plane to another city far from home to be served up with the same uniformity in stores is not exactly what people are looking for. Social trends that at that time were moving towards uniqueness, self-fulfilment and authenticity made this model untenable. Also do not forget the malpractices that go with globalization, such as the mass outsourcing of the production of products in sweatshops, which played a role in this mind shift. I remember what an eye-opener Naomi Klein's book 'No Logo' was to me. I must admit that before that I was barely aware of any harm. By reading Klein's research and work, I have become more critical of well-known global brands myself, an attitude that is not a bad thing, I think. Even though the book is now more than 20 years old, I still recommend it to everyone to read if they are not yet familiar with the downside of globalization.

Learnings from history

Today, people are looking for authenticity, genuineness and local anchoring and they will hold brands accountable for their actions. The pandemic has made (some of) the people realize that buying local is better. Better for the local economy, better for the climate and better for social cohesion. They were already looking for this before the pandemic, but it has become even more prominent. What department stores did on a large scale, boutiques do on a small scale: they are 'a microcosm offering its customer something exclusive, being advice, service, *warmth, and uniqueness'.* The boutique look and feel is entirely back and even large concerns like IKEA, Apple and Zara are using *'the boutique as a motif'* as a differentiation strategy. Zara and Apple choose A-locations for their stores and they like to inhabit beautiful (old) buildings. Once inside you get a lovely mix of the existing architecture with sophisticated new furniture. Today retailers *'translate their identity into the design of the store interior'*, indeed, as I will elaborate on in Part II of this book, retailers becoming *'a brand on its own'.*

In a way, IKEA adopts the 'boutique as a motif' as well, by creating smaller bubbles of different atmospheres within one store. The house mock-ups can be seen as such bubbles, as the smaller shops (Danish corner, corner with Persian carpets) IKEA is experimenting with. One mistake that IKEA made is linked to *'glocalization'.* IKEA thought that their formula could be copied throughout the world. But they learned the hard way that local adaptation is needed. The first time this happened was when they opened a store in the U.S. The company initially tried to replicate its existing business model and products, but it had to customize its products based on local needs. American customers, for instance, demanded bigger beds and bigger closets. IKEA also had to make a number of changes to its marketing strategy in the U.S. Similar problems arose when they entered the market in China, though they were better prepared. IKEA had to adjust its store location strategy as most consumers in China use public transportation. Rather than the usual stores in the suburbs, IKEA sets up its stores on the outskirts of cities which are connected by rail or metro networks. Also the renowned catalogue had to change into digital communication via Chinese social media platforms. IKEA learns from their mistakes and continuously adapts to the changing environment, through trial and error, which not many companies are able to do, because it is very costly when mistakes are made.

B. The emancipation of retail design

I t is clear that throughout history shops have literally become larger, more complex and increasingly international. In addition, more and more products came onto the market that, in the long run, differed little from each other. The first hoover or the first TV had little competition and sold itself. But that pole position obviously does not remain as soon as more brands sell these products. The role of the store and the retailer as a brand in the sale of products therefore became increasingly important. Indeed, the start of the retail design discipline really emerged when design companies and retailers jointly developed a type of store that established appropriate perceptions in the retailer's targeted customers. Terence Conran was one of the first proponents of this approach with his design of the interior of the '21 shop' in Woolworth's department store in 1961. From the 1960s to the 1980s, retail design was viewed as a discrete activity in the store development process, though with its very own practice. In the 1980s, the profession of an interior designer was emancipated, and interior architecture / interior design became a discipline in its own right. This had implications for the emancipation of retail design as well. At that time, retail design became more and more claimed as a domain within interior architecture, with furniture makers and interior decorators often leading the way. Store design became about relating consumer behavioral needs to functionality and branding. As stores are a reflection of society, the emancipation of the discipline of retail design is a result of the interplay between need and offer, society and retailer, and designers who connect both. I was lucky to get my education in retail design in the period when the emancipation of retail design was really taking off and to witness this surge in popularity firsthand. Both society in general and consumers more specifically, design agencies, and retailers have played a role in the development of the discipline.

The role of design agencies

It all started in London

As mentioned in the introduction, retail design as a profession, or as a discipline, has only really been known since the 1970s. Earlier, it was more an intuitive expression of commercial acumen. It was only then that people realized that designing stores required expertise, and that as a designer you could make a business out of it, with London as the place where it all started. The first designer to rethink the design of the store and the high street was Terence Conran in the 1970s and 1980s. He started his own design practice 'Conran Design' in 1956, designing a store for Mary Quant. His designs for Habitat were a true translation of the retail brand in the design of the exterior and interior. Focusing on young marrieds and singles, products and store design were brought together. With great passion, he was selling not needs, but wants. Habitat stores offered a place where shopping for homeware was as pleasurable as shopping for clothes. Rodney Fitch, mentored by Conran, also played a vital role in this. By buying the design side of Conran design – Terence Conran sold his design company to continue with his homeware chain Habitat – he founded his own design company Fitch and Company Design Consultants in the 1970s. Rodney Fitch was distinguished by his lively interiors in the 1980s, with Topshop and Marks & Spencer as examples. Though the economic boom of the 1980s played a role in the rapid expansion of the Fitch company, Fitch's designs were well placed – by the late seventies – to shape the coming zeitgeist of 1980s consumerism. Besides the fact that Rodney Fitch practically invented the business of retail design – making money out of designing stores – and gave it credibility, there are three points of change in the perception of the role of retail design, instigated by him, that were crucial for the development of the discipline.

In Fitch's view, shopping, being one of the most important cultural indicators of the modern age, should be fun, rewarding and entertaining.

A first change was the shift towards the idea of retailers not merely being distribution channels for third-party brands, but being brands of themselves, as I discussed above. Approaching a retailer as a brand and designing the store as a whole changed the British high street in the 1980s. The function of a store evolved from a necessity to becoming a place that should facilitate buying experiences in a rather innovative or creative way. The designer (and his/her skills) became increasingly important. When consumers started to buy products as an extension of their lifestyle, increasing the importance of brands and image, target-group oriented strategies proved to be profitable. Knowing the target group, what they want and how they were best approached was the primary knowledge necessary for a designer to design a matching store. Both Rodney Fitch, with Topshop, and Terence Conran, with Habitat, were designing stores where product and store came together to create a lifestyle offer.

A second change was the thinking, in an analytical way, about how merchandise needed to be presented and lit and how customers would flow through the store. Rodney Fitch always aimed at designing better places to shop for ordinary people which was reflected in his book 'Fitch on Retail Design' (published in 1990). The book made this knowledge common to every other designer providing them with design tools of how to create 'good' retail environments. I remember reading that book for the first time when I was getting educated in retail design at the Piet Zwart Institute in Rotterdam in 2003 from the man himself. I was immediately impressed by his analytical mind and I never thought of design having an analytical side to it. I was trained as an interior architect with the focus on creativity and knowledge, knowledge of materials, construction and visualization. Rodney's insights and spark immediately grabbed me and ignited my love for retail design. Suddenly it wasn't about taste anymore but about brands and analyzing them. Understanding the brand and then providing a design solution for the fans of that brand. Decisions were made based on thorough analysis and knowledge of the brand, the customer and the products on offer.

A third change came from the Fitch's belief of 'shopping being the purpose of life', leading to a shift in the way all stakeholders in retail thought about what retail and retail design should be about. In Fitch's view, shopping, being one of the most important cultural indicators of the modern age, should be fun, rewarding and entertaining. This message was widely spread by his design company, with offices (at the time) in London and New York. His involvement in the training program in Rotterdam also resulted in a new generation of specifically trained retail designers.

A multi-disciplinary field

By recognizing that retail design is more than just designing a store's interior, Rodney Fitch set the tone in creating a business that crossed over various disciplines, and incorporated retail design and architecture, alongside product and packaging design to offer his clientele a particular design service. This idea of a multidisciplinary design agency became the norm during the last decades, mediated by the impact of the digital (r)evolution, causing a turn in retail design. It became widely known that retail is a multi-channel business that must integrate a whole range of sales channels. Because the number of different designers or agencies working on a project can cause problems of dissonance, design agencies started to combine forces, once more offering the entire service to their clientele. So, instead of separate specialists such as interior architects, visual merchandisers, graphic designers, web designers and so on, each designing their proper part of the retail experience, the retail business has evolved into the design of a wholly integrated customer experience for which specialists from diverse disciplines need to work together. I was lucky to experience this myself when working at Fitch. For each assignment, a team was put together consisting of team members from the various disciplines needed for that assignment and which were best suited (in terms of style, for example) to the type of assignment (at that time 48 people were working at Fitch). That could be one or more web developers, together with one or more graphic designers, one or more retail designers, and a trend watcher with one person leading the team. We worked and thought together as much as possible, with a briefing and debriefing session every day. This way of working creates physical and digital spaces that are consistent, coherent and above all, complementary. It was a well-oiled machine and the client was always presented with a total package. It was a very instructive time for me and with a pace of a new project about every three weeks, the learning curve was extremely fast.

Besides employing many differently trained designers to be as complementary as possible, design agencies nowadays also employ psychologists and sociologists to better understand the people for whom they are designing. Because of the importance of such a customer-oriented approach, product design offices and service design firms are also moving their services into the retail design industry, designing stores with a more user-centered approach.

The role of retailers

Retailers have also played their part in the development and importance of retail design. Their drive for innovation and differentiation has ensured that designers have been challenged (which, since this century, also happens in reverse, designers challenging retailers). In the 1980s, products were key, and a design only needed to be complementary and never eclipse the products on offer. However, later on, with the commodification of products, store design played an important strategy to differentiate oneself. I would like to take you through several innovations that I observed and that, in my opinion, took designing for commercial spaces to the next level.

Starbucks: the design of a third place

A first major player challenging retail design was Starbucks, created in 1971. After some tumultuous years with ups and downs, Howard Schultz purchased the company in 1987. Inspired by a trip to Milan, he envisioned Starbucks to be more than a coffee selling store. Committed to the café concept he saw in Milan, he added sales of beans, equipment, and other items in Starbucks stores. Store employees were trained in customer-friendly sales skills. This new Starbucks were the first to offer what is described in the literature as a 'third place'. A place between work and home where you can relax, meet people and even work (Starbucks was also the first to offer free wifi to its customers). From a design point of view, the requirements for designing such lounge areas are therefore higher than in a regular café. There was room for coziness, more luxurious materials, and sofas. Starbucks pioneered in blurring the boundaries between retail and hospitality, something we take for granted today, with their coffee for take-away or drinking-in, again challenging the designer with different sorts of customers. Starbucks not only challenged designers in the 1980s; more recently, in 2008, when the company was struggling, they decentralized the design of the shops, creating eight design studios across the U.S. and 18 around the world, with each one tasked with developing a look reflective of the local flavor. Another reference of Starbucks' journey of acting local (indeed, following the glocalization strategy) by adapting its design to local tradition is Starbucks' journey in China and Japan.

Although forced to act local in order to survive in these countries, the Ninenzaka store (Tokyo), opened in 2017, does serve as an example (see sketch). By incorporating elements of traditional culture and history, customs and architecture in a 100-year-old traditional house in Kyoto, they really changed pace again. The exterior of the building has been left untouched to preserve its historic character. Not even the green, twin-tailed mermaid Starbucks logo is outside. There are many other examples to be found in China. They are now even preserving a heritage site in Tianjin for their flagship store. This seems to be the way forward for Starbucks but also for many other brands, local anchoring can really make a difference in acceptance and succes of a global brand. Starbucks keeps inspiring me. During the last decade, they started their Starbucks Reserve store to compete in the high-end coffee market. With the Starbucks Reserve Roastery, of which they have six at the moment, in my opinion, they created a truly immersive coffee experience with coffee bars with tastings, areas to observe the roasting and brewing processes, a bakery and local art shop. I visited the one in Milan and in terms of design it is mind-blowing. The choice of materials, the luxurious details, the tastings and even the restrooms all contribute to the high-end coffee experience.

Calvin Klein & Prada: leveling products up to pieces of art

Another key player in the evolution of retail design is Calvin Klein. With the choice of John Pawson as its designer for the New York store, Calvin Klein took a different path in store design in 1995. A path where products were given more space, where perhaps for the first time the revenue per square meter was relaxed a bit. Pawson designed a store where clothes were presented as arts as my sketch illustrates. As a lofty former banking hall, the space referenced an art gallery with its enormous height, white walls and its presentation of the mainly black and white clothing. Pawson's minimalist sensibility and Klein's modern tailoring resulted in a perfect fit, challenging future retail design and slowly leaving the idea of only thinking in turnover per square meter that became the norm during the modern age. In fact, they might have been the forerunners to link art with experience, something we see more and more today. More and more brands are positioning themselves through art, but more on that later.

Prada also continued this path and even went one step further with the launch of a new type of store in Soho in 2001. Mrs. Prada's suspicion was that shoppers were getting bored of the typical luxury shopping experience. She came up with the idea of the 'epicenter', a rejection of what she called the flagship syndrome. She invited Rem Koolhaas to design the Soho store (and as we know, much collaboration followed). For Koolhaas a flagship store was 'a megalomaniac accumulation of the obvious'. So, Koolhaas aimed for an architectural statement and designed a half-pipe shaped wooden curve that connects two floors (the basement and ground floor) visually, making the architecture of the store more important than the products – which are sold in the basement in a rather cramped environment. Koolhaas has put the brand Prada literally on a pedestal and a stage, elevating the merchandise to the level of art objects. Mrs. Prada's urge for disruption and Koolhaas's creativity and boldness set a new era for shopping – one in which selling ideas is as important as selling a pair of shoes. Something we call storytelling today. People love stories and stories help to make a connection between people and brands and between people. A side effect of the cooperation between Rem Koolhaas and Prada is that by retailers increasingly asking high profile architects to design commercial buildings and spaces, the discipline of designing for retail got more attention and more respect.

We saw a store emerge that abandoned the idea that stores mainly serve to sell products and generate high turnovers; it was used to sell and promote the brand.

Niketown & Samsung: designing brand experiences

In 1996, we first saw a store emerge that even abandoned the idea that stores mainly serve to sell products and generate high turnovers; it was used to sell and promote the brand: Niketown Midtown East NY (since 2018 Niketown has been on 5th Avenue). The designer was now given the space to incorporate more experience. Experience in the form of testing products in sports cages. Customers were triggered to spend time with the brand as a pleasurable activity. Moreover, while Nike is promoting an 'active store' that is more about brand identity than bottom-line sales, it succeeds in engaging its visitors and in building fans. Nike has completely abandoned the idea of revenue per square meter here, since the store was far from profitable. This is also why a significant portion of the marketing budget goes to these stores. Niketown blurs the boundaries between promotional, sales and educational spaces, making the first flagship store (see further down for more explanation of this store typology) happen. Nike, and the many followers afterward, deployed flagship stores as a communication channel. Although Nike was unable to maintain this strategy and adapted the store to a more profitable one several years later, it left its mark on current retail design.

One short leap ahead brings us to the Samsung experience store at the Time Warner Center in New York in 2004 (the precursor of the current one in Meatpacking district). This store took the brand sales strategy one step further. The store was designed only for customers to get to know the brand since no purchases could be made. By showing and letting customers experience the latest development of Samsung's digital vision in a homelike setting, Samsung hoped to build up a relationship with the user. Customers who wanted to buy a Samsung product were referred to the nearest Samsung retail outlet or an outlet in the customer's hometown. Without knowing it, Samsung had already introduced the concept of show rooming, even before its time. The current Samsung experience store in Meatpacking District still operates on the same principle of not being able to buy anything in the store, with the difference that today the products can be ordered online with one click.

Comme des Garçons: the start of ephemeral retail spaces

What was not expected at that time, but left a huge stamp on retailing today, was Comme des Garçons' guerrilla store in 2004. The first Comme des Garçons was located in a former bookstore in the east of Berlin (see sketch), followed by one in a former slaughterhouse in Cologne and a pharmacy in Helsinki. The guerrilla philosophy is simple: the label accepts proposals from fashion lovers around the world to 'occupy' a space for one year, with a minimal budget for the interior design. Locations are generally chosen in marginalised areas and are advertised by word of mouth. Though the store was made with a minimal budget and composed with mediocre materials, they were selling upmarket collections. 'Temporality' was the new thing about this format. Only Comme des Garçons' community knew of the existence of this store, increasing the value of uniqueness and exclusivity. Soon, other brands started using this form to lift the status of the brand.

So what started as a guerrilla store has now grown into the current popular pop-up stores (see further down for more explanation of this store typology) that can be found everywhere. Today pop-up stores are used for many different reasons. They allow retailers or brands to create unique experiences, by its location, its ephemeral character or by selling exclusive products developed to this end. Also newcomers use the typology to experiment with whether they are valid. But let's be honest; although it left its mark on the development of store typologies, the pop-up store requires an interior architect at least. This is a place for experimentation.

Apple: the store of the people

Without intending to be exhaustive, there is one more brand that has managed to be distinctive and create a legacy in store design, over and above product innovation – Apple. Although it may not have been clear to everyone at first what the purpose of these stores was, or what role they could play in the retail landscape, the impact on brand perception and generating fans is clear. The bright open store excites the customer to explore products. In addition, people can go to the genius bar for questions and attend free sessions to learn how to use Apple apps and the Apple software. Thus, every Apple store in the world has a simple layout. Also the materials used (wood, metal, tiles, plexiglass) in the store are rather sober, businesslike and plain. This way, Apple applies its product design philosophy in retail. Although it was not the first Apple store (more or less the 150th store), the store on Fifth Avenue, designed by Bohlin Cywinski Jackson in 2006, is the most well known. Here Apple did not only have a surprising interior, but also an extraordinary exterior, making a statement with the architecture on the outside. I am talking about the glass cube on Fifth Avenue which only holds the entrance to the store that was located underground, beneath a public plaza (see sketch). A store with premium products in a premium place with no shop windows or view of the interior of the store is pretty surprising. What Apple has been doing since then, more precisely opening stores in heritage buildings, receives respect and admiration from architects, designers, retailers and consumers all over the world. Look at examples like the formal theater in Covent Garden in London, Carnegie Library in Washington, and Grand Central Station. Apple's strategy to preserve and restore historic buildings pays off quite well and makes us wonder and challenges us to rethink the role of a store, and a brand for that matter.

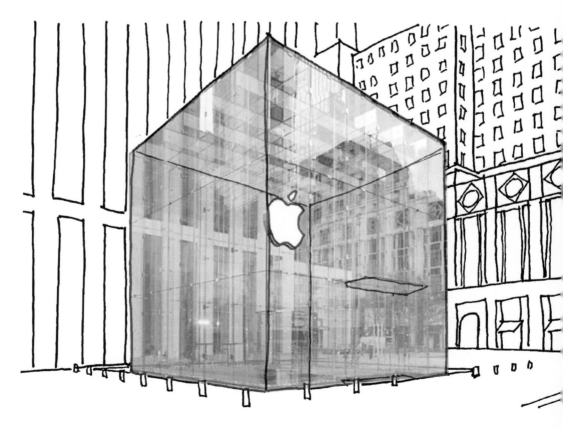

Reflecting on previous innovations, there are two innovations that we did not even know about in the previous century, one being the pop-up store, and only by the end of the previous century, and the other being the flagship store. These are two distinctive typologies that have left their mark on today's retail landscape and are worth discussing more in detail.

Pop-up retail

There was a time when we were surprised to see a pop-up store in the street. It attracted our curiosity and encouraged exploration, knowing that it was a temporary store with a unique collection. It was their temporality that was part of the innovation that allowed retailers or brands to create a unique experience. Not only its ephemerality, but also its location and often the exclusive products developed to this end created a buzz around the hosting brand. I remember even traveling around Europe to see these pop-up stores. Studies in our interior architecture/retail design Masters program were also very interested in this phenomenon and it became a hot topic in their graduate research.

After Comme des Garçons many other brands launched their pop-up initiatives in many different forms and locations, ranging from one-week stores in subways to pop-up restaurants on top of skyscrapers. However at one point, the 'guerrilla factor' (they were called guerrilla stores in the beginning) disappeared and what was once exclusive and unique became more mainstream and multi-purpose. Take the Bernhard Wilhelm Tokyo flagship boutique (2006) as a first example of using the pop-up concept for another purpose. The store resembled the pop-up style but was not at all temporal. The designers were asked to be resourceful with rubbish and hired the conceptual artist Cyril Duval as director. He collected a variety of discarded items in the dense and decaying areas of the city to create the store. Apart from almost being a social study, the store uses the pop-up concept as a motif by cleverly adopting its characteristics: crudely assembled interiors thrown together overnight, the ephemeral character, and mediocre materials.

A second purpose pop-up stores have been given is launching start-ups. Via pop-up stores entrepreneurs can experiment with their retail concept first, before taking a big leap and make large investments. Most certainly in times of economical crisis this is a strong benefit pop-up stores offer.

Third, cities have also discovered the potential of pop-up retail and use it for city-making purposes. Attracting new ideas or hot brands to the city can make the increasingly abandoned streets vibrant again. An example in Belgium that illustrates this is the Box. This formerly empty retail outlet was renovated to host both retailers and chefs. To this end the space is fully equipped with a kitchen and some basic displays. The idea is to rent out the space for low prices during a couple of months to attract new entrepreneurs. When proven market-fit, they are stimulated to rent one of the empty premises in the same street to grow further. But if the concept were to fail, the entrepreneurs would have no financial hole to fill. The Box (originally established by Stebo) combines the temporary spirit of the pop-up concept with an infrastructural investment in the street to revitalize it by dealing with the vacancy problem. The Box started with one outlet and since then opened seven locations in Belgium.

Besides cities, real estate owners also recognize the benefit of hosting temporary stores: they help to attract possible long-term tenants. Though very popular, pop-up stores hosted in (always the same) vacant buildings have lost their unexpectedness and their ephemerality.

The multi-purpose use of pop-up retail has caused the concept to change from unique and trendy to a mainstream and commonly adopted store typology. But besides retailers, cities and developers adopting and adapting pop-up retail, as well as the experience seeking consumer have contributed to this transformation. Our online buying behavior has definitely played a role in how we want to shop offline. If online is cheap, convenient and quick, offline should offer something else, something more: experience. Retailers are therefore forced to stand out to get the consumers into their stores. Pop-up retail can make that difference. Strangely enough, it is also online retailers who seek their success in offline retail by means of pop-up stores. Pure players like Amazon and Zalando have tested their offline marketability via pop-up stores.

The success of offering the idea of temporality to lure customers to the store.

The success of offering the idea of temporality to lure customers to the store is illustrated by Boxpark in Shoreditch (openend in 2013), London. Here not one store, but 61 striped and refitted shipping containers are the attraction point. The containers are stacked to create a complete open air shopping centre where 50 carefully selected brands have found a home. Though located in a remote area of the city, at a former railway goods yard which had been abandoned for 40 years, it attracts thousands of people. Though the temporary character is, again, a bit lost – the developers originally had a contract for five years, but they are still there... – it does not miss its goal in revitalizing the neighborhood. Other sectors have also adopted temporality as a way of being.

Today, pop-up stores have definitely lost their pioneering role; they evolved on the one hand to a 'new' store typology that is here to stay, and on the other they are reduced to several characteristics which are adopted to regular store design. Look at & Other Stories as an example. & Other Stories was born out of the concept of stories. I remember their first website that told stories about clothing lines. A line could be from a blogger or a designer. Sometimes there were also lines around a certain color or motif. Every few weeks, the story would change and you could find the collection in the shop, grouped by story.

With this concept, the parent company H&M Group wanted to appeal to a different, more sophisticated customer. At & Other Stories you will not only find clothes, but also lingerie, beauty/cosmetics and many accessories such as shoes, bags and jewellery. The store also fully embodied the idea of stories and fast-changing collections. In fact, it still does. The website still tells stories, but in a different way. The interior of & Other Stories today is the same as it was at the start in 2013. It radiates temporality through the light furniture. Everything seems to be movable, as you can see in the sketch. Especially the corner with the jewellery and cosmetics seems to be a pop-up shop. Also the signage seems to be temporary because of the clips used to attach cards to the shelves. What I find most striking are the white canvases scattered around the store. These look like empty paintings, meant to make a story. Your story. The canvases are also used to indicate the collections/stories via the same simple clips with a card and a picture. By adopting the pop-up store characteristics, the brand indicates that it is dynamic. Following the trends and always with new stories to discover.

Workplaces, housing, hotels, etc. are popping up when and where needed. Even hybrid forms have appeared. A hybrid store combines different products with services or activities. The combinations that are made are often not obvious. Indeed, because the consumers expect ever newer and more challenging forms of experience and brands do this with the aim of distinguishing themselves from the competition. In 2018 this trend was at its peak. A nice illustration of this is the phenomenon of the luxury branded club used by Hermès. It was a temporary 'club' offering a select product range; it was more about the experience through a mixture of other services such as a bar, a night club, a place to hang and experience the brand. It was meant to bring a community together. They are temporary and traveled around. As far as I know only Yves Saint Laurent Beauty and Prada followed this example. They only traveled to world class cities such as Paris, Madrid, New York, Shanghai, Tokyo and Hong Kong.

Some years ago, design students of the Politecnico di Milano, TUDelft and Hasselt University participating in our summer school Seamless Retail Design came up with this idea of pop-up stores being there on demand through the concept of 'crowdretail' – using crowdsourcing to find out where pop-up stores are needed and which products they should sell. This way, the journey of creating the store and going to the store becomes part of the whole experience, creating a relationship between the community, the store, the environment and the range of products. The inspiration came from crowdbuilding.com where new ideas for empty buildings are proposed, seeking to be approved by possible inhabitants. Entrepreneurs could use the same strategy to find out online where their success offline lies and what kind of store they should open.

Flagship stores

With Calvin Klein and Prada, and later Nike, the concept of a flagship store was born. A flagship store has changed over the years. The first flagship stores in the early 2000s were stores on key retail sites around the world, designed to impress their visitors and offer them a brand experience. Although these stores were larger in retail size and held the most volumes in merchandise, they did not aim at selling products but at selling the brand. Many of these stores were not even profitable. It was during this period that international brands sought partnerships with respected architects. Until then, architects were not really concerned with commercial properties. But the impact on the urban fabric and the attraction a building could have when designed by star architects was clear. Look at Bilbao, with its Guggenheim Museum designed by Frank Gehry. Artists have also taken on this role. Dover Street Market in London (opened in 2004) aims at making a visual statement. The invited artists each designed a level of the store showing their artistic creativity. As the sketch shows, it looks almost coarse with raw concrete floors and cash desks housed in rickety wooden sheds. But in essence it was/is the most trendy place. This takes us back to the time when store design had more of an artistic approach, as I mentioned earlier in this book. I think flagship stores might have a little more freedom to make a statement. Especially since, in most cases, they are not supposed to make a profit. In fact, for the first time in that period, the funding of these shops came from the marketing budget of the big brands.

This indicates that the store is really a part of branding and marketing and not just seen as the end point in the buying process, where the purchase actually happens. In 2013, Doug Stephens said in his book ('The Retail Revival') that media is becoming the store and that stores are becoming media. Seeing and designing the store as a media channel is key. It is the ultimate point to engage

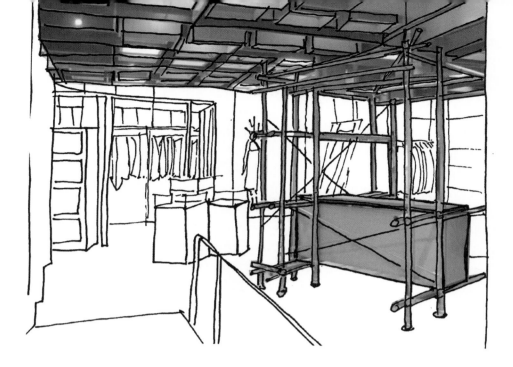

in dialogue with the customer, to show them who you are and what you stand for. When flagship stores arose this was their ultimate role, but today, online shopping has made the need for this way of thinking increasingly necessary, and not just for big brands this time. Smaller retailers would do well to adopt this way of thinking. The days of being a stock of products with a salesperson present, are over; this type of store is not coming back.

Online has become a thing for big brands as well, in addition to the digitization of the stores themselves. Flagship stores as show-offs of a brand therefore made the transformation to digital hubs. The quest for an omni-channel brand happened mainly in these stores, with brands like Nike and Burberry as frontrunners. The artistic freedom of flagship stores made room for a more knowledgeable approach to the design.

Variation within the typology of the flagship store has become more diverse since then. They are no longer necessarily large impressive shops. Smaller and smaller variants are making their appearance, and in some cases a mix is made with the pop-up store typology. Impressive temporary installations appear and disappear without losing their effectiveness on brand immersion. I will discuss some examples in the last chapter when reflecting on what is yet to come.

The role of consumers and the society at large

Although the role of retailers and designers in the development of the retail design discipline are clear, it would not have been able to flourish if people weren't ready for it. As mentioned, the Industrial Revolution played a big part in the evolution of products, which became mass produced, and stores, which became bigger and more global. But the biggest shift that caused retail design to become a discipline on its own happened at the beginning of the 21st century with the shift in our economy which made the consumer the focus of attention. A consumer is no longer seen as solely a buyer of products; he is also seen as a consumer with a proper personality, feelings and longings. This perspective requires different, more sophisticated (marketing) approaches and new retail concepts with more attention to the designed environment. Also that same society became one where shopping and looking for new experiences are essential activities. Pine and Gilmore referred to this phenomenon as the Experience Economy in their book of the same name in 1999. They talk about three stages. The first stage being the addition of an experience to a product or service, thereby increasing the value of the product or service. The customer has a passive role in it. The second phase is aimed at selling the experience as the main activity (and, indeed, even ask money for it, although that never was a great success). The third, the one were are in today, being a more interactive experience where retailer and customer take equal roles.

As experiences have become more important, the store environment has changed into a place where you can buy products in a space where interactivity, socialisation and communication are key. A place that is fun, rewarding and entertaining, as Rodney would say. Designing such places requires knowledgeable design, both in terms of quality and approach. Let's not forget the widely adopted use of the Internet. Consumers started spending a lot of time shopping on the Internet, searching information in order to compare products and prices, or making real purchases. This changed the consumer from a passive unaware partaker, to an informed, active participant.

To sum up, the the first decade of the 21st century was an important period, or even a catalyst, for the development of the discipline of retail design. That leaves us to have a closer look at what the discipline is today and to try to define it.

There are three stages in the experience economy:

The first stage being the addition of an experience to a product or service.

The second phase is aimed at selling the experience as the main activity.

The third being a more interactive experience where retailer and customer take equal roles.

Chapter 2

WHAT IS

A. The discipline of retail design in the 20s

The academics among us are always looking for definitions, descriptions, frameworks, and so on, to start from. Often, there is a general understanding of terms such as value, branding, experience, and so on, but the meaning is subject to the spirit of the times. The term experience is a very good example of this. When experience was first described around the year 2000, it described a different experience than the one we see today. Which is logical, given that society is changing, and consumers and their expectations are also changing. In this chapter, I want to define the concept of retail design. Here, too, we see that the definitions that existed were colored by the spirit of the times. So my definition of retail design today is also temporary, although the basics obviously do not change. The discipline of retail design is still relatively young and strongly influenced by what happens in society, and to the stores. It is therefore also important to understand what the role of the store actually is today, and what role the consumer plays. So in this section, I want to frame the diversity and difficulty of the discipline of retail design and link it to the current challenges.

From designing the space to facilitate the selling of goods...

The term retail design consists of 'retail' and 'design'. I will explain both so that you fully grasp what we are talking about when referring to retail design. In a very basic manner, as the encyclopedia says, the word 'retail' means the supply of services and products to the end user being the consumer. So, retail 'design' should be about designing the space to facilitate the selling of these goods. This seems like a very straightforward definition, with both the supply of physical goods including fashion, food, DIY, decor, etc. and services supplied by banks, travel agencies, post offices, ... If I look at this definition, some questions arise. Restaurants also sell products and services at the same time, just like hotels. Should they be included? Are they retailers? What about amusement parks and music festivals; they sell experiences – are they seen as retailers?

Retail designers should supervise and direct the design of all the touch points.

They would definitely not consider themselves as retailers. But in fact, they are partly doing retail and meet the definition. It is therefore not illogical that retail techniques, such as branding, circulation, flow, experience... are used by hotels, festivals, etc. The difference, however, is that the aforementioned players have made selling experience and a good time their core business, so that they fall into a different category, called the entertainment sector, in the case of parks and festivals; and hospitality, in the case of restaurants and bars. But are they really so different? I use the word 'experience' very deliberately, because that is what binds all three sectors together. In a retail era where retail was purely transactional without experience, the distinction might have been clearer, but now that retail also has to focus on experience, they are coming closer together and are increasingly competing with each other. I had a discussion with Nicole Srock.Stanley from Dan Pearlman (brand architects) about this. She made a very good point, saying that retailers should bring the leisure key performance indicators (KPIs) to retail. And that is so true. The competition of retail in the near future is not other retailers, but leisure. It will not be about money any more, but about spending time. Where will customers prefer to spend their time? At places that are immersive and engaging. Indeed, In this case offering 'experience' equals offering leisure(time). And consumers choose where they want to spend their time. So, although very closely related, I do consider them to be different for the purpose of this book. I do believe retail can learn a lot from the entertainment industry, but more about that later.

So, for now, retail design is about designing the space to facilitate the selling of products and services. This adds a new term though, the term 'space'. Again, in the previous century this was clear, but today, the concept of space has changed with the introduction of the world wide web. Whereas 'space' used to refer to a physical store environment, nowadays, 'space' has become a broader concept with the development of e–tailing. It includes virtual spaces – web shops, but also Facebook, Instagram and other platforms that retailers and consumers continuously use to buy products. Due to this multi-dimensional approach of space, being a retail designer (or a retailer) has become increasingly complex since there are many channels where a consumer can be reached and which, as a consequence, should be designed properly. Indeed, as I explained earlier when retail design offices were starting to include different expertises in one office to be able to offer the whole package, this should be the norm today. Does this automatically entail that a retail designer as we have known them for many years, should also start designing web pages and web shops? No, of course not; that is impossible. What I do expect from a retail designer is to be able to supervise and direct the design of all those touch points. I will discuss this further at the end of the book, when reflecting on the future retail designer. Remember that evolutions in technology and society cause the rules of the game to change at an increasing pace, leading to a growing complexity of the retail discipline, making it difficult for a definition to be accurate and remain truly up to date. Indeed, just like retail is the mirror of society, retail design definitions in the past also reflect the spirit of the discipline at that time, making it interesting to have a look at them to fully comprehend the evolution and what it stands for today.

...to emphasize its strategic level...

The first definition of retail design I could find, coming from the field, was only developed in 2000 by Rasshied Din in his book 'New Retail'. As it shows, it still emphasis the art dimension, though completed with attention to brand value and efficiency:

> 'The role of contemporary retail design is to link instinct, art and commerce...to come to efficient (in terms of space, flexibility and cost) and effective (to communicate the retailer's brand values and encourage consumer activity) retail environments that meet the ever–tougher consumer demands. Therefore a designer's task is to combine his expertise and the retailer's knowledge of the market with elements of psychology, technology and ergonomics'.

With this description, Din considers design at a strategic level and applies it to every aspect of a retail space. He also indicates that retail design is multi-disciplinary as it is a result of contemporary design processes drawing the consumerist, psychological and aesthetic elements together.

Michel van Tongeren from the design agency SVT Branding and Design Group confirms this strategic level in his book 'Retail Branding' in 2003 saying that the design of a store is:

> 'A creative representation of the interplay of the rational and emotional elements of the brand and its formula'.

According to van Tongeren, design shapes thoughts. So, thinking is, and should be, the primary action when designing stores. He continues by expressing that a deep understanding of how brands work, how the formats are organised and established, is necessary. This needs to be related to what consumers expect from a brand. So, a retail designer designs for the retailer and the consumer. A designer must place himself in the aura of those two.

In 2006, Jeff Kindleysides came up with a definition for the Design Council platform. His definition shows the semi-public space a store actually is. In Kindleysides' view, retail design is:

'an understanding not only of what will work aesthetically within the space, but how it will perform functionally and commercially, and how it can be built to budget and meet all of the regulations governing the use of a public space.'

Kindleysides indicates that designing commercially and for public spaces requires more skills than purely interior design. Indeed, as a semi-public space, a store needs to be inclusive to different people with different social, personal and even different cultural backgrounds, each experiencing a store differently. So, it is not the amount of design that makes a successful shopping environment, but knowing of the effect of it on the consumer.

...and its relationship with the customer...

What I miss in these definitions so far is what the role of a store design should be. Although price, brands, quality and location are important choice determinants (and for some stores, the most important ones), the answer seems to lie beyond. I would like to refer to what Kevin Roberts says about products in his book on 'Lovemarks', published in 2005. A lovemark is about a relationship. To Roberts, lovemarks are brands with which consumers have a special emotional connection, which generates loyalty beyond reason. I like to adapt this idea to stores. Thus, a retail space ceases to be merely a merchandising outlet and instead becomes a place where passion is shared. The difference between a space and a place is exactly that emotional connection.

...and its uniqueness...

Another thing that changed: instead of functioning as a background to products, as was the case in the beginning of this century, retail spaces have taken on their own properties. Indeed, in today's global market it has become difficult for retailers and brands to be perceived as 'different' from competitors. One of the key roles for design has thus become to 'make the difference': while being aware of the merchandise carried by competitive retailers, the design of a store becomes more important when the merchandise itself is increasingly perceived as similar. Creating a unique retail environment thus almost has become a necessity for customer binding. The drive to uniqueness (for increased market share), other retail forms have entered the market. I talked about pop-up stores, brand installations and flagship stores. The latter two often have the purpose of selling the brand, rather than just products. To this end, I do feel I need to expand the definition from products and services to the brand.

...to a new definition

So, defining the dynamic field of retail design is quite a challenge. Retail and society influence and change each other constantly making it hard for retailers to stay relevant in relation to our changing habits. Although retailing as commerce is timeless, retail design is one of the most challenging new fields of design, embracing both design disciplines of architecture, industrial design and communication design as well as social science disciplines such as environmental psychology, sociology, cultural anthropology, marketing and management. So, a definition of retail design seems always to fall short, because it changes over time. Still, I would like to define the retail design field as it is today as follows:

> Retail design refers to designing spaces for selling products and services and/or offering a brand experience to consumers. It is interdisciplinary in its intent to create a consumer–valuable experience with the brand's DNA1 in mind.

For the purpose of this book I focus on designing the physical outlet of a store, without neglecting an omni-channel approach.

---

1 the DNA is a term used to express what a retailer/brand stands for emotionally and rationally as will be explained in part 2.

THE BIG BOOK OF RETAIL DESIGN

B. Designing the physical store space

To better understand what designing the physical store means, we must first consider what exactly the role of the store is and how people see and use the store. The aforementioned evolutions have made designing for commercial purposes complex. Each step in the past (crises, technology, the pandemic, but also the aging population) has left its mark on retail design and added an extra layer each time, so to speak. Looking back, we can dissect these layers one by one and peel them off like an onion to analyse them, but we cannot simply add them up again to arrive at a clear answer of what designing the physical store is today. More than ever, designing the built environment is about understanding the user. Architecture and interior architecture, product design, city planning, etc. have never been so consumer-centered as they are today. Stores are part of this and should even be at the forefront of it because they are interwoven with our daily lives. Shops are the ideal place to experiment in this regard. Compared to other buildings, there are a lot of people visiting them every day, which means that playing and testing certain (design) interventions can be done relatively quickly. In addition, shops are part of our routine, making them the ideal place to introduce people to new products (as department stores did) or, more contemporarily, to certain evolutions such as the need to be more sustainable. As the historical overview made clear, shops have always been at the forefront of certain developments in the past. Even now, they should do so by example. How do you treat people and the planet? But also, how can we even better understand people – customers in this case – and connect with their environment? Shops have an important role to play here, as I will further expand on in Part III of this book.

Understanding the customer

To understand how to design physical stores we must understand the customer. Actually, customer expectations are higher today. The customer has so many choices. In terms of product choice, in terms of purchase channel, in terms of brands and retailers, the world is in his hand. Why would a customer be satisfied with less if he can get more for the same effort and cost? In other words, the customer no longer accepts the fact that a retailer is not there when he is needed or when things go wrong, that the store does not look nice, that products are out of stock (and that they cannot be ordered through the store but can be ordered via an online competitor), and so on. Such obstacles send negative stimuli to the customer's brain that in turn determine the overall image of the retailer. If the balance between negative points and positive points tips over, the customer will choose another retailer. Keep in mind that negative aspects outweigh positive aspects.

Also note that it is increasingly complex for the customer as well. As mentioned in the introduction, the spectrum of knowledge, incentives, accessibility, possibilities, have increased tremendously. We have never known so much about man and earth and even the universe as we do now. Just because we know so much it makes it harder to navigate. However, with more knowledge, the desired result can be obtained better and the chance of success can therefore be increased. That does not leave out the possibility of experiencing choice stress (or just indifference?), of being tempted to overindulge (or simplify), of wanting more and more (or less is more?). People need help to make choices. Retailers that tap into this need will flourish.

Understanding the role of the physical store

It is important to realize that everything we see around us is a result of the Industrial Revolution. Cars, roads, buildings, mass produced products, fast fashion, etc., and so are the stores. So it is only natural that stores have been the same for decades. But, with the revolution of technology, this needs to change. We find ourselves moving from the industrial era into the digital era. Consumers walking around all day with a smartphone as an extension of their arm is the most visible expression of this. We have the world in our pocket, we can call helplines, look up information, and even buy elsewhere than the store we are in. That world in our pocket will only expand. Look at the augmented reality apps that are already available where you can put a seat in your living room (virtually) and where you can try on shoes. Indeed, this technological revolution revolutionized the way we buy (and sell) our products. I cannot discuss the role of the store without talking about technology. To illustrate: imagine a consumer, let's say Angèle, is looking for a product, having little time and having the product choice already decided for.

It is important to realize that everything we see around us is a result of the Industrial Revolution, but we are moving into the digital era.

Most likely the purchase will then be online. But imagine Angèle a week later, having a bit more time and being a little more hesitant about the purchase, then a trip to the store might be preferred. And, even again a couple days later (or even just a couple of hours later) when Angèle does not need a product, but passes the store after having lunch with a friend in town, she may at that moment be triggered to step into the store by the window display, for example, or by a personal message she received from the store when passing it. If privacy regulations were not in the way, she would get personal offerings and suggestions on digital screens when she enters a store or neighborhood. Those who have seen the movie 'Minority Report' know what I mean. (The movie, released in 2002, apparently had a very realistic look into the future. In one scene the main character walks through a neighborhood with a lot of screens that play personal advertisement through eye recognition). The technology is there. But, my point is, for all these moments a retailer must be ready. If not, this customer will find a retailer that is. More so, we know that the pandemic has boosted online shopping. During the lock-down, people had no other option than to order online. Because of this forced move to online, everyone has been able to experience the convenience of it and any reservations about it have been completely dispelled. Online shopping figures have risen since the pandemic and online shopping has become an inherent part of society. Experts indicate that the pandemic has accelerated the process of online shopping by four to six years. This means that we are in a state of flux and retailers, and their shops, must adapt at a fast pace.

So, Angèles' example also shows that the reason that customers visit one of the multiple channels is different and alters over time. So, inherently leading to what the altering purpose of each channel could or should be. Not every channel has to be a place to sell and communicate and educate and inspire, but a strategy linking certain channels to certain purposes is necessary. Indeed, the purpose or multiple purposes of the store does make a difference in designing it. My point is, the role of the physical store is no longer limited to a place where you buy products, it is just one of the places where you can buy products, and it should not be the only one. Remember what Doug Stephens said: stores are media and media are stores. The store is only a part of the entire business model of a brand or retailer. The store is just one of the channels and thus plays its part in the entire chain. Along the same lines, I also heard Doug Stephens say that a store is there to commit people. So stop thinking only about sales, but about range. Although we are talking about the physical store here, we obviously cannot neglect the virtual version of brands and stores. This is a 'body and mind engagement', as Michel van Tongeren says where the strategists, designers, managers, et cetera, have to create one holistic concept that the consumer can intuitively make sense of and find appealing. Holistic means that the sum is in fact more than the parts. The whole thing can be unraveled, but it cannot be developed or even experienced step by step. Indeed, the customer literally enters the store and senses the entire shopping experience at a glance.

Again, a store does not function in isolation. A beautiful store with beautiful, fairly priced products can be ignored because the staff is not friendly. But the reverse is also true. Good products at a good price, in an outdated store design will still attract, but only until a competitor offers about the same, but in a new, more attractive store. So, it becomes relevant to understand the role of design and experience.

The role of 'experience'

Whereas in the past first selling products and later selling brands and experiences might have been the biggest difference between stores at that time, I see that today the need to differ has increased under the influence of the pandemic and other crises. Differentiation in experiences, brands or products are now added with differences in store typologies and shopping purposes. Basically, as a retailer you choose to either be hyper efficient and serve the customer in a safe way and as simple way as possible, or you choose to offer entertainment to the consumer so that they can spend a nice time with you. Everything in between will disappear. Either way, efficient and frictionless shopping is highly appreciated nowadays, but it is not yet entirely clear how this should be done. Online shopping now fulfills that role to a large extent. Smart retailers are trying to do both, frictionless shopping in an experiential environment, so they can serve both shopping purposes. This, of course, has to go beyond combining an in-store pickup point with an experiential store. The ideal mix is created when you can shop without friction in stores where touching products is highly valued, such as in the fashion sector. For the time being, we have to make do with self check-outs, which is quite a step in this sector.

Macy's and Nike are examples where a mobile check-out is used, where you can pay via an app on your mobile phone. Decathlon, a French sports store chain, has also been experimenting with this for some time. In high street fashion stores I have only seen it at Zara. There is effectively a dedicated space with a few check-out counters (which apparently lead to an increase of +14% sales). In food, this was adopted some time ago (remember Amazon Go).

During the lock-down I saw some retailers thinking creatively. For example, I went to a fashion drive-in, the ideal combination of online shopping, immediate gratification and personal contact. This mix of online shopping and having access to a physical store is what brands like Coolblue (a Dutch company offering a wide assortment of consumer electronics) and Amazon are going for. They recognize the need for social contact and a place to turn to when troubles with products or deliveries arise. Indeed, online sales go up in regions where physical stores are opened. So again, recognizing the role or purpose of the store helps in making decisions on how to design them. Coolblue is not aiming for experiential stores (yet). The stores are there to communicate with customers. They are moving away, as retail should, from transactional services, adding more emotion through personal connection.

At the other end of the spectrum, when entertainment becomes key, a lot of examples of premium brands pop up again – the same brands I discussed in the section of pop-up stores. An inspiring example – a bit more realistic for local retailers – is Casper's Dreamery, where one has to pay to test the products. It is a perfect example of combining the last two stages of the experience economy as described by Pine and Gilmore. Since its founding in 2014 as an exclusive e-commerce business, Casper has tried multiple partners to go physical.

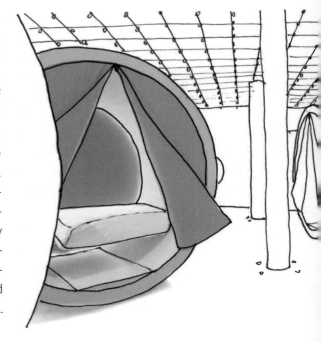

THE BIG BOOK OF RETAIL DESIGN

Although they have opened pop-up stores of their own where people could test drive the mattresses for 20 minutes, the Dreamery focusses more on selling solutions to sleep problems. Customers can schedule a nap break at The Dreamery to enjoy 45 minutes of rest in one of its nine Casper-equipped sleep pods fully decked out in Casper beds, sheets and pillows (see sketch). It costs you 25 dollars, and includes a cup of coffee in the lounge, the use of bathrobes, ear plugs and makeup wipes. You actually do not pay to test the products, you pay for a good nap. Selling the product seems almost collateral damage (although we know better). This last example illustrates perfectly where retail might be heading.

The role of design

The role of design or its impact on society at large is underestimated. No one pauses to consider the creativity and research that preceded it when they put on their favorite sneakers, or when they are drying their hair with a hair dryer. When we see an impressive building, we might think for a moment about the architect and engineers who came up with it. But do you have that reflex when you walk past a typical house in a row? Or when you walk across a square? In short, everything around us is, to a greater or lesser extent, designed. So too are the stores. People are often amazed at the knowledge and creativity involved when you explain it to them.

Jos van der Zwaal (design firm Milford), once succinctly described what retail design should do:

'In modern Western society, design has become as ubiquitous as air and water. We hardly notice it anymore, confrontations with highly innovative or mind bending examples excepted. A retail environment is the surrounding 'par excellence' where all functionalities of design are confronted with the public appreciation. Here design is challenged, tested and judged on its effectiveness without a jury, without a casebook and without mercy. The retail environment does not worry about academic divisions between graphic, interactive, product or environmental design. Here design just has to do its job. It has to be functional, physically as well as mentally. It has to communicate the targeted position and the quality level of the retailer. And it has to contribute to the reputation of the retail brand and the company behind it.'

'Design doing its job' is not as easy as it sounds. Maybe in the past it was more simple. When generations were distinct and marketing and store design was specifically aimed at certain generations or ages and could only be reached via a store and analogue advertisement. Today, target groups are no longer definable by generations or age when it comes to shopping. Everyone shops everywhere, it's just how it suits them at the time. So yes, the (grand)mother might just shop for shoes in the same store as the (grand)daughter, something that was unthinkable not even that long ago (about 15 to 20 years).

We even see that the attention to design and layout of stores has increased. Shabby stores with vague propositions or underdesigned discount supermarkets are no longer mainstream. Design has become mainstream. With the Retail Design Lab, we have worked on a B to B distribution brand of hardware, fasteners, construction hardware, tools and personal protective equipment. Even they noticed that even construction workers appreciate a nice environment to shop in. They would even drive extra kilometers for it.

As more channels are used and the expectations of the customer are higher, the next challenge arises: design management. Just as retailers should manage communication, i.e. convey the same message across all channels, the same applies to design. As I mentioned before, the design of the website/webshop, Facebook and Instagram page, advertising messages... and the store should all elicit the same visual message. And let that be the challenge, although I urge design offices to include people from different disciplines to offer the whole package, the truth is that often for the design or control of these platforms, different consultants or designers are still hired. And if no one manages the design of all these channels, each platform or channel transmits its own message. An example: a customer is orienting himself/herself online and arrives at a beautiful, brand new website of a retailer. The atmospheric photography, warm colors and trendy products appeal to him/her. He/she decides to visit this retailer and, in doing so, ends up in an outdated store that exudes nothing in common with the website. How do you think that this makes this person feel?

Will he/she proceed with a purchase or turn right around? The reverse can also be equally damaging. If in the online orientation phase there is no stimulating website, or other digital trace, that attracts this customer's attention, while a beautiful new physical store awaits him, the customer will not even come to the store, nor the online store. Design management is therefore together with communication management equivalent to expectation management. Creating and fulfilling expectations is one of the big challenges in retail (design) today. Design can do that, but one has to know how.

Now back to the physical store. I made it clear that this asks for much more than a designer to translate a retailers' identity into a store design, and that it goes beyond mere functionality and efficiency. Even more so now that a commodification of products, brands and retail is occurring. The ever-changing expectations and aspirations of the consumer, that are above all paramount, have made retail design a fast-emerging discipline with a sophisticated design approach. Store design is now emphasized in retailer differentiation strategies and retail positioning. Creating a competitive, strongly differentiated retail store, asks for designers with an in-depth understanding of retail's contexts and parameters.

The role of technology

Definitely not my field of expertise – there are other experts specialized in this – but technology does play a role in the future of stores and I would like to take the time to reflect on it and share what I see happening. As mentioned, we are moving into a digital era. I do have to acknowledge that there is a difference in the adoption of technology in different countries and even more between different continents. Everybody is looking at what is happening in China. They are playing in a whole different league. Technology, the metaverse, avatars, virtual influencers and robots are much more adopted. So is mobile shopping. What is very hot in China and Asia for that matter is live shopping, shopping through live-streaming. Thirty-year-olds are massively adopting this trend. Although it was predicted that mobile shopping would conquer Europe as well, Facebook and TikTok have decided to pull out the plug in Europe. I must admit that I am not surprised by this. Of course, we operate at a different speed, but there is a reason why Western Europe and China are where they are. It concerns an enormous cultural difference as I mentioned in the introduction. It is because of this difference in development and scale , I do not believe that Europe is heading in the same direction as China. Of course, Europe can learn from what is happening there, but copy-pasting does not work.

Technology is also helping us out in acting more sustainable.

From making a personal connection....

What strikes me is that online they know everything about you, but in a physical store, you are a question mark. To me, that means the technology and knowledge is there, but there is a huge bottle neck in data management. So much more can be done with the things that are already there today. If you want to be relevant to a customer, there is a goldmine waiting here. Let me start with a simple example of using customer data to make a one to one connection with each customer, which already happened to me 10 years ago. But I still remember getting the first personalized ads in my letterbox (yes, letterbox, not mailbox). The one that has stayed with me the most is the letter I received from my Mini. One day, my Mini wrote me a letter asking me to give him a nice treat. It had already clocked up X kilometers and its tires were worn out too. Time to take it in and pamper it. I must say, I was moved. Moved that my Mini asked me to do this so sweetly. Very smart of the Mini garage, because they know that people who buy a Mini love their car. A Mini is a treat car; nobody buys a Mini for functional reasons. By sending such letters, you affect the owners because they love their car. This example is a very simple one in terms of technology and use of data. Today, much more is possible to make an emotional connection with the customer by means of technology. Nike might be one of the frontrunners in this. In their SoHo (NY) store, they have upgraded their experience shops as we know them from the 2000s where you can test and try products before you buy them, with a layer of technology that makes the whole experience personal. Around the basketball court, cameras are set up to record the action from multiple angles, and the hoop is equipped with sensors that capture body movements. The same goes for the treadmill (see sketch), allowing in-store assistants to analyze the results and recommend the best pair of sneakers. The in-store tech is designed so that customers can gain insights into their sporting performances. Customers can later access all footage recorded of them through their online Nike accounts. The next time the customer comes in, the experience is tailored to him, to recommend specific products. Even when customers walk out without making a purchase, their data is stored and accessible (for them and for Nike) so they can buy the best suited product for them at a later stage. This store offers experiences that consumers can't get online. Even more, they use the advantages of having data to empower the store experience. And that is the power of technology enriched physical retail.

...to serve us

The role of the store is undoubtedly intertwined with technology. I do wonder about what role technology will play in the near future. Judging by what we see today, I dare say that technology will be there to serve us. It will make the whole shopping experience easier for all stakeholders such as customers, staff and the retailer himself. Technology has already proven its worth in optimising logistic processes. Stock management, production processes, payment systems, omni-channel management, etc. are examples of the usefulness of technology in the back-end of a store. Technology is also helping us out in acting more sustainably. Products and their manufacturing process can be traced back, educating the customer on where it came from. But technology is also used to optimize production processes to create less waste or to produce products that are easily disassembled so the materials can be recycled. So, the role of technology could be huge in this regard in the future, but what we will 'see' of it on the shop floor is less. There will still be screens and interactive mirrors that provide atmosphere. But the rest of the technology will largely remain invisible. The best examples in my view remain the ones where you do not see the technology. It's there but it's supportive. That to me is, first and foremost, the future of technology: it optimizes the retail experience for all stakeholders. To give one example: Burberry, although already there for a decade, still represents what technology mixed with experience can be. Burberry is using the technology to improve the customer experience. Each product is equipped with an RFID tag (radio frequency identification). This is a technology for remotely storing and reading information from so-called RFID tags that can be attached to products. So, it has the advantage of being able to communicate in two ways, giving information but also receiving information. Originally coming from the automotive sector to track all parts of a car in a factory, but now adopted in the retail sector, it offers legion opportunities. Each code is unique. No physical contact is required and no line of sight is needed (as with the barcode) to read the code. Hundreds of codes can be read in one or a few seconds, which is very efficient in terms of inventory and stock management. Burberry uses this technology to enrich the customer experience in the store and to enable the personnel to offer seamless experiences. For example, such a RFID tag can react when brought close to an interactive screen or mirror. For example, when a customer comes close to a screen with a handbag, he gets to see a film about the creation process of the handbag. In the fitting room, the interactive mirror will react and, for example, suggest clothing combinations with the handbag. In the entire shop, no cash register or counter is visible. Each staff member is equipped with a tablet. This tablet is used to make payments, but also to view the stock, to find products and their location, to place orders, and so on, as not all Burberry products are present in the store. In an omni-channel world where service is key, this has become a must for such luxury brands.

Where do we go from here?

Despite the digitalization of retail and technology being an integral part of our lives, the physical store space remains the most important channel for retailers to connect with their consumers. In today's saturated retail market, differentiation by price or product no longer holds ground. Designing attractive and up to date stores is what has become the new standard. Also, although a lot of retail transactions are happening online, pushed even further by Covid, the physical store remains a very important communicator with the consumer. It is the most direct way for a brand to bond with a customer. To maintain this role, stores do need to adapt to the 'ever connected' customer, who does not care about on- or offline. A retailer just needs to be there (let's say wherever his customer goes). Within this mix of on- and offline presence a physical store can take on many different roles. It is important to understand the role of the store and place it in the entire marketing approach. It is the role of the store that determines how it should be designed, as I will explain in Part II. Here we focus on the role of the store in the context of a retailer's entire strategy. I am not questioning the role of the retailer in society just yet; I will get to that in the last part of this book.

A retailer just needs to be there.

Chapter 3

WHAT WE KNOW

What we know

Now that we have a better understanding of the role of the store and the role of design in it, it is time to get a better grip on all the different aspects of a store, and more specifically the design aspects. It is often thought that retail design is the same as designing the interior of a store, but nothing could be further from the truth. The interior is only one of many aspects. Communication (tone of voice, packaging, signing, etc), sensory aspects, the exterior (parking lot, façade, signing, etc.), and the entire visual identity is part of retail design. Each aspect plays a role in a larger whole. The whole of the store and how it comes across to the customer. Because that's what it's all about. A customer experiences the store as a whole. And, as mentioned earlier, the store is not experienced in isolation. Personnel, location, products, social media, ...all play a role. Even the spirit of the time plays a role. However, how far the skills of a retail designer should stretch is less clear. Obviously, when I was trained as a retail designer, it was quite simple. The skill set of a retail designer was focussed around the physical store space. Advertisements and catalogues were part of the marketing strategy. Later, when websites and webshops arose, and in the next step also social media, other experts were hired (within a company or as discussed earlier within design agencies) to also cover that and to safeguard consistency throughout all touch-points. This does not answer the question of what skills a retail designer should have, and I am happy to go into this in more detail in the last part of the book because this is, after all, a very existential question that I do not want to go into lightly. But for now, we focus again on the spatial translation of a brand, in whatever form (pop-up, flagship, one off,...).

I like to compare the spatial translation (let's call it the store) to the inside of a mechanical watch. All cogs (shapes, colors, scents, lighting, door handles, singing... every little detail of a store) need to be precisely in sync; when you change one of them it affects the others. It requires knowledge and insight to tune the mechanisms of a store. And the customer only 'sees' the total outcome: the time, so to speak. Then again, each store has its own inner mechanism with an awful lot of cogs. Science tells us that there are certainly similarities in the construction of the inner mechanism and the ratio of the cogs, but no two watches are exactly the same. So, through science we can figure out as much as we can about the mechanics of a store in order to make more knowledgeable design decisions to increase the success rate of a store.

A. Scientific research

The WHAT

Scientific research is characterized by its positioning anchored in studying and thinking with an inherent aim of advancing knowledge. It gathers knowledge in a methodological way (= systematic) where the design and procedures are accurately described (= transparent), with the aim of being able to replicate the research. As a consequence, academic research is most often associated with educational institutions such as universities. At its base, two types of scientific research can be distinguished: fundamental research and applied research. Fundamental research is that part of science that focuses on basic mechanisms and fundamentals. The goal is to create knowledge for the sake of knowledge, without the need for a concrete application in prospect. One of my colleagues did her PhD about theorizing the experience economy. Through her research she developed a framework conceptualizing the phenomenon as such via a thorough screening of scientific literature and studying customer experiences with the help of ethnographic interviews (informal interviews that take place in a natural setting – a store in this case) with retailers, designers and customers. This contrasts with applied research, the part of science that aims to solve a problem or develop a technology, product or service. Scientific applied research is inspired by questions from practice that require solutions or answers. To continue with the example of studying experience, we received funding from the university to take the conclusions from the above PhD one step further to see how we could develop insights to aid practice (designers and retailers) and come up with a solution to help retailers and designers to develop better (experiential) stores. As a part of the study we organized 60 eye-tracking studies combined with in-depth interviews to analyze how people perceive (the experience of) a store, how they act in it and questioning the why behind it. A lot of new insights were gathered from this study which are shared throughout this book. For those who do not know eye-tracking, it is a technique that allows a researcher to follow and track a person's eye movements while walking through the store. It reveals in what direction a person looks, what that person is looking at and for how long. The great advantage of eye-tracking is that it measures both conscious and unconscious gaze behavior. Although people can very well decide where to look and for how long, details of those movements are mostly out of people's control and occur unintentionally. In my opinion, a very honest and valuable research method.

Although people can very well decide where to look and for how long, details of those movements are mostly out of people's control and occur unintentionally.

THE BIG BOOK OF RETAIL DESIGN

What I have always found to be a challenge is the fact that scientific research takes time, something that the business of retail usually does not have. Indeed, shifts in retail are occurring fast so doing scientific research following trends is hard. To give an idea, a typical PhD study takes three to four years. Experimenting also takes time because elements like 'the newness factor', seasons, marketing actions, etc. might have an impact so you need to measure for long enough to exclude such impacts. Also pre-testing and analyzing the results need time. The goal of such research is to get to generalizable results that serve a larger purpose than one retailer. So a study is therefore preferably conducted in different stores or with so much data in one store with a 'mirror store' (a comparable store that is not manipulated) so that the results could be generalized.

The HOW

Does all research need to be scientific in order to be relevant? Of course not. When specific questions are asked by for example a retailer wanting to know how customers behave in his store, whether or not before or after a design change, this question can be studied more simply and purposefully. Note that these results only apply specifically to this retailer in that particular store and that they cannot be generalized. Should there be the opportunity to involve several retailers who are facing the same question and who are subjected to the same study one by one, these results may well be generalizable, as long as the sample is large enough. With the lab we do both, but we will aim to generalize as much as we can so more people can benefit from the knowledge gathered.

From studying the customer...

Studying the customer can be done in various ways. I have talked about eye-tracking studies and in-depth interviews. They both are qualitative in nature as discussed. Other examples are talking to people, observing them, case studies, etc. In qualitative studies the how and why prevails, not the data. When a study is based on data, it is categorized as a quantitative study. Eye-tracking can also be applied in quantitative studies. In that case one needs a multiple of 60 persons. Setting up experiments, conducting surveys, analyzing sales data, etc. are examples of quantitative research. While quantitative studies are very common in the field of marketing, qualitative studies might be more linked to the field of design. But, in retail design research, both are needed. Indeed, on the one hand, understanding the how and the why helps to understand why certain cogs in the watch are bigger or smaller and how that impacts the perception of the watch. On the other hand, quantitative data is needed to understand how one cog impacts the other.

Make no mistake, retail design research is still in its infancy as the design discipline has only just come into existence. I was the first person doing a PhD in interior architecture in Belgium back in 2006. Just like other PhDs in other disciplines before me (there were studies from sociologists, marketeers,...), research relating to store design happened in a rather fragmented way and there was no common ground to start from. The closest related discipline is marketing. Research in marketing is more established and the discipline itself has been around for a long time – it can be traced back to the 1960s. So, building on the results of marketing studies research in retail design is finding its own merits. Gradually, it is becoming clear what we could do as a research field; doing applied research that is relevant and also somewhat timeless, or adaptable to the times. We can be proud of where retail design science already stands today.

As you can see, the boundary with marketing is vague since both disciplines are looking into the customer. It is therefore no coincidence that we often work together on research, from joint PhDs where the impact of design (or design aspects) is measured through experimental studies to helping retailers out with questions they have on measuring their store experience, for example.

...to understanding retail design processes

So besides doing research to understand the customer better, with the lab we do research related to the design process, usually to come up with tools or guidelines to aid designers. Such research starts with looking at and analyzing existing frameworks, either theoretical or from practice. One of my PhD students looked at the ways the design process of stores happened by interviewing 27 retail design practitioners internationally. Another one of my PhD students lat-

THE BIG BOOK OF RETAIL DESIGN

er interviewed another set of designers to do an update of the design process. Indeed, stores and store design are evolving at a rapid pace, so we have to keep up to date with how these stores should be best designed and how that might impact the design process. Based on both studies we developed the Retail Design Process Model (see Part II) which we use as our guidance to develop tools. In the same study we also had a look at what experience today means because if experiences change, then the design process might also need to change. Pine and Gilmore already talked about different phases that evolved over time. Since their books were written some years ago, it is time to estimate or define where we are at today. My PhD student as well as marketing literature, state that retail experiences today need to be valuable. And value can only be derived from the customer. If he or she values it, it is a valuable experience. So this also means that it is personal and varying over time and circumstances. Indeed, one can derive value from an experience at one time, but not at another time. Now, today, a valuable in-store experience combines:

offer & service (including the operational needs of the staff),
physical environment (balance between functional – i.e. routing, store organization – and experiential – i.e. sensory, digital – store design factors, relating to the store location) and
'some delight' (e.g. something going beyond what the customer expects)

The newness about this is the 'some delight'. It makes sense though; experiential retailing is not something that you design once and then leave be. In that case people will only come once. So experiential stores are hard work. It is an investment in time, means and people. Also designing them is not something you do overnight. Of course, there are different levels of experience and many different options to play with. In Part II tools and guidelines are given.

The WHY

Why do we need more knowledge? First of all, because of a specific need. I already discussed that designing stores is not an obvious task and that this has become more and more complex over the years and consequently requires more knowledge. That is why the need for scientific knowledge and research is increasing. Where previously experience, intuition and personal taste were sufficient to make important decisions about the concept and design of a store, today this is no longer sufficient in most cases. The discussion is increasingly shifting from taste to science. A design based on science gives a higher chance of success because through science one knows more about which cogs of the watch have which effect. Indeed, this is not an exact science, but it does help to make more knowledgeable design decisions. Good retail design consists of the combination of knowledge and imagination. Of course, a lot of knowledge is already present among designers and retailers, but the problem is that this knowledge often remains with these parties. Scientific research can provide insights to which everyone can have access. On the other hand, scientific research is increasingly being used to make this implicit knowledge – of designers and retailers – explicit, so that this knowledge can also be disseminated.

Thus, scientific insights should be widely disseminated, but unfortunately this is not always the reality. Scientific knowledge often continues to circulate within academia via the so-called scientific journals. People outside academia do not have access to these, simply because these databases are unaffordable and also not very accessible because if you are not used to reading academic papers and research – it is almost impossible to do so due to the multitude of studies and papers. In addition, people who are in practice usually are interested in the results, but not in the whole set-up and method of the research, which takes up most of such an academic paper. So there is a need for an extra intervention, so to speak, to bring this scientific knowledge to practitioners. This is called the valorization process in the academic world. The process of creating added value from scientific knowledge and expertise outside the scientific field. This is where the Retail Design Lab at Hasselt University plays an essential role. It is precisely our ambition to carry out that process and share the knowledge with practitioners in order to professionalize the discipline. In this case, through this book.

Second, to help people. Yes, helping people. In the medical world, helping people is the obvious reason and this is rarely questioned. It is even taken for granted. Research in retail and retail design is often viewed differently and the idea that if a human is being helped, then it must be the retailer who wants to take more money out of the consumer's pockets, right? This reasoning is understandable and of course stems from how people have looked at advertising and marketing for years. But extending this reasoning to retail design is not entirely correct. The more time passes, the less this will be, since a store is no longer solely the place where you buy products, but that aside. Yes, research is used to better understand the relationship between the customer and the store. Yes, it often includes the buying behavior component, because that's the real dealbreaker. If one really wants to know how a customer feels in a store and if it is appreciated, that is the only thing that solidifies this note of appreciation. And, people don't always do what they say and say what they were really thinking of doing, so asking about possible behaviors or emotions says not enough about the success rate of the store.

A store could be seen as the theater of a retailer, but one you can just enter, without paying.

The only truth is what people really do. After all, you're not going to question the success of a theater or performance by asking how people feel and if they would come back. A theater or theater company or any artist for that matter can only survive if people come back or encourage other people to do so as well. Taking this analogy a little further, for a theater performance, you even have to pay in advance, before you have seen it. A store could be seen as the theater of a retailer, but one you can just enter, without paying. You are not even obligated to buy anything. It is only very much appreciated and even hoped for, because that is the only way that the retailer can survive. Also, don't forget that the retailer has probably already had to make heavy investments to make those products available to the customer, and then again to do it in a good way. So of course the retailer will do everything possible to entice the customer to make a purchase. But you can't give him more power than that, more power he doesn't have. So to move back to research, research can be used to help retailers sell their products and services. As mentioned, customer expectations are so high that retailers also need to be advised by experts (designers, marketeers) on this matter. And in turn, these experts also need insights. So why do researchers do what they do? To help these people. But secretly, we're helping the users too. Because just like going to a theater performance, shopping is also increasingly seen as a relaxing activity (grocery shopping aside). That's one of the reasons consumer demands have increased so much. They want to find entertainment while shopping.

So one may think retail is a 'dirty' business, but it is one of the cornerstones of our society. This is not to say that we should just continue to do as we are doing, heavily under the influence of today's consumerism and materialism. On the contrary, retailers, retail designers and consumers have a responsibilities here. But I will come back to that in the last part of this book.

B. Some truths

We can do a lot of research on the impact of certain design aspects on the customer, but everything still starts with analyzing basic human behavior in stores. Paco Underhill, an environmental psychologist, is a clear founder of this. In his books ('Why We Buy' 1999, 'Call of the Mall' 2004) he unravels human behavior in stores and thoroughly describes what he has seen and learned through his observational studies. Since his books, we are a lot further on in the development of knowledge, but a number of truths have remained unchanged. It is my pleasure to summarize Paco's findings because we still refer to these and use these in teaching retail designers:

- We (still) need to consider the human scale and capabilities, and the fact that these can change with age. So, don't let older people stoop to the bottom shelf to take their products (Paco's famous stay-of-my-butt factor, meaning that when you stoop in too narrow aisles people rub against your behind when passing), and no, don't let them stretch to the top shelf either.
- That same person and their scale sees 'nothing' for the first few meters when entering a store. We are then busy orienting ourselves in the newly entered space and are busy deciding which way to go. So don't put products, baskets or important communications in this zone. Later I will refer to this as the acclimatization zone.
- Something else that Paco Underhill already highlighted as important in his book in 1999, but where people still manage to mess up today, are the fitting rooms. The place where the decision is made whether or not to buy, they sell the deal! Why does this still happen so often in a poorly lit and too small a room? Not enough space to hang all the clothes and spotlight on your head, which causes large shadow spots on the face and makes it impossible to see

a skirt or pants properly, has not yet seduced anyone into buying. The fitting room should be a place where one feels good and where one looks good (and preferably without deception by angled mirrors). This helps to sell clothes and have happy customers.

- The importance of the cash register/pick-up point/info point is also still underestimated and often poorly executed. Both its placement in the store, as its ergonomics (a person only has two hands, so a surface to put a handbag or previous purchases on is handy), and its potential to make the wait more pleasant remain a problem in many stores.

- Another truth is people's orientation. We are trained to drive on the right (in most countries, anyway), the majority of people are also right-handed, which makes us inclined to start our route on the right when we enter a space. Thus, where people are left oriented, conflicts arise between these two currents. The London subway is the perfect example of this. You can easily separate the tourists from the locals based on which side of the staircase they choose. Bringing it back to the store, designing a route counterclockwise is therefore the best solution for right-oriented countries, and clockwise for left-oriented countries.

- A final truth we found in Paco's book is that when customers are busy searching, they are not busy shopping. Even multi-taskers fail to do this. So make it as easy as possible for the customer to find his way around (in the broad sense of the word). Use eye-catchers, for example. These can be used for navigation (visually we are stronger than with letters) and, in strategic places, eye-catchers will stimulate the customer to further explore the store.

I will go deeper into these truths and how to tackle them in the next part of the book. Meanwhile, science has not stood still and we too have already gathered a great deal of knowledge through observational research with the Retail Design Lab. The eye-tracking study mentioned earlier laid the foundations on which all further insights, design guidelines and tools in this book are based. What we learned from this study is that a store design has to start from a retailer's/brand's DNA. Consumers are very sensitive to the message a retailer sends out, and the store is an ideal communication medium for this. We can say that when the functionalities in a store do not meet the basic requirements (e.g. having accessible shelves, restocking sold products, making sure all interactive systems are functioning) the experience does not reach the customer simply because the brain is dealing with these issues. My sketch visualizes what I am trying to say: work from inside out. Very concretely, we found that a store with a clear DNA, good functionalities and a limited investment in experience (but an experience that matches its DNA), scored higher in appreciation by the customer than a store with a very high investment in experience, but a not so clear DNA and/ or functionalities that are not in order. Thus, when people are frustrated about inconsistent messages or products they don't find, they will – literally – not have an eye for experience.

In concrete terms, this means that all tools and guidelines discussed in Part II start from this principle, the DNA. Given the importance of this, in Part II I will also start with a tool to capture and name the DNA of a retailer.

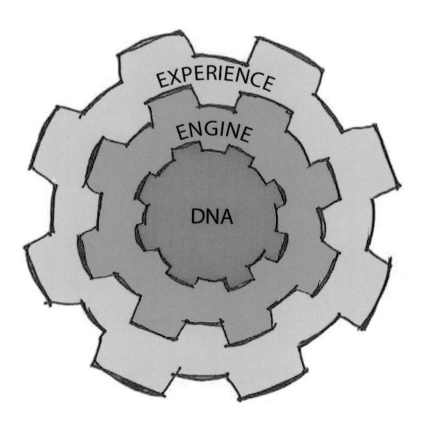

PART
2

Let's move the discussion from taste to science

Y ou would be surprised to learn how often the discussion about designing a store interior is about taste. And this is totally understandable
when it comes to one-man stores where the interior is sometimes an
extension of the owner. But when you want to establish a brand, it is no longer
about taste, at least not that of the CEO or owner, but about the brand and the
target audience that needs to be addressed. I have sat at the table with CEOs of
large chains where an idea can be brushed off the table by the CEO because this
person really doesn't like the proposed color. Indeed, it is not wise to dismiss it
on a personal note. Likewise, we train our students to never use 'because I like
that' as an argument in a retail design process. You always design for someone
or several people with their wishes being paramount. They count on our taste

to bring the whole thing to fruition. So design is definitely about taste, but not about personal preference. But the nice thing about science is that we can rise above taste or measure something that is tasteful to come to insights about what preferences certain (groups of) people have. As I mentioned earlier, science helps us better understand how people interact with spaces, how they react to them and how we can elicit certain emotions and behaviors. A store design today still consists of a good dose of creativity, intuition and science, where the latter is gaining ground.

In the following part, I want to take you through the scientific insights that exist today to design more successful stores. To collect these insights, we received funding a few years ago with the Retail Design Lab. We collect all available scientific insights from scientific journals and books. We sifted through more than 300 reported studies and translated them into guidelines relevant for use by (retailers and designers) and created models to support the design process. In what follows I start by dissecting the design process to then assign tools to specific design phases. Before embarking on the step-by-step development of a store design, there is a set of rules to follow. These rules form the basis or background against which the tools function, independent of the sector, retailer or brand.

Chapter 4

SOME RULES TO PLAY THE GAME

Some rules to play the game

The question on everyone's mind is what kind of store design gets the best store performance. Unfortunately, I do not have the answer to that question because there is no one-size-fits-all. Each brand, each retailer will have a different fit, or even several fits. As mentioned, store design is no exact science. At this moment we do have a good idea of what makes up the inner of the watch, as referred to earlier, but not every detail is known. However, it is about understanding the watch, how it works and what components can and need to be designed. That is what I will discuss next. It is tempting to use this part of the 'big book' to make statements about ergonomics, ideal aisle widths and so on. For the spatial designers amongst us, the Neufert of retail design, so to speak. But that would take me too far. Besides, the Neufert is still a good source for humans and size. Designers are trained in this, so this knowledge is not unique to retail design. So, in what follows I highlight design aspects that typically are part of the domain of retail design. Indeed, retail design is still seen as a specialization in interior architecture. So it is with that lens that the following steps are discussed.

It is good to know that although people change, society at large changes and trends come and go, I have seen some rules to play the retail game that did not change during the last decades. If anything, they just became more outspoken.

Rule #1 is about the DNA

Rule number one in retailing: everything starts from the DNA of the brand. It has to be clear who the brand is and what they stand for. Indeed, we know from our research that a brand's DNA has an impact on who they attract. Also the store has an impact on who is attracted to it. So, it is clear that a retailer should design the store according to its brand DNA for getting the best results and so that a causal relationship can arise between the DNA, the store design and the resulting target group. Consumers are increasingly expecting this. They want to get to know the company, what their values are, so they can check this against their own values. If there is a match, a retailer has his foot in the consumer's door. Standing out as a retailer/brand with such DNA increases this opportunity otherwise one risks becoming a plane Jane, disappearing into the crowd. Why? Because we live in a world of abundance. Abundance in products, but also in stores and services. So, to even get noticed it helps to be different by explicitly expressing who the retailer is and what they stand for, giving the consumer a reason why they should shop with that specific retailer and/or brand (and not with someone else). This process of making retailers, small or large, into a brand is actually the process of branding.

Indeed, further in this book I will only talk about retailers as being brands. I will make no distinction between product brands (usually single brand stores like Nike, Apple, Aesop), retail brands (usually multi-brand stores like most of the food stores, boutiques, but also chains like Target, ASOS) and single stores (bakery, bicycle shop, jewelry store, pharmacy etc.) because once we talk about store design, there should be no difference in how to design them, indeed starting from its DNA. Moreover, we have rapidly moved from the store as a space where products are sold into a place that sells experiences, reinforcing the narrative of the brand. Even in multi-brand stores, the overarching brand (the retailer) is the one the customer will relate to.

Now, how do you build a brand? I am not an expert in marketing nor branding, but there are plenty of experts who are and who have produced clever and useful diagrams, tools and schemes. I have put some of these (well known and often used) diagrams together (e.g. Sinek's golden circle, Kapferer's brand prism, Keller's brand equity pyramid, van Tongeren's retail formula) and looked at them from my (academic) retail design perspective. So, focussing on what a designer needs to know before designing a store. The result is a summary diagram, the Brand Behavior Model, in which the most important aspects a brand needs to pay attention to are set out.

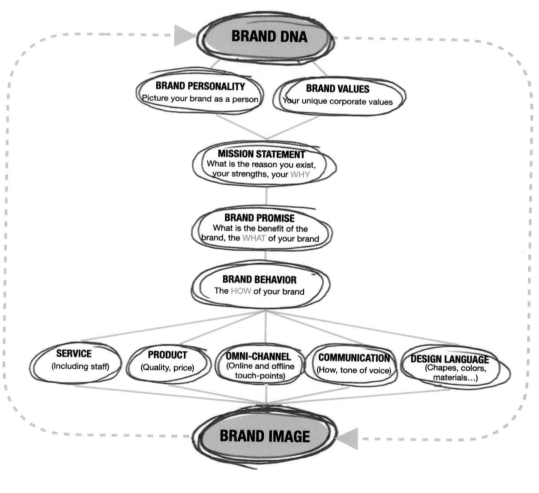

It starts with knowing who you are...

Just as every human is unique, via a genetic code in the DNA, we strive for this uniqueness for brands too (hence this reference to DNA). A brand's DNA consists of a rational side and an emotional side. The rational side is about the (unique) values that a company puts first, the corporate culture. They go about how you interact with customers and other stakeholders. These are values that are mainly communicated internally. Think of values such as responsibility, quality, innovation, transparency, etc. The emotional side is about personal values. Try to imagine the brand as a person; what kind of person would it be? Typically, personality traits emerge here such as energetic, friendly, strict, formal, ... To keep it simple, let me take IKEA, which everyone knows, as an example. IKEA's rational values are 'people, planet positive, ethical'. These are terms you can find on their website. These terms define IKEA's corporate culture. If we then look at the emotional brand values, we start imagining that IKEA is a person. So what kind of person would it be? I see IKEA as someone who is smooth, relaxed with a playful touch, yet also organized and distinct. And, someone who values family.

It is a fun exercise in itself, turning brands into people.

It is a fun exercise in itself, turning brands into people. Let's do another one. Think of Amazon, which is a whole different person to IKEA. I see Amazon as a bossy person, wanting to be the best all the time (a bit annoying sometimes), but also a curious person who thinks big. Their rational values are customer obsession, inventive, operational excellence, long-term thinking. As you have probably noticed, for brands with a strong DNA, this exercise is easier to do than for brands that are more vague or less pronounced. Note that also for new brands the same exercise needs to be done and because there is no legacy yet, it offers the opportunity to be very specific and unique in this. A clear set of values forms the basis for everything that follows: whenever decisions need to be made about marketing strategies, communications, design, etc. it should be done with this set of values in mind.

...to WHY you exist...

The next aspect in the Brand Behavior Model is THE WHY behind the brand. Why does the brand exist? What is their strength? I call this the mission of the brand. Some examples of a mission are: putting food products first that are all organically grown or raised; or being there to make the world a little greener; or making sure your clothing is timeless. Also, don't forget to do this in accordance with the intended audience. What are they lying awake over? What is going on in society at large (or in the place where the brand is based)? If I may refer again to IKEA, their reason for existence, the one thing that makes them unique today is that they offer affordable interior design solutions that are also compact. More than 55% of the world's population lives in cities. So most of them live compactly. And most people want to make their homes cosy with affordable design that, above all, also makes our homes better (organized) from a functional point of view.

...and WHAT makes you relevant...

Once the mission is clear, look at THE WHAT, what does the brand promise to the customer. In other words, what benefit does the customer get from shopping with this brand? Some examples: a promise to always have fresh local produce; a promise to sell only green cars; or the promise to only offer quality basics for one's wardrobe. Looking at the examples you see that the three missions mentioned earlier have a link with the three promises (the first example of a mission links with the first example of a promise, and so on). So the promise is a consequence of the mission. Again, do this in relation to the target group. What problem can the brand solve for them? Referring to IKEA, they promise a better daily life for as many people as possible. The relevancy of a brand can often be found in their advertisement. IKEA always show daily issues in a house with a family (indeed, the family being the target group). They show that they have solutions for daily problems like stacking, organizing, cooking, etc. without compromising on space and coziness.

...putting it all to life in HOW you behave

This is where it all comes together. If the DNA, the mission and promise are clear, the brand behavior can be determined. This is about THE HOW of the brand. How is the brand going to establish all of the above? How will the brand behave in the world? This behavior translates into five sub-aspects:

- What **service** is offered? Think about the level of service as well as how the staff should behave. This is an extremely important aspect of a brand's behavior. Offering a certain service can make it unique. Just as the people who work for the brand and interact with the customers can do too. Note that service can also imply organizing events, offering education, or hospitality. Service is about how you stay relevant to the customer. IKEA's services have expanded during the last decade. From a pure self-service retailer they added services like kitchen advice, having products delivered and even having them installed, and loans. Hospitality, their restaurant, was there from the beginning.
- What **products** are sold? What quality is pursued? What is the pricing strategy (note that only one can be the cheapest, so the rest must use a different strategy). If I zoom in for a moment on retailer brands (leaving aside product brands for a moment) that sell different brands or that offer a lot of depth within a product segment (many variations within a segment, such as a plant center) or that have a very wide range of products (many types of products as a hypermarket does, for example), the selection of products on offer is very important. Everything is available online, so a store cannot handle this competition. There is no point in offering as much as possible, it is about offering carefully selected products. A retail brand should act as a curator. Somebody who knows his way in the world of abundance and picks just the right products. By doing that, he earns trust from the customer, whether it is about quality, uniqueness or taste. He guarantees a good selection. I think that is still a retailer's strength today. I like to think of them as passionate curators.

If they do their job well, they will create a fan base. Brands who produce their own products, like IKEA, the brand itself should focus on products relevant for their target group without losing who they are as a brand. IKEA has been expanding its product range step by step, without making too crazy leaps. For instance, offering a variety of mattresses is a logical consequence of offering beds, and offering taps and kitchen appliances Is a logical consequence because it closely matches their kitchens. Now that a move into electrical supplies has been made, IKEA could safely take this further by also offering other electrical appliances that can be used in and around the kitchen. The stronger the brand, the greater the product elasticity.

- Through which **channels** is the brand available to the customer? Which channels are deployed as sales channels and which as communication channels? It is certainly not the intention here to offer products everywhere and at all times. Align this with the target group. Which channels do they use to communicate and/or buy? IKEA is another great example of this. Although we are going digital en masse, IKEA still published its very distinctive catalogue until 2020. And even now, people are still asking for it. A big chunk of their target group wasn't ready yet to go fully online (it needs to be said that another chunk was waiting for it). But the digital evolution combined with sustainability made IKEA decide to stop doing this anyway. They are now betting very strongly on inspiring online. They have even become one of the frontrunners in augmented reality through their app which helps customers to see a piece of furniture in their homes. Indeed, one has to go where the target group goes.

- How is the customer **communicated** with on each channel? This could be in a very smooth way or humorous or just very polite. This is referred to as the 'tone of voice'. The tone of voice is determined by the brand personality and the target audience. Of course, it makes sense to try to connect with the latter. Note that the tone of voice can change per channel. It is accepted that people use a looser language on Instagram than on a website, for instance. But it should still be consistent with the brand. For example, IKEA, being proud of their origin, addresses its target audience worldwide with 'hej' in a mail, which means 'hello' in Swedish (and this is also neatly explained at the bottom of the mail with an asterisk). Concerning the names of the products, they stay very close to themselves. Did you know that each product has a name of a river, a stream, a puddle or a place in Sweden? Given the extensive collection of products, girls' names and boys' names have also been added. Although most people don't understand it and don't make the link, it does convey the atmosphere and culture of Sweden.

- What **design language** suits the brand? This involves both colors, shapes and material choices for all channels and touch-points (online and offline). As mentioned earlier, this needs to be consistent through all channels. I will discuss this in great detail when we tackle the subject of designing for retail.

The five sub-aspects of brand behavior play a role in how the brand comes across to the target group. In other words, they determine the image of the brand, being a result of public perception built over time as a result of every experience (big or small, from an ad to a store visit) with the brand. In the ideal situation, this image corresponds to the identity of the brand. So what a brand wants to be is also perceived as such by the customers. If this is not in line, something went wrong somewhere in how the brand behaves. Of course, it is also true that a brand needs to make every choice and decision involving this Brand Behavior Model with the consumer in mind. For IKEA you could summarize the how in: making it easy and fun for customers to shop.

Note that the physical store is one aspect out of the omni-channel strategy, interlacing communication and design language. So, if the design of the store is not in line with the DNA of a brand (which happens a lot actually) the other brand behavior aspects (service and product) are becoming more essential to communicate the DNA. This is not insurmountable, but if the store plays its part (read: shows DNA), it strengthens the brand's message. Store design is a means, not an end in itself. And within this design, even what might seem to be a small detail that is not in sync with the (future) identity may distort the image of the brand. Which brings me seamlessly to my next rule.

Rule #2 is about coherency, consistency and detail

Again, this is not something new, but retail is more and more about coherence. The more channels, the more touch-points, the more the need for coherence. Every stimulus that the customer receives from a brand must fit within the DNA of the brand. This is often a huge challenge for both large and small brands. Remember the example I gave about small brands often having the problem that for different channels, they call on different experts who each give their own vision and translation of the brand into a store, or website, or advertising, etc. If the brand then doesn't act as a design manager as we discussed earlier, things go wrong. But large brands are also faced with similar problems because different people within the company have different opinions and responsibilities, usually each working with their own team so the brand message can easily be lost. So coherence is about making sure the same brand message is broadly communicated, across people and channels.

Consistency is about doing this rigorously, down to the smallest detail. Again, this from all channels to the plinth in the toilet. Let me illustrate with an example on the shop floor that what might be seen as an insignificant detail to the brand might have a huge impact on the customer. It just so happens that you are a customer in an expensive boutique looking for a beautiful dress for your cousin's wedding in the summer. When you take your silk dress to the fitting room it turns out that the curtain of the fitting room feels like an old shower curtain. In addition, the place where everyone grabs the curtain is also dirty from the many touches. The curtain also closes badly so there is always an opening. And don't let me even start about all that goes wrong with lighting in fitting rooms (I will do that later, don't worry). Does this sound familiar? Or when you are trying on shoes and there are only mirrors available that only show your legs from your knees down. And the one big mirror that is there only allows you to stand 1 meter away. I'm sure you also know of a toy store where your child is not allowed to go to the bathroom. Minor detail? I don't think so. Customer service can hardly be called a detail. And who is the customer in a toy store? The child indeed. So, know the customer! Over to rule #3.

Rule #3 is about knowing the customer

Use data as a basis...

Customers – that's what it's been all about for as long as we've been in business, although they have never had so much power as today. What causes that, we all know by now. The Internet. Consumer power rose the moment people could share their opinions online. And not just within their circle of acquaintances, but with the whole world. The impact of such opinions is huge. Indeed, the impact of negative feedback is ten times greater than positive feedback. So it is best for a brand not to generate negative feedback. And if it does, it should respond to it appropriately. Now, the Internet also helps us get to know the customer better. So much data exists around each person that it is sometimes grim how much you can find out about someone. Anyway, using data smartly is easier said than done. Without a proper data management plan, one gets nowhere. And, the European General Data Protection Regulation (GDPR) and the California Consumer Privacy Act (CCPA, which impacts all of America) doesn't make it any easier. But it is all out there. Step one is definitely starting a customer database digitally.

...but it's really about empathy

Although we have more resources to know consumers, they have become more complex. Knowing the customer is not so obvious these days. There are several reasons for this. I have already discussed the fact that generations have long ceased to be generations (in terms of shopping behavior). But customers nowadays have become very complacent and lazy; they do what suits them best. I can't blame them because the world is at their feet. There is abundance in everything, so why go to more trouble than necessary? We even experienced this literally. A few years ago we conducted an experiment in which participants were asked to shop in a simulated supermarket. The idea was to let the customer choose products from differently lit shelves. We expected that each time the customer would choose the product that looked best (i.e. under better lighting conditions) over the product that looked inferior but nothing was further from the truth. No matter what setup we used (each rack was duplicated so we could vary the lighting), the customer always took the product from the first rack they encountered. Well, why would they take another step for the same product (even if it looks better)!? I guess often the same goes for choosing the store for shopping for necessities. Most people will naturally choose the nearest location (proximity is a clue in itself) UNLESS another store has something more valuable to offer (e.g. better quality, nicer service, etc). But, as soon as that value disappears, or gets overruled by another store, people will change their preferred choice. This choice can even be overruled by pragmatic reasons like time constraints, special price offers, but even social reasons like the occasion one is shopping for (daily groceries versus shopping for a candlelit dinner or a party). As

THE BIG BOOK OF RETAIL DESIGN

a result, customers are not only less loyal, they are schizophrenic. One day they are this and another day they are that. One day they feel great and are in for a shopping treat, and another day they might be frustrated and sad so not really in for a jolly holly shopping experience. When the involvement of the shopping changes, like buying a dress for a wedding party, the motivation changes, and so does the behavior. For high involvement products people will take the extra time and effort to find it. For low involvement products convenience might come first. I realize I am not making it sound like there is a way to understand the customer let alone to design for them, but there is. The power of good retail design often lies in the empathy (= understanding feelings, not just sympathizing with them) of the brand and the retail designer. If one understands and knows the customer, the ideal store can be designed. As will be explained further down in the 'optimizing the retail design process' section, shopping motivations and personas are ideal instruments to empathize with the customer.

One day they feel great and are in for a shopping treat, and another day they might be frustrated and sad so not really in for a jolly holly shopping experience.

Rule #4a is about an image saying more than a thousand words

From product presentation....

We all know the expression: an image says more than a thousand words, yet we don't seem to realise that the store design and resulting look and feel of a store does exactly the same. A store paints an image about the who and the what of the brand. When customers enter a store, what they see is also what they expect to get. A neat store where the products get all the attention they need tells a very different story than a store where (even if only at the end of the day) it is a mess and the same products are mixed up. Where do you think the customer is willing to pay most for the same products? Every product evokes a certain level of willingness to pay, but so does a store and its product presentation. This is why discount brands are very fearful of making their stores too fancy or too designed. Customers may then think the products have become more expensive. Products and store design should best match in terms of price perception. But it's not just about cheap or expensive, it's also about the love of a product. A brand that is crazy about their own products will display them in a different way than someone for whom this is just doing business. If a brand does not treat his own products with love and respect, why would a customer? And why would they want to pay for it?

...to the design of the store...

There is more than just product presentation though. Materials, colors, shapes, lighting, details,... all make up the total image you see. And they each have a role to fulfill in communicating the brand story. The word 'image' suggests that it is about the visual. And that is, of course, true. But everything a person feels, smells, hears and experiences in a store also plays a role in the mental image we get of a store. So a store and its design should largely tell the story of the brand itself, without interference from the staff. Mind you, it is not easy to make a customer understand a store the way the designer intended it to be. It takes a fair amount of skill to know how a store will be perceived by the target audience. Besides understanding the target group, this also requires understanding how materials, colors, shapes and any other stimuli come across to people. But more on that later.

...and the care of the shop

Apart from design, orderliness and cleanliness also play a role. A beautiful store design where clutter takes over obviously misses the mark. Think of poorly maintained shops, unpacked boxes in aisles. Of course, when someone from the staff is standing by and working on it, this does not pose a problem, but boxes just sitting there for several hours is actually bad. Although this is temporary, a new customer may come in just at that moment. What image do you think that person will have of the shop? There are a thousand examples of such flows. For instance, I have already come across retailers who advertise that they sell TVs and come to install them at home, while the cables wriggle in a tangle on the floor in the store. That doesn't exactly inspire confidence, does it? Or kitchen dealers where no attention has been paid to detail in the showroom so work-tops are crooked and skirting boards are not made to measure. But there are also supermarkets where stock trolleys (empty or full) are left standing in aisles for hours, lingerie shops where the lingerie looks like it's on sale all year long due to unkempt presentation and overstuffed shelves. I could go on for a long time, but my point is clear, I think. At any time of the day, a store should look perfect (whatever that means within the brand story). Why? First, customers are increasingly bothered by this. We recognise from research that the basket of negative incentives is filled more quickly than it was a few years ago. Custom-ers are less and less tolerant meaning that the bar is getting higher and higher. When a brand does not reach the bar, they will switch to another brand, which does reach the bar. As John Furner (CEO of Walmart) says: loyalty is the lack of something better. I would not go so far as to say that, but there is some truth in it, but as long as you do not give the customer a reason to look elsewhere, you are safe. Second, any time of the day new customers can come in. Indeed, just like we judge people we meet for the first time, we judge stores exactly the same, leading me to the second part of this rule.

At any time of the day, a store should look perfect.

Rule #4b is about having that one chance only

Any second of every day could be somebody's first time in the store. That first moment can be at 10 o'clock in the morning, but also at five to six in the evening. Whatever time of day it is, that image must be the same, just as orderly, just as filled with products, just as nicely decorated,... I would also like to emphasize that very first image a customer gets when walking through the entrance of the store. The image, when entering or looking inside the store must be designed with the necessary attention. Research shows that the view through the door was a bigger determinant than shop windows for entering a store. What does the customer see when entering or having a peek in the store? Everything? Or do you attract attention by placing a presentation table right at the entrance? Do you want the customer to see the cash register immediately or just barely? These are all questions that need to be served with a thoughtful answer. A customer who sees something he doesn't like will simply walk through after peeping in or even turn around when standing in the doorway. So make sure to lower the threshold by opening shop windows, use visible lighting that is clearly on when the store is open, and make a strong first impression. This again leans towards expectation management as cited earlier. This is even more so when customers have certain expectations due to having seen the website, or shop window. Make sure that that very first encounter with the physical store counts.

Chapter 5

DESIGNING FOR RETAIL

Designing for retail

When designing physical stores or outlets we always start from the golden triangle: customer – retailer – designer. It is the retail designer's task in this triangular relationship to bring both the needs of the retailer and the customer into balance in the store design. This is specific to retail, making the design process slightly different from the design process of, say, a house, with the biggest difference that for designing a house you design for one family and for a store you design for thousands of families. The difference in client also plays a role. With a house the client is often the same as the end user. With a store, there are many more stakeholders involved. And the client is only one of the users. While in most interior design assignments, understanding a building and its (future) occupants is the starting point and subject of investigation, in retail design the brand and its (future) customers are the starting point, and the building or site often comes later. Indeed, retail design has more similarities with designing for public buildings, such as museums and cultural centers, and also hotels and restaurants since all have to deal with a variety of users and stakeholders such as the staff and the users of the space. As designers it is essential to take everyone's wishes and needs into account when designing these spaces. But, what makes designing for retail different from the previous examples? Apart from the difference in the type of experience they offer as I explained earlier, I see two additional differences, the time a user stays in the space and the purpose of the space. The time a user spends in a retail space is on average much shorter than the time spent in museums, hotels and restaurants. In addition, the purpose of the space is also different. Stores are there to allow products to be experienced and make profit out of it. Especially the latter makes the difference very clear: a store in most cases has to bring in money, some-one has to be able to live from it (within only a relatively short time of interaction). So the combination of **time X purpose** makes this sector unique. Again, this is not to say that there can be no cross-fertilization between the aforementioned sec-tors. On the contrary, museums are increasingly being run commercially and are adopting design principles from retail. The other way around is also a fact. Stores have, as seen in the past, adopted museum settings to display their merchandise. Aqualex (see sketch) took it one step further by mixing an art gallery with a show-room, elevating the water tap to the level of art. The line between hospitality and retail is also becoming increasingly blurred. On the one hand, these functions are often mixed in concept stores, on the other hand, we should also see the retail sec-tor more and more as a service oriented sector. But more on that later.

Before I explain the retail design process, it is of importance to understand how customers perceive a store. Based on our research we have gained insights on how different design aspects have a different impact on the total store experi-ence, or how a customer perceives a store. Because in a retail context every per-cent counts, there is an ever-increasing trend towards measurability and quan-

THE BIG BOOK OF RETAIL DESIGN

tifiability. We have spent years with the lab developing a research method that can map the shopping experience as objectively and reliably as possible without spending a lot of time and money on customer research each time. Although the retail experience is holistic in nature, it is possible to make statements about different layers of a design, or the cogs of the watch I referred to earlier. As such, the following sketch shows the spatial implementation (literally everything outside the fixed elements such as the building itself) makes the biggest impression on the customer, namely 40%. Second in line is the sensory experience with an impact of 25%. Less obvious is the impact that communication can have on the customer, namely 10%. I notice that this is an often forgotten layer when architects or interior designers not specialized in retail design a store. By 360° experience, 9% of the total impact, I mean the integration of online and digital tools, but also the uniqueness of a store involving products, the staff and the concept, and the earlier mentioned delight factor. The interior shell (floor, ceiling and walls) and the exterior (the facade, signing, accessibility) each play a role of 8% in the total customer experience.

Building further on this knowledge we have developed a tool consisting of a scoring grid comprising more than 90 questions, each with its own weight in the total score. So, instead of doing a lot of customer research, an expert can now use the tool to scan a store experience, which takes about one hour. We have called the tool REXS, which stand for Retail Experience Scan. In short it is a science-based tool that allows all relevant components of a physical shopping experience to be mapped and scored objectively. It is based on 15 years of research at the Retail Design Lab added to research around retail design from universities worldwide. And although the scan does not query the customer, the customer and their experience was always at the center of its development. So REXS is indeed , based on research with customers.

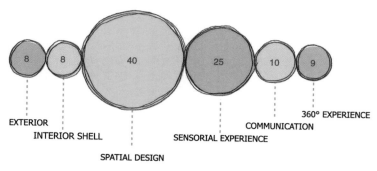

EXTERIOR

INTERIOR SHELL

SPATIAL DESIGN

SENSORIAL EXPERIENCE

COMMUNICATION

360° EXPERIENCE

A. Understanding the retail design process

To understand the complexity and uniqueness of the retail design process, the Retail Design Lab team mapped out the design process after having numerous interviews with designers in Europe. My doctoral students concluded after analyzing and synthesizing all data that six design phases can be distinguished. The analyses and the research behind them has been published in academic journals so I don't want to talk about that now. I want to show you the result, which the following sketch visualizes.

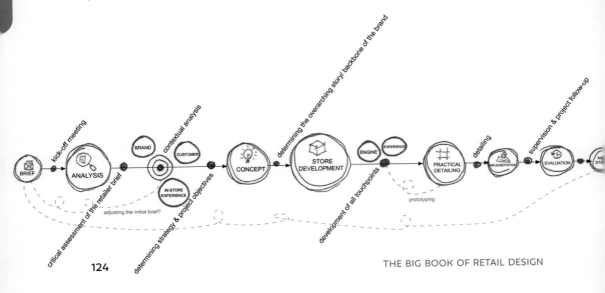

THE BIG BOOK OF RETAIL DESIGN

The retail design process is divided into seven phases: defining the need, the analysis of the task, the concept design, the store development, the (practical) detailing of the design, the implementation, the use and evaluation (and maybe back to the drawing board again). Note that designers do not work in clearly de-limited phases. However, this subdivision makes it possible to give a clear over-view of the designer's main activities.

It all starts with a thorough design brief...

The first phase starts with the retailer who experiences a certain need or prob-lem. After having defined a retail strategy and a project objective, a creative partnership can start between the retailer and the design agency. In the best cases the retail designer receives a design brief with an exhaustive overview of information concerning the retailer's project objective, the market, the target group, the defined brand DNA, the retail strategy and the practical and financial constraints. But there are also a lot of brands that are not (yet) that far advanced strategically and for whom this is quite an exercise. In that case, retail designers often take the time and responsibility to figure this out and shape it further. The strange thing is that this does not depend on the size of a brand or its age. We have worked with brands that already had quite a few shops (more than 100) but where a clear WHY and HOW were simply missing. And we also see SMEs that do know very clearly what they stand for and where they want to go. Anyway, a design brief will both inform and constrain the retail designer as it gives a con-text from which to work.

...but usually, more research is needed...

When the brief is given, a second phase starts, the analysis phase. This is a phase in which happens a lot. It is also a phase that you can make as long or as short as you want or as needed. The steps that need to be taken are: critical analysis of the design brief, analysis of the context, and determining the strategy. This step is the most subject to time and budget. As a minimum, in this step a designer must first gather and analyze (additional) information. It is a phase in which em-phasizing skills are key. Designers must immerse themselves into the customer and the brand DNA, while already considering the in-store experience.

Regarding the customer, it happens that brands ask retail designers or creative agencies to do more research into the target group for example. Or the afore-mentioned eye-tracking studies were also part of this phase. Indeed, retail design projects consist of an important research component, which is related to disciplines such as marketing and social sciences that impinge more and more on the domain of retail design. It is definitely also the phase where the brand and the design brief are challenged. Designers have a good critical eye and are usually well informed about what is going on in the retail landscape. That is exactly what makes them a good party to work with. Another relevant skill of designers is that they are traditionally 'specialised generalists', who have learned to accept the uncertainty of 'not knowing everything'. This skill is needed to cut knots and make (design) decisions in the creative process. For me, analysis is part of the creative process because it inherently goes hand in hand with decision-making and ideation. Not coincidentally, 'empathizing' and ideation are two key steps in the very popular design thinking workshops given to companies worldwide.

Regarding analyzing the DNA, it may happen that due to all the knowledge gathered, the initial design brief needs to be adjusted. It once happened that the analysis that we did for one of our clients needed to be updated after they briefed us on their brand DNA. But our analysis showed that in the mind of the consumer these traits no longer matched how the brand was perceived. We discovered that the brand had evolved from the bottom up due to initiatives introduced by various retail managers at different locations, that influenced the brand perception. Luckily, the image had changed for the better, so it was a matter of getting corporate on board again with these newly acquired traits.

Maybe somewhat surprisingly, or new for many designers is that considering the intended in-store experience should already take place in this phase. Remember that I mentioned that one of my PhD students has been studying this phase and the role of the physical store and has come to the conclusion that in order to attract customers, the store must provide a valuable in-store experience which combines offer and service, with a physical environment and 'some delight'. The latter pushes retail designers to reflect on bringing a sense of difference, novelty or discovery to the store. More importantly, is that this is not designed at the end of the design journey, but in this early phase. As a first step towards bringing something delightful, retail designers might want to look at what is happening in the retail landscape and world at large – e.g. what their brand competitors are doing. Next, retail designers should also look beyond what already exists and focus on the future. Note that not every retailer has the ambition to be innovative, though to stand out moving forward is key.

It pushes retail designers to reflect on bringing a sense of difference, novelty or discovery to the store.

So, simultaneously with the analysis, the first conceptual ideas might arise, usually without making them explicit yet. This is the moment that interesting things happen and that is often perceived as being complex. The complexity originates from the triangular relationship between the designer, the retailer/brand and the customer, as mentioned earlier. Translating the values of both the retailer and the customer into a store design, taking into account boundary conditions such as budget, retail legislation and commercial policy – which have a huge impact on the proliferation of retail formats – is key. Remember that usually other designers/consultants are also included, such as marketers, (digital) communication designers, product designers, etc ., and that they can be part of the retail design agency, part of the brand or be independent.

...to come up with the concept...

In this phase, the third one of the creative process, design teams engage in brain-storming sessions, in which they are free to dream without restrictions (in a later phase, designers gradually shift from abstract to more concrete conceptual ideas, which should be practically and financially feasible). It is also the most difficult part in the whole process because at this point, the big idea, or the concept is formed. It is here that the skills of the retail designer are tested. It is probably the most mysterious phase as well. A phase where all the magic happens. I would like to compare it to cooking. All the ingredients are there, but it is the chef who decides what to do with them and which magic happens when using these ingredients. A designer is therefore similar to a chef. An idea needs to rise from all the gathered knowledge and insights (ingredients). So forgive me as I cannot give a tool or method to do this. Neither can a chef when he starts cooking. After the magic happened, one can explain what was done, but there is no formula, just a healthy dose of creativity. When studying retail design in Rotterdam, this was the most difficult part in the beginning. Coming up with 'the big idea' is harder than it sounds. Usually as an interior architect you have several ideas, one for the cash desk, one for the fitting room, and so on. But in retail, to get people on board and to communicate the brand's message, a sum of loose ideas won't seal the deal. I learned to start with a big idea for the overall concept, that is then translated into the cash desk, fitting rooms, etc. So it is really working top down, starting with the brand DNA, figuring out 'the big idea' and then making it work throughout the design. Never bottom up – you will get lost that way.

...which will embody the design...

Designers shape the big idea, defining aesthetic, atmospheric and functional retail design variables.

During the fourth phase, the embodiment of the design, designers shape the big idea, defining aesthetic, atmospheric and functional retail design variables, as I show in my sketch, relating to the exterior, the interior, the furniture, communication etc. It is the designer's task to orchestrate these design variables consistently and coherently into a holistic store experience, which is in line with the defined brand DNA. During the last decade I noticed a shift in store design. I was trained as a retail designer making sure that the design of the store operates as a backbone, or support, for making the products shine. I was trained to never design an empty store, to always draw products in to see how the store made the products shine. Today, the design of the store itself receives much more attention. The architecture of the store can create an experience in itself. This is fundamentally different from a decade ago. Today, I train my students to understand that the design of the store must radiate what the brand stands for, even without the products in it. This is also always an interesting exercise for brands when they are thinking very product focused, even in terms of store design. I ask them to imagine their store without products in it; does the customer still see what the brand/store stands for?

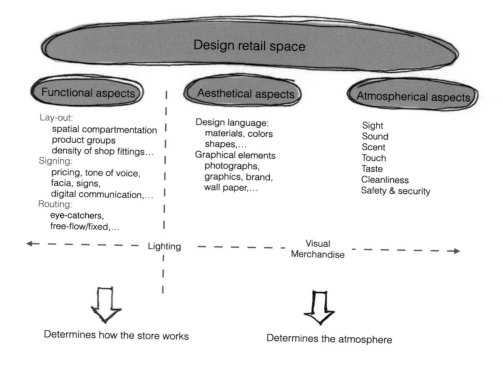

The sketch visualizes the different aspects of design, that is, the aspects that a retail designer will probably encounter and needs to answer during the design process. Although a design for a store can be clustered in three aspects: functional, aesthetic and atmospheric, the division between them is not strict. Just like visual merchandising can function within all three aspects, concrete designerly considerations and choices such as lighting, for example, can too. On a functional level product presentation and lighting are both needed to make a store work. On a next level, beautiful product displays lit with crisp bright lighting have an aesthetic value. If general lighting is alternated with accent and indirect lighting, this clearly creates a certain atmosphere (beyond the purely functional). Product presentation can also be more than just pretty, by involving more senses in a display and by doing so in different places in a shop, product presentation transcends the functional and aesthetic.

Note that these elements do not function in isolation, but together generate the holistic experience of a retail space. This holistic aspect has become increasingly important and includes integrating every aspect very consciously and consistently.

...till the smallest detail...

The fifth phase is characterized by detailing the design and finalising the solution. In the case of a one-off store, the design drawings are made immediately. In contrast, when designing for chains, before detailed drawings are made, the conceptual store design must be translated into the actual spaces. This due to the fact that designers tend to work in a conceptual space, a white box, which represents the ideal store environment. Once the conceptual design is signed off by the brand, the agency continues to translate the design into the different locations. This is also the phase in which prototyping happens. Sometimes design agencies make mock-ups to test specific elements, furniture or spacial organization. However, brands also often do this in-house. Many of the larger brands experiment quite a lot in simulated stores. This goes from actual labs to virtual simulations. Anyway, prototyping helps to see whether the design meets the expectations. If not, it means going back to the drawing board.

Depending on the nature of the design task, the retail designer's role might stop at the conceptual design. In this case, a concept manual will be composed and handed over to the brand, who will further manage the production and the implementation of the concept. Such a manual can contain more general information or can go really into detail, from how to use the logo in the space to determining the floor, walls and furniture.

Some retail design agencies or consultants, as we are in the Retail Design Lab, already end the process with the presentation of the concept. So to get to the detailing, another actor is needed (could be an (interior) architect or a contractor or even a carpenter where drawers take over). It's fair to say that just delivering concepts is very fine; that's what we are trained for and where my heart lies. On the other hand, from that point on, you do relinquish control so the advice or concept may not always stand up 100%. Costs, different insights from the parties taking over, time constraints, ... are all reasons why concepts are sometimes diluted.

...constructed on the shop floor...

When design agencies offer the full service the final phases kick in. During the sixth phase, the whole concept will be implemented and constructed on site. This process is not very different from other construction processes. The importance of like-minded, competent and trustworthy partners are all key to the successful delivery of a project. Usually via a tender process such partners are found. What might be a bit different in retail, or what is more pronounced due to the impact, are deadlines. Especially when shops undergo a full remodeling, it has to be done as fast as possible considering the store is closed during that time. It is therefore normal to act here with strict deadlines and accompanying clauses to minimise losses. One such clause, for example, is a penalty for the contractor for each day the completion is late. And these are serious amounts. This is why it is so important to work with partners and contractors who can handle this and who have the right scale to be able to work in this way. But even with new shops, time is money.

What I regret here, but understand, is that sometimes time is more important than quality. Due to the often short delivery periods, certain materials are already simply not used because of drying times (think of a cast floor that needs to dry for a week) or because of availability of a material. Thus, choices are sometimes made that weaken the design. This is also sometimes accompanied by a negative impact on sustainability. Unfortunately, it is sometimes faster to get a material from China than a locally sourced material. As I will explain later, in Part III, sustainable retail design asks for a different approach in which both brands and designers need to take up responsibility.

...ready to be evaluated

The store will be subjected to a profound in-use evaluation in the last phase of the process. But is it really the last step? In the past it definitely was. Today, I see a different view of the design process and what a design agency delivers. So where before the process ended with an evaluation of the store to inform the retailer and the designer if further optimizations and adaptions of the store concept (for the design itself or for future store developments – roll outs) are necessary, it is now more a starting point. Indeed, the delivery and opening of a new store should not end the retail design process, for the obvious reason that a store will always remain subjected to the changing market and customer. There are several reasons why I say this.

The delivery and opening of a new store should not end the retail design process.

The first reason is that the store is only one aspect of the whole customer jour-ney and it is not always easy to assess what its role is exactly. It is only when the store starts playing its role that it often becomes clear how it impacts all the oth-er touch-points. Things can be so well thought out, but the reality is sometimes just different. And in my opinion, that's also totally ok in today's society. We are still exploring the role of the store in the digital society. And when we think we know, there are new developments. So it's ok to test and experiment. That also means that a design process does not stop at the (first) design delivery.

A second reason is that in order to compete and stay relevant, stores need to be able to adapt quickly. Given everything changes so quickly, a store should be able to do the same. To this end, flexible furniture that allows a retailer to play around with and to surprise the customer each time with such changes is the way to move forward. A design process should not end at the design delivery, but should question the design again, including customers in that process. This in contrast with having a store renovated every cycle of seven years, leaving the old store's interior to the scrapyard.

Thus, designers need to look at their designs differently. One of the great exam-ples in this is Brinkworth design from London. They started to question whether a store should remain the same and for how long? Brinkworth approaches a store as an 'activation space for retail'. It is apparent that a space created needs room to grow and breathe with its evolving function. To this end a store needs some level of flexibility so the brand is given the option of staying ahead of the competition and anticipating future change. Inevitably, as Brinkworth also does to some extent, design agencies will also have to start thinking more in terms of services. The execution and delivery of a design is only part of their service. Another important part then becomes follow-up, evaluation and adjustment. Call it a kind of maintenance service.

B. Optimizing the retail design process

To improve the retail design process and make informed design choices, we have developed a set of tools to help at each phase of the process. The tools are designed based on the combination of academic knowledge and practical insights. The result is a toolbox that can be deployed and used in different ways. It has been extensively tested over the past years with different target groups in different contexts (students in different international universities, professors who want to teach retail, workshops with designers, projects with brands and retailers). For each target group (education, designers, and retailers) specific preconditions and information have been added in what follows so that you can see the use of the tools as a manual or even a menu. Note that I only discuss the tools that are specific for retail design. General tools, like moodboards for example, are not discussed. The same goes for design knowledge; only specific retail design related aspects are discussed. The tools are focused on the design phases of the process (so up to Phase 4). Apart from our REXS experience scan that I mentioned earlier, which is situated at the end of the design proces. REXS can be used to evaluate the store design once completed or it can serve as a starting point of a (partial) remodeling.

Besides developing these tools, in recent years we have archived reports of research into retail design published in scientific literature. From these studies (such as the impact of scent on consumers, the importance of branding in shops, the role of design on customer perception, etc.), we have formulated 130 guidelines that help brands and designers make informed choices when developing a store design. Our guidelines are included in this section, and they appear on our Retail Design Lab website. These can be quoted and are numbered explicitly.

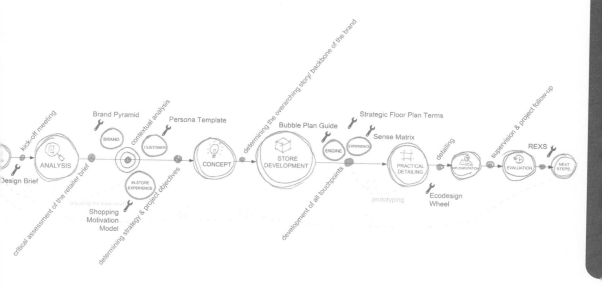

Toolbox#education

In recent years, I have taught one-week retail design workshops at several universities in Europe and South Africa. We have also been organizing an international summer school of retail design on our campus every year since 2014, which students from all over the world come to. The tools have always been the core of these courses. This has allowed me to fine-tune them and test them for effectiveness. In this context, the Design Brief, the Brand Pyramid, the Bubble Diagram and the Sense Matrix are the most popular. We have even received feedback from both students and professors that these tools can also serve within other sectors such as hospitality, museums and other public buildings.

 Want to teach students how to design for stores? Then be sure to read the 'how to teach this tool' parts, indicated with this academic cap.

Toolbox#designer

As a trained designer, I understand all too well the uniqueness of each designer. As such, it is not our intention to curtail or fix the design process so that creativity cannot prevail. The toolbox is just an instrument from which you as a designer can choose which tools you need, and which you don't. The tools can be used to improve your own knowledge or as a means of communication between you and your client. The Design Brief, the Brand Pyramid, the Sense Matrix are the most popular tools when it comes to tools that retailers and designers can use together.

Toolbox#retailer

As a retailer, you may be less wary of the design process. You just outsource design because that's not where your expertise lies. Yet it is good to understand how retail designers work. What steps they take and how long these take. To get a kick-off meeting with a designer off to a good start, filling in the Design Brief is already a good exercise. Understanding how your DNA can take shape in a store design through different senses is also essential. Both the Design Brief and the Senses Matrix will help you with that.

Phase one, designing the brief

The Design Brief tool is actually the first tool we developed. Based on a lot of interviews with retail designers, we put together the ingredients needed for a good first meeting with a client. We use it ourselves with our clients and with our students. Students use it as an analysis tool. We ask them to map existing brands. With our clients, this is a document to be completed by them first after awarding the contract. This then forms the starting point for all subsequent steps in the process. The clients with whom this works best are SMEs. For larger chains, one of my PhD students has developed a larger version we call the Retail Design Kick-off Platform which goes much further in questioning this matter (and for that reason will not be discussed here). Note that the Design Brief asks some primary straightforward questions that need to be deepened further down the process. The design brief can save a lot of time when already filled in by the brand before the kick-off meeting. This way the design agency has more time to go into depth during that first meeting.

There are five large pillars in the Design Brief: brand, target group, product offer, competitors and a final part on the anticipated role of the store that needs to be designed. A template of the Design Brief can be downloaded from the Retail Design Lab website. But let me explain each pillar separately here.

Brand

All retail design projects are the result of a strong collaboration between a brand and the design agency. Indeed, a design process starts with a good brief. The designer and the brand sit down together to shape the design brief. Because this does not always run smoothly, the document we designed contains a number of essential questions that a brand should try to answer in advance. I have noticed in conversations with brands that the question of who they are as a brand and what their unique DNA is, is often difficult to answer. Some brands have an idea, some know perfectly, but others have no clue. To help streamline this the brand question is broken down into three parts with visual aids each time. The first part is about pinning down what a brand's core values are (referring to the brand values of the Brand Behavior Model). These are values that a brand carries within the company. How a brand manages their business. We have developed a word cloud to offer inspiration and to show the variety in these values.

All retail design projects are the result of a strong collaboration.

These are not the same type of words used for the second part of the DNA, the personality traits a brand wants to communicate to the customer. What story a brand wants to tell. Remember, to get a grip on these kinds of words it helps to imagine the brand being a person. Also for these, we have developed a word cloud.

Finally, as a visual aid, a choice needs to be made from a range of wine bottles that connect to the personality traits best. This step helps the brand to think visually and the designer to understand these visual links. The full list can be found in the Design Brief template online; I only show a few here.

The choice of all these brand values (core values and personality traits) should be made with great consideration. After all, this forms the basis for the entire retail design. As I mentioned earlier, a store is the place to communicate with the customer, where one shows who they are. Within the Retail Design Lab, this is the starting point of every cooperation.

Target group

Defining the target group may seem easy, but it is not. The most common mistakes are referring to an age group, or claiming 'everybody' is welcome in the store. Does this mean you cannot refer to an age group? Yes you may, but be aware that age is fluid. People are less and less defined by their age. One could speak of generations, but still, each generation is not very cohesive. So, even within one generation, a more precise target group needs to be defined. Studies into generations tell what values this group holds and how they are in life. But within this group there is still great diversity in buying behavior and specific interests. It is at this level that a target group needs to be defined. Think for example of fashionistas. Even though the majority comes from a specific generation, it is not limited to that generation. And, not everybody in that generation is a fashionista.

I do understand why brands say they are there for everybody. That might be a noble cause, but it is not reality even for brands that do seem to reach everybody like brands typically in the supermarket sector or in electronics. But if you think of it, there are people shopping in supermarket brand A that have never shopped in supermarket brand B. The key is to understand why supermarket brand A is preferred. If you do, then you know the WHY behind the brand that should lead you to a more precise description of the target group. In the Design Brief we ask the brand to visualize this group in one image. I advise looking for an image that shows the target group in action. Preferably an action related to the type of store. For example, a young family playing in the garden if active young families are the target group of a garden store. Or a group of people enjoying a meal together if the target group are food lovers.

Product/service offer

To start the design process it is key to know what products or services are being sold. The difference between the primary product group and the secondary is also important to know because it has an impact on the design of the store since there are some insights on what should be placed where, as I will explain in the Bubble Diagram tool further down. Also additional services, like offering retouches, for example, should be made visible in the design because this might be a differentiating strategy for the brand.

Competitors

Knowing who the competitors are, what they do and what they are offering, can help a brand to make their products, services and retail design stand out. Also which brands offer inspiration is useful information to understand the WHY behind a brand. Indeed, knowing the big disruptors in the field helps one to think strategically about the role the brand wants to play. I notice that smaller retailers do not consider online platforms or online players like Amazon as a competitor simply because they never looked at them. Competition can come from all directions, not just from stores within a 20 km radius of the store.

Role of the store

The last section of the Design Brief handles the role of the store in the whole retail strategy. In case of an already existing store plotting what its strengths and weaknesses are might impact the new design. To ensure an omni-channel approach, it is key for the designer to understand what role the store plays in the midst of all the other channels. Does the store serve as a click-and-collect point? Is it a store aimed at selling the brand more than selling products? Does the design needs to be able to be replicated in other stores or is it a one-off? Indeed, the design takes a whole different approach when the store needs to function as a flagship selling the brand or as a first in a series of many stores that need to be rolled out.

The Design Brief template helps students to understand a brand and to empathize with it. If the goal is to have students take their first steps into branding, it is a good idea to ask them to use the Design Brief to study a well known brand. I use the Design Brief in both theoretical courses where students learn what it means to design for retail and in design studio projects. In a next step I ask them to use the Design Brief again for their first retail design assignment in which in our case students have the freedom to design a multi-brand store, meaning that they have to develop their own retail brand. This is a more difficult thing to do, but by forcing students to go through the steps of the Design Brief, they are able to make choices early on in the process. This forms the framework for the students and the teachers to build the design from there on. To synthesize the findings of the Design Brief in one visual I then use the following tool: the Brand Pyramid.

Phase 2

Synthesizing

While the Design Brief is more about gathering information, we use the Brand Pyramid to synthesize information. However, more in depth study is necessary. The elements that can immediately be taken over are the brand values, the personality traits and the target group. The other aspects (mission – the WHY, behavior – the HOW, and brand promise – the WHAT) emerge by analyzing the brand (see the Brand Behavior Model in #rule 1). With this pyramid, everything is clear at a glance and it becomes a good tool to communicate with all stakeholders. Even the staff in the store could benefit from it. I don't want to say one should hang it in the staff break room, but it wouldn't be a bad idea.

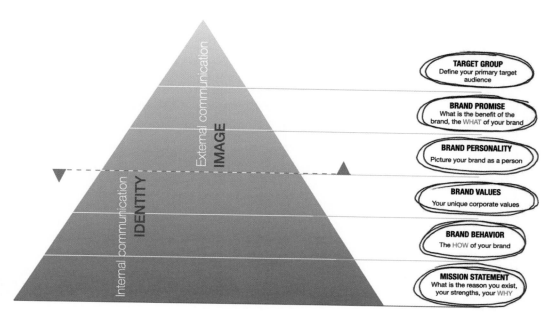

Note that the pyramid needs to be filled out from the bottom up, starting with the internally communicated aspects (DNA – bottom three). The top three layers are about what a brand wants to communicate to the world, leading to the image people will get from the brand. It is important that each aspect of the pyramid is filled in as specifically as possible. Also avoid using the same words for different layers of the pyramid.

In case of cross-disciplinary collaborations (that even occurs within one company) the pyramid's importance has been proven. Indeed, it is not evident that all stakeholders – brands, marketeers and designers – speak the same language (again, not even within the same company). Missions, visions and values are typical terms that are interpreted differently in different disciplines. We are only at the verge of developing a common language. Using the same tools will aid that process.

When teaching this pyramid to design students who are taking their first steps into the retail world it is best to have them start filling in the pyramid for a well known brand. They can search online to get the necessary information. I also use this pyramid when teaching economics students about how to understand a brand. Usually they are familiar with branding, but have never formulated a brand's characteristics in a concise way. No matter what the background of the students is, the brand pyramid is always a challenge because it is so concise.

As an illustration, I will use the example of IKEA again. The explanation of each line can be found in the explanation of the Brand Behavior Model. The only thing I haven't discussed yet is the target group. You can usually see the primary target audience in the advertisement of a brand. In case of IKEA that is young families. Of course students and older families also shop there (they form the secondary target group), but as mentioned earlier, there is always a group targeted directly. The rest are secondary target audiences. Be aware, just naming who the target group is, is not enough. As a designer you really need to understand them. So that is our next step.

THE BIG BOOK OF RETAIL DESIGN

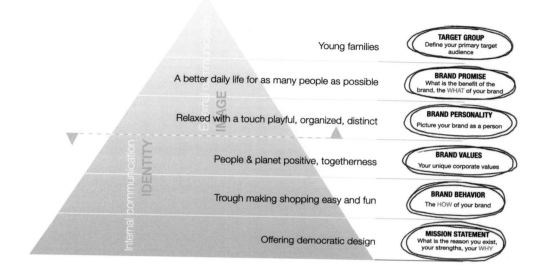

Understanding the target group

...by defining archetypes...

Both the Design Brief and the Brand Pyramid call for a description of the target audience. But that is, of course, on a very broad level. A target group could be, for instance, 'young families' or 'food lovers' but no matter how concrete that description may be, it is still too broad to really grasp for whom exactly one should create a design. This is why personas are often used. Personas are fictional profiles representing a group of people. It is a technique used in many different disciplines and sectors, with one goal at hand: facilitating the process of empathizing with the user (the customer in this case). Personas make customers tangible by literally putting a face to the variety of people targeted. Via personas personal characteristics, pains, gains, mindsets, love brands, etc. are being grouped and appointed to one single persona that represents a cohesive group of people targeted. Indeed, it is much more tangible to talk about 'Daniel', who just graduated and has just started his first job and is eager to invest in himself and his joy, is crazy about technology and is therefore totally into digital media and technological gadgets, than to talk about a target group that is young and still has little purchasing power. There is no strict rule on how many personas need to be defined. In my experience it ranges from three to six.

In some cases, a brand has these already at hand. If not, there are many apps and websites to help you to make personas. They range from simple three-dimensional descriptions to complicated eight-dimension templates. However, as I use them for the purpose of empathizing with customers, ultimately visiting stores, six dimensions seem to provide enough information. The six dimensions are: persona details (including a photograph, a quote and basic demographics), short bio or scenario, personality dimensions, needs, frustrations and lovebrands as the following figure shows.

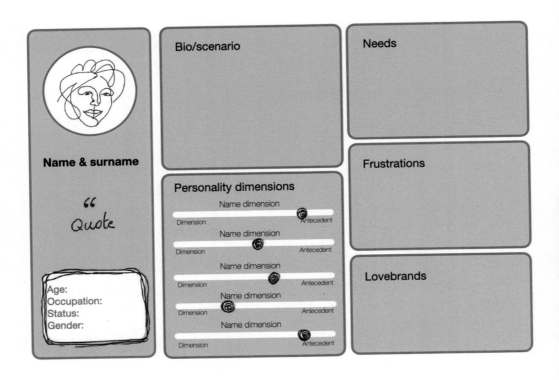

Creating archetypes:

The idea of making up personas is to define archetypes that represent the target group (primary and secondary). Everything you choose to define a persona is fictive, however based on knowledge. Knowledge of the targeted costumers. Indeed, ideally before you start making personas you do some research into the brand's customers or targeted customers. Studying the customer database or conducting some interviews are possible ways to do this. Give each persona a fictive name, choose an appropriate photograph and complete the demographics. Sometimes I add a quote – it is optional – but it is a nice way to describe somebody's life motto or something that typifies the persona. The bio could be an elaboration on that. Sometimes however it is helpful to describe the interaction with the brand and/or store, like a scenario. That way you can highlight why that person is a customer of the store or brand.

Everything you choose to define a persona is fictive, however based on knowledge.

Defining personality dimensions:

Maybe most difficult to define are the personality dimensions. My advice here would be to link those dimensions to both the brand values as well as the personality traits. By linking I mean making sure that they relate to each other. It is not a one on one copy of it, though. For example, if the store is about convenience, then you might consider taking 'taking (or having) time to shop' as a dimension with 'taking no time' and 'taking a lot of time' as the opposites. Other typical dimensions are related to mindset (e.g. open minded/traditional), character (introvert/extravert), budget to spend (a little/a lot), trend (-follower/-setter). Again, this is best funded with research into the target group.

Understanding emotions:

To define the needs it is what the target group expects from the brand, what they can gain from the brand. So for 'Daniel' the gain needs to be different than for 'Selin', for example. Daniel might be looking for service while Selin is very efficient and does not want to be helped. The same counts for their frustrations. They lie awake for different reasons, their pains are different. Again, Daniel might be frustrated by the many choices a store offers so he needs advice. Selin, on the other hand, might be frustrated by all the friction she encounters while going to a store to buy necessities.

To understand and define the relationship between a persona and a brand, it is wise to also list other brands, brands that are seen as lovemarks. This gives some insight into what the target group loves to buy as well. Choose brands from all sectors, from cars, to shampoo, to fashion and food. Again, giving the opportunity to place the brand in question within the other brands and to explore whether the brand in question is (up for a race to become) a lovebrand as well. Remember, if a specific store manages this, are seen as lovebrand, it can count on a loyal customer.

Again, as a starting point to get familiar with the template I advise starting with existing brands. I have students working with real brands in one of the theoretical courses. They have to empathize with the target group by interviewing several people. Based on these talks, they make up the personas. When working with fictive brands or made-up brands this is an easier job to do. Making personas is useful for students because it is easier for them to design the entire customer journey for each persona, understanding the different needs and wants from each targeted group. Indeed, it helps them to empathize with the target group. For examples of personas I refer to the last chapter of Part II: Walk the talk.

THE BIG BOOK OF RETAIL DESIGN

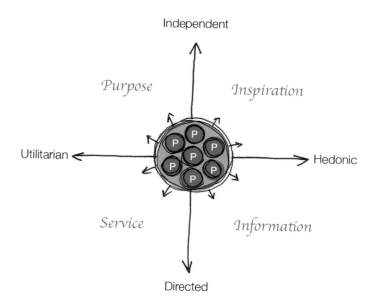

... and understanding shopping motivations

Sometimes personas simply don't do the trick. This might happen when the target group is too diverse. Also in product oriented stores, like for example DIY, or when more services are added like electronic stores, or even B2B stores, it is sometimes more wise to use a different strategy: shopping motivations. Picture our friend Daniel coming to the store one time, let's say an electronic store, to get batteries because he ran out of them. This should be a quick errand so Daniel expects the store to be efficient so he can easily navigate his way to the batteries. The next time Daniel comes in he is looking for inspiration because he does not know what he wants to give his partner for New Year. After spending quite some time in the store he finally makes the choice to buy a smartwatch. An expensive gift for him, but after consideration, he decides his partner is worth it. Daniel returns home happy and excited to give the gift. Although his partner is very happy with it, the smartwatch appears to malfunction. Imagine the disappointment Daniel feels when this happens. Such an expensive gift that he spent so much time picking out. Daniel will have to return to the store to exchange the watch. He won't be that happy anymore because it takes up precious time again.

We expect stores to be efficient so we can easily navigate.

Indeed, the store will see a whole new Daniel entering. When designing stores these different versions of Daniel need to be considered. Daniel was first a purpose driven shopper, looking for batteries, then he became inspiration oriented, then ended up as somebody with a complaint. And whether it is Daniel or Selin who picks up something via click and collect, the behavior is similar. This also applies when exchanging broken items or filing a complaint. Irrespective of the persona, one is not in a state of mind to search the store. They come for something purposeful and it is difficult to get them to change their minds, unless when this first task is done, when the 'pain' is taken away, there might be an opening to get them to browse. Note that when it comes to advice-seeking and browsing, the differences in personas do come out. So, yes, it is an option to mix both strategies and have the personas fulfilling different shopping motivations when drawing up the customer journey.

As my sketch shows, four different motivations are defined: coming in to buy in a targeted way (whether or not with a (selection of) product(s) in mind); seeking inspiration; seeking advice or information; coming in to pick something up or exchange/return it (whether or not accompanied by a complaint). These different shopping motivations have an impact on store design. It should not only be something the personnel needs to encounter by trying to estimate Daniel's mood when coming in. The store design should and can facilitate this as well. To this end, based on the Shopping Motivation Model, design choices can be made.

Purpose driven shopping

As people are coming in with one goal in mind, buying, the store should facilitate this process. Think of logically structured product categories, proper signage (in larger stores), good overview of the store, easy paying systems, etc. A good example of a store that is solely directed at those customers is the aforementioned Amazon Go store. It is frictionless shopping, just the fun without the hassle.

Just browsing

In stores where customers go in with a mindset of 'just looking', the focus shifts more to being able to explore the space and discover the products and/or services. Although it might sound as if they do not need structure, the opposite is true. It is often a balancing act between providing enough variety through incentives and surprises, and unity structure. The stores of Paul Smith are an exquisite example. Most of them are located in old town houses where you have a mix of Paul Smith's clothing with art (his own collection) in highly decorated rooms. Because each space looks so different, curiosity is stimulated and people want to explore. Because the rooms are part of a house, there is (a known) structure present to help us navigate.

In need of information

It often happens that people are looking for a particular product or service, but have not yet decided which brand, model or design it should be. In the store, they expect to be able to get advice around this or gather extra info. Typical showrooms are an example aimed at such behavior. Think of car showrooms or bathroom showrooms. However, showrooms more often turn into experiential stores, showing off their products. Look at Samsung experience in the meatpacking district in NY I mentioned before. It is literally a showroom; there is nothing on sale, just to experience. But the goal remains the same, offering extensive product information and product testing.

Solely service

Stores directed at customers needing service or picking something up should pay more attention to the service area. Design attention needs to go to how user friendly such areas are, making sure that they function for all users (personnel and customers). A typical example is the earlier mentioned Coolblue. They started as an online store but now have multiple service centers internationally where people can buy or pick up products, but more importantly, have somebody to talk to, ask advice and can turn to in case of problems with a product. Although the latest service centers are becoming more store-like, offering a lot of products on the shop floor, just a couple of years ago the service area was the main area and just a handful of products were offered. If you start looking at service-oriented brands (like banks and postal services) there is much design work to be done. In most cases they are quite functional with no attention to how people behave and use a space. In Part III I will show some nice examples, though.

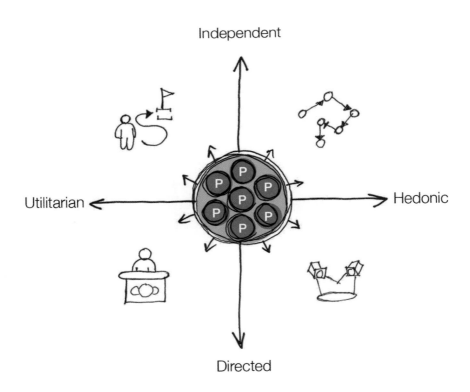

THE BIG BOOK OF RETAIL DESIGN

Although I gave typical examples to design around all four shopping motivations, it is a good strategy to try to incorporate all four, or at least the ones relating to the target group. Let me again illustrate with an example: Apple. Apple incorporates all those four dimensions into one design. Customers who are more goal oriented can easily manage to find a product themselves. The stores are open plan and give a clear overview of where to find what. If they are in for getting a nice experience, Apple provides that with their architecture that allows people to explore the space and enjoy its nicely designed features. Apple very often chooses heritage buildings or makes architectural statements on public squares. This in itself is a reason to visit the stores. If people need help or assistance, a whole bunch of employees are at their disposal to help them out. It is not even necessary to look for someone, they will come to you. Finally, people immediately in need of (technical) assistence can turn to the genius bar, a tech support service offered in store. It is designed as a bar where customers can interact with the personnel in a very relaxed manner.

The shopping motivation model is a very straightforward model that is always handy to use or to check whether a design offers an answer to all four shopping motivations, when they apply. They are the most direct link to make design decisions regarding the flow in the store as I will illustrate Phase 4 of the design proces.

Phase 3, the concept

Now that we have come to understand the brand and target audience, we can move on to coming up with the 'big idea'. I wish we could develop a tool for this too, but that is impossible. As mentioned earlier, this is where the creativity of the designer plays its part. I advise our students to think in metaphors. What image should the store evoke? Suppose you are designing a store for a brand that wants to act out its sustainable nature then you could have the big idea of having the store be like a 'walk in the woods'. Or suppose a brand sells 'sleeping comfort' then a possible metaphor would be that the store should feel like you are in heaven. Of course, a metaphor does not always have to be so obvious but it helps to create an initial mental picture. A next step is then to visualise this mental picture. We always do this through a concept board. I call it a concept board because it is not the same as a mood board or a materials board. The latter is something that clearly belongs more at the end of the design process, in the embodiment of the design. A mood board usually shows several images to inspire the design. There is not necessarily a recognizable whole in this. They are different moods visualized. Usually this is the starting point of the creative process. So, what is a concept board exactly? A concept board does require an unambiguous image. This is to ensure coherence or consistency throughout the design proces. Such an image shows how the metaphor is given a visual translation. Making such an image requires slightly more skills and expertise. Anyone can create a mood board via Pinterest, for example, but a concept board is more often put together using a programme such as Photoshop.

 For an example I refer to the last chapter of Part II: Walk the talk.

Phase 4

Organizing

The basic of any store is the engine. If the engine isn't running, you can't get anywhere. The most important thing is to establish a good in-store customer journey. How do you guide people around the shop? Which product groups go where? Ideally, on the one hand, people can find everything very easily, should they be looking, and on the other hand, people who are exploring should be able to discover the whole store without much thought. The latter is a challenge in larger shops. Did you know that research shows that a good store design contributes as a catalyst to the desired shopping behavior? But what is 'good store design'? Well, one that puts people at the center. This means both the visitor (customer) as well as the user (staff). I will get back to the customer later, but for staff a good design makes their job easier. I often encounter awkward situations in shops where I see that the store design does not work for the staff. This often happens in smaller shops. For example, I see bakeries where staff get in each other's way because the checkouts are in the most awkward places, or checkouts right next to an (automatic) door so that in cold weather, staff stand behind the checkout with a thick scarf, or even a jacket. In larger stores, the stock-distance dilemma arises. Of course, it makes sense for large products (on pallets, for example) to be close to the stock so they can be replenished quickly, but unfortunately this is not always the best choice from the consumer's point of view. In short, creating a good design is a complex story where managing products, people and space is key.

So, let's go through the different steps to start the running engine, seen from the customer's point of view. Indeed, each store will have its own challenges concerning logistics, so that is something that needs to be taken into account and done in accordance with the brand.

Starting to make a good floor plan based on the big idea from the previous design phase is the most difficult step to take because the idea needs to be made real. The first thing to do is to structure everything, the entrance, the products, the checkout, waiting areas, fitting rooms, stock, toilets,... all the functions needed for a particular job. In what follows, I will take you through a step by step plan.

Bubbles first

It is important to decide what goes where. Ideally, this exercise should be done independently from a floor plan. It is best to start from an ideal configuration where the links between certain functions and product categories have been studied. It is only later that we will look at how this sits on the floor plan. The danger is that if you go straight to the floor plan, you are immediately caught with the limitations of the building and so very quickly it is decided that something cannot be done. It is a better strategy to not dismiss things too quickly and still explore the possibilities.

So what to do? Make an inventory of all that is needed in the store. Start listing the different areas that need to be included in the plan: counter area, fitting area, restrooms, stock, café, the different product groups,... everything of importance. Also estimate how much space these elements might take up. This determines how large the bubbles need to be. Once that is done, start drawing these bubbles on an empty page, taking into account how they should relate to each other.

Try to do this with the customer in the back of your mind. What would be the ideal in-store customer journey? And yes, even for smaller stores it is wise to think about this. Even if only three bubbles do the job.

One bubble that is fixed and needs to be there at all times is the landing-zone bubble or acclimatization zone located at the entrance (remember Paco's truth). This is a zone where people take the 'time' (a fraction of a second) to orient themselves in the store. This involves taking a quick look around the space, gauging its size and building a mental map. Our brains are processing information and stimuli to build that map and we genuinely do not see anything else. People scan the space looking for identifiable objects that help create a path to start following. So this is not the place where we read signs or find shopping baskets. Also, people need that space to adapt to the new situation. It might be rainy outside and they need a moment to close their umbrella or wipe their feet. Or the sun is shining very brightly so that when entering a store their eyes need to adapt to the lower lighting levels. So it is wise to place nothing important in this area, not even shopping baskets because they will be missed (put them throughout the store). There is no mathematical formula to decide how large this area needs to be, but it will be somewhere between one and a half meters for tiny stores (less than 20m²) to 45 m², like IKEA is doing. Indeed, IKEA only wants their customers' full attention when the inspiration rooms start, usually on the first floor, after the customer has taken the escalator.

One bubble that is fixed and needs to be there at all times is the landing-zone bubble or acclimatization zone located at the entrance.

The 45 m² is no luxury knowing that you are walking a fixed route for the next 2 km. Also theatrical stores like Selfridges need more square meters of acclimatization because people are overwhelmed when they enter so you need to give them space. If you do not, people will stand still after entering to absorb all the stimuli. But that is not what you want, people standing still in the doorway. Also bear in mind that the location of the store also impacts the size of the landing zone. Stores located in shopping malls need less space than stores in a high street because the conditions do not change that much since you are already inside and the acclimatization happens when entering the shopping mall. Stores located next to an arterial or collector road or a big common parking lot typically need more space because people came in cars, so they need more time to adapt.

As you can see on my bubble plan, which I drew up for a cookery store also selling fresh flowers, books, pottery, paints and dry food. Next to the entrance they offer advise and work-shops and to complete the experience they also have a bistro. The location I drew this for had a separate entrance and exit. In the bubble plan the entrance is the landing zone bubble and from there on I started to think of a logical order in which customers would encounter the products and services. This is just an exercise to explore the connections between the functions. Also color coding the bubbles helps to decide where what goes and what the possible connection are.

While making such a bubble plan, reflecting on the rules of the game. There are some key questions you need to ask yourself:

- Based on the retailer's DNA, what does the customer expect when entering the store? What do you want them to see or explore first? Remember that first impression that needs to be managed. This is one of the reasons why supermarkets put their fresh products, fruit and vegetables, first – those products have the biggest potential to show off.
- How do customers shop? What would be a logical route for them to explore the store? So which products/functions should be adjacent to each other? Or do you mix some products to inspire customers? Indeed, the key concern should always be the customer and how to get him around the shop in a natural way. Remember Paco's truth that in countries where people drive on the right side of the road, they will most likely intuitively turn right after entering a store. Indeed, in places where people drive on the left they prefer to turn left when entering a store. This is a matter of how our brain is programmed.
- Also think of the location of the counter and service areas; the Shopping Motivation Model should help you to decide how close or far these need to be from the entrance. Also how large both (if they are separate) need to be, or if you even need a counter – paying systems are getting more and more contactless. In case of click-and-collect options, you will definitely need a service desk near the entrance. Remember, people on a mission need to be able to fulfill this mission asap.
  Be aware that where you place the counter influences how customers perceive the brand. It can be a deliberate choice to have the counter near the entrance so one has the opportunity to greet each customer. This also has the benefit that if you have a click-and-collect service, it is easy for customers to have a quick in and out to get their package. The downside of having the counter in the front of the store is that if many people are waiting in line to pay, new customers coming in are confronted with that and may decide to leave. Having the counter in the back of the store leaves the customer with more freedom to browse. They will feel less watched when entering the store. Indeed, the downside here is that for quick services, customers have to walk a bit further. So it is really about the message you want to send out.

- In the case of fashion, what purpose do the fitting rooms have? Just for independent fitting? Or is service key? What level of privacy do the customers expect? Answering these questions leads to the needed size and location of the fitting rooms.
- If there is a bar or café, should it be at the end of the customer journey? Should the bar be able to function independently (so best visible from the street with a proper entrance) or is it a part of the store? Definitely also consider whether the brand itself should operate this or if it should be outsourced.

Also the retailer will have a lot of input in terms of logistics for example. This is certainly the case for product oriented stores like DIY and food. Remember bigger products might be best situated near stock so that shelves can be efficiently replenished. Retail design is teamwork. All stakeholders will have a say and should have a say. Note that to this end the bubble diagram has a rather functionally oriented approach. This might slightly change when the first designs are made. However, only when all bubbles are in place you can go to the next step, in which we look at the building the store will be located in. Indeed, ideally, only after the completion of all previous design phases do the plans of the store come into the equation.

 In students projects, this is the point that we hand out the plans of the building to our students. We usually do this after six weeks, out of the thirteen weeks they have in the retail design studio.

Cut & paste

Now the time has come to have the bubbles and their connections with each other fit within the plan, taking the location specificities into account. Take a thorough look at the location. Are there elements present that could determine the route in the store? Think about structural elements that might be very prominent and give direction to a space. It is better to use such elements, such as heavy beams on the ceiling, because they help customers to make directional choices more intuitively. Daylight and differences in height (floor or ceiling) can also help determine how best to arrange a space. About differences in height, in evolutionary psychology, one speaks of the 'prospect and refuge' principle. With 'prospect' referring to those landscape elements and configurations that enable the individual to overview the environment in an unimpeded manner. 'Refuge' refers to places or landscape configurations where one can hide, rest, or find protection. In retail contexts refuge could mean having separate, dimly lit spaces with a cosy atmosphere in which consumers can have a rest. Prospect can be evoked by creating spacious areas, raised ceilings, wide and open views on surrounding spaces, building on an elevated site, etc. Refuge areas seem particularly relevant for stores in which high-involvement decisions have to be made (e.g., a car, luxury accessories like bags or jewelry).

While we are respecting the properties of the property as much as possible, we obviously do not intend to recreate the entire bubble diagram. The most creative solutions arise precisely when there are challenges and constraints.

It is good to look for a story in the design, or an idea making it easier for customers to understand the store design.

THE BIG BOOK OF RETAIL DESIGN

I mentioned earlier that the bubble diagram often grows from a functional mind-set. When we are pasting the bubbles into the floor plan it is good to look for a story in the design, or an idea making it easier for customers to understand the store design. I will never forget my very first contact with working in this way. It was during the time I worked at Fitch. Fitch was very good at strategic store design. I learned how to logically put together a customer journey, really from the customer's point of view, starting from the big idea. One of the first concepts I worked on was the design of a flagship store for a major telecom brand. The big idea was using the theme of one of the events they are lead sponsor for as the theme for the store: formula one racing. So the design language was set on racing and red (including a pit stop, using communication as 'refueling', etc).Remember Paco saying when a customer is searching, they are not buying. So, simply adding layers to the design, such as the idea of placing the heart of the store centrally, where interaction could take place, and then dividing the products from low service (mobile phones with accessories) at the front of the store to high service (subscriptions) at the back, was enough to give the design a framework and make it legible for the customer.

The front part of a store is always busier than the back, so it makes sense to offer more service and privacy at the back. Although this is a very simple example, there are others. Look at IKEA, who have a very clear logic in their shops: first immerse yourself in the world of IKEA for a whole floor, then load up your trolley with all the nice stuff you already saw in the first part. Finally, you take the large products out of the warehouse yourself. Ingenious, isn't it? That is quite a different story from a DIY store where I saw the drills next to the cleaning products or the bikes (yes bikes!) next to the lawn mowers. The latter being a typical example of retailers who are product-oriented and who have been dividing the store into categories (with accompanying category managers) for years. It is therefore literally very difficult to look beyond the categories and experiment with new product layouts that are more attuned to how a customer thinks and shops. Another ingenious example was Topshop, a multi-brand store *avant la lettre*. They are unfortunately no more, but they started to group clothes by style, not by brand (in the late 90s this was still possible). Within a style, you could find 30 euro trousers next to a 300 euro jumper. This would still work today, maybe not by style, but in offering combinations of brands and mostly price ranges mixed together. This is how consumers often shop today.

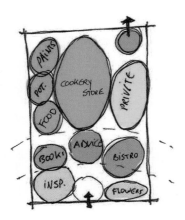 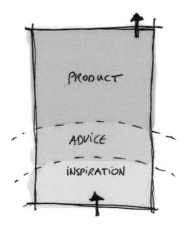 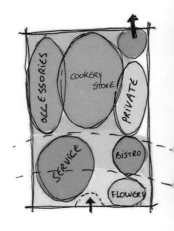

So now back to my example. Adding some logic to the journey a customer encounters is smart (see sketches above). The first one shows my attempt to paste the bubbles in the floor plan. Because of the two entrances/exits the location offers, I needed to shift some bubbles around. Next I started looking for some logic and noticed that offering inspiration in the first part of the store would make sense, followed by a part where advice is central. Near the exit, it would make sense to display the products. Maybe just like IKEA does, inspiration first, stocking up next. As my third sketch shows, I tried to place the bubbles according to that new layer I added to the design.

Choose a flow strategy

It might seem redundant, but it is key that a flow strategy is chosen to start with. Each flow strategy links with certain design elements needed for the flow strategy to work. We can define seven different flow strategies.

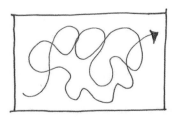

- Open plan: This type of strategy offers a continuum of open space. Physical separations between selling departments are rare. Only mobile fixtures, by means of a change in height or direction, indicate the different departments. Signage and graphics are vital to enable customers to orient themselves. Flexibility is key to this store plan. This asks for continuous floor materials and ceilings. Typical example: Zara and Apple, but overall quite common in fashion.

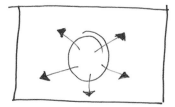

- Centre core plan: this type of strategy is orientated around a core in the store. The core can contain central escalators, an atrium or an open vertical court, possibly crowned by a skylight. The core could also be a service point being at the center of the store. This core is used to define a central base from which the customer can move to all parts of the plan. Typical example: department stores of the 19th and early 20th century.

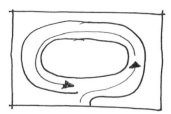

- Loop plan: In a sense this strategy is a combination of the open plan and the centre core plan. This plan assures a traffic flow throughout the whole store. And it limits the depth ratio per department. The departments or circulation can be indicated by differences in floor finishes, ceilings or lighting fixtures. Nowadays this technique is used less because it limits flexibility. Typical example: the lower floor of a department store selling perfumes and cosmetics, also many bigger sports stores (e.g. SportsDirect) are set up this way.

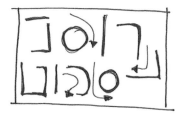

- Free-flow plan: this strategy forces customers to browse. The use of curvilinear, amorphous forms adds interesting perspectives at every turn. The customer is guided via attractive, highlighted selling points. Typical example: Usually the Comme des Garçons stores are designed this way, certainly the one in NY.

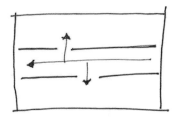

- Linear plan: a central traffic avenue divides the store into two sides with smaller traffic pathways. Straight on the main path, it can subdivide each side. This type provides clear access and visibility throughout the store space. Sometimes the path is clearly visible by a change of floor material. But as mentioned, this reduces flexibility. Typical example: any supermarket, Decathlon.

- Zone and cluster plan: associated products are clustered together in separated, physically divided zones. Within the zones flexible aisles are used. The zones provide the opportunity to create variety, for example life-style related, between the zones. Typical example: IKEA.

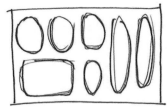

- Shop plan: the ultimate expression of each department is key. Each zone or department is designed as a separate boutique or shop. Another possibility is defining each brand separately, resulting in a shop-in-shop concept. This is clearly the most expensive and the least flexible of all types previously described. Typical example: De Bijenkorf and Selfridges still work this way, but less pronounced than back in the day. Indeed, a retailer needs to brand himself making the overall look and feel increasingly important.

It is not because certain floor plans are associated with certain types of shops that there cannot be cross-pollination. And, variants and mixes can be used. There is a trend towards more open floor plans anyway so that the customer can explore on the one hand and the retailer has the necessary flexibility on the other. More flexibility means more options to surprise the customer. Also note that the bigger the shop floor the more need for structure. Again, links can be

THE BIG BOOK OF RETAIL DESIGN

made with more efficient and functional shops that might be served better with a linear plan and a store that wants to stimulate browsing behavior will tend more towards a zone and cluster plan or free-flow plan. Do not forget that each strategy needs certain design elements to make it work. Indeed, a choice of a strategy comes with consequences. If you ask me, that's where the bottleneck lies. In product oriented stores we usually see more open spaces with lots of shelving in a linear plan. If the accompanying design elements are not implemented, this configuration quickly brings to mind a warehouse. Indeed, independent of the sector, customers need more inspiration, excitement and surprise.

 Steps 3 and 4 often go together. The bubbles are given a place and, of course, you also take the circulation into account. This interaction determines the general layout of the plan.

Optimizing

Now that we know how functions and product groups relate to each other and we have also determined the strategy we will use to send people about, it is time to further develop the current bubble diagram into a strategic floor plan. A strategic floor plan shows two things: the customer journey of each persona or customer motivation with the associated eye-catcher; and a first conceptual representation of the use of space in the interior (product density). To get to this point several steps need to be taken.

Calculate

So this is the step where you need to calculate. Indeed, the running meters of products that a retailer has specified for each product group must now be set up in space usage. This is an initial sketchy infill of the bubbles with the correct area utilization, taking into account the desired product density. Product density is usually something determined by the client, but don't forget that often running meters are specified on the basis from what is known. What they are used to from another store for example. But this is the moment to question (again) what the relationship between product and space should be, just like the relationship between product and experience, or product and services.

Now, the discussion will be different in a supermarket than if you are designing a flagship store for a fashion brand. But a critical look at what is being asked is never wrong.

Of course, you cannot calculate space utilization if you have not yet made choices about the height, length and depth of shelving. In this phase, that will begin to crystallize. This is really a process of sketching, measuring, shifting, checking and fitting until everything falls into place. Remember that in a design process, going back and forth between steps is normal. It is an iterative process. The proposed bubble diagram will certainly be tweaked a few times and that is ok (as long as the idea behind this is preserved). It is important, however, that every choice is made on the basis of the DNA of the brand and the customer for whom the brand is doing it.

Designing a flow

A good 'flow' is created when people shop intuitively and are able to do what they set out to do: explore the shop, ask for advice, pick something up,…. The term originates from positive psychology, a flow state, also known colloquially as being in the zone. It is the mental state in which a person performing some activity is fully immersed in a feeling of energized focus, full involvement, and enjoyment in the process of the activity. In essence, flow is characterized by the complete absorption in what one does, and a resulting transformation of one's sense of time. That is exactly what we are aiming for in retail. Getting customers in a flow state so they are immersed in the store. Linking it back to shopping motivations, the one where customers are looking for inspiration and are interested in just browsing the store, is the one where 'flow' is essential. Indeed, more functional motivations, like returning or picking something up, are easier to shape and highly rely on their location in the store. Customers in a relaxed state, just exploring, need guidance, subtle guidance. A customer should not think about where to go, but should be guided where to go. Indeed, at the end of exploring the store you want them to feel satisfied, that they have seen all. You don't want them to have to make considerations about where to go all the time. Let alone that they have to think whether they have seen a specific part of the store or not.

THE BIG BOOK OF RETAIL DESIGN

A good 'flow' is created when people shop intuitively and are able to do what they set out to do: explore the shop, ask for advice, pick something up.

Did you know that research has shown that observations of shapes in the ceiling or on the floor stimulates physical movement along these shapes and that they also lead to emotional joy due to the extra stimuli they provide? So, by having curves, lines or different colors or materials in the ceiling or flooring (for example, to highlight zones or walkways) you can lure people in, make them follow a certain path. Be careful though with lines on the floor because we also know from research that they can form a boundary which people do not dare to cross. Personally, I'm not really a fan of lines on the floor that delineate paths or zones because this also often lowers flexibility. Shapes of lights on the ceiling, or placing lights in a certain way to give direction to a space and the flow in it, have less of that.

When designing a flow, one thing to take into account is to create tension in the journey, no flat line. Indeed, too boring is not the way to go, but neither is too intense. It is a matter of continuity versus eye-popping stimuli. To offer continuity we need to set a baseline. The baseline is the level of design (or experience) the entire store should at least meet. I refer to this as the look and feel of the store, as I will discuss in the next part. Within that baseline, which offers continuity, eye-popping stimuli can be added.

Now, there are two important preconditions to design a good flow. One is making sure that no disruptive factors or irregularities play a role in the customer journey. The other is making sure that customers are drawn from one spot to the other in a store (like playing pinball). Let me zoom in on both aspects.

Play pinball with your customers in the store.

1. Avoid irregularities

Irregularities#logistic-affairs

To offer customers a good flow, all irregularities need to be avoided. One of such irregularities could be the placement of logistic affairs, such as toilets, access to car park, personnel entrance, entrance to stock, etc. The bigger the building – as big as an entire shopping mall – the more likely these functions are there and take up considerable space. It is not always a free choice when you are renting a place, but if you have the option to decide where such places go take into account to never let logistics cross the customer journey. When there are situations in which access to toilets or personnel spaces do cross the customer journey, make sure they blend in. Doors to stock and personal spaces do not even need to be visible so make sure they are as good as invisible. Well designed shopping malls, like Westfield, London, for example, are a nice inspiration. Next time you go there have a look at where all these logistics affairs are located and how they are designed. Toilets, entrances to car parks, they are all there, but never in a disturbing way.

And then there are staircases...the ones for personnel and the ones for customers. Staircases for personnel should be 'invisible'. Nothing is more distracting than a staircase that looks very inviting and then has a rope blocking the way. Why not place a mannequin or some other nice display to indicate that a floor is not accessible (in case the staircase is there in a rental)? In newly designed stores, such staircases are preferably out of sight. This is in contrast to stairs that are intended for the customer. They do need to be on the customers' path and they need to be as inviting as possible. The most efficient way to make it part of the experience of the space is to use escalators. Of course, this is not always possible. But do use them, when it is an option. It's not easy to get people to go upstairs – people are lazy, remember? When designing a staircase or escalator, it should fulfill more than just a functional role. It should be visible, attractive and inviting and be part of the experience of the store. So give the customers something to encourage them to go upstairs. Make it attractive. Look at what department stores did with their atria. Thought was given to vistas so that the customer was always encouraged to explore other parts of the store. Also in smaller stores such vistas are key. I have seen designs where, with the best of intentions, the store continued in the staircase and the mezzanine. If you ask me, though appealing, this does not always create a safe situation. Indeed, the stairs have to be twice as wide as 'normal'. After all, three flows of people need to be able to cross each other: people going up, usually also the ones going down and those who are standing still in front of the products. So this illustrates that designing for retail is really about knowing how to deal with flows of people, using your common sense and empathizing with them. Remember it is about managing people, products and space.

Irregularities#dead-ends

Another irregularity is dead ends. Customers do not like to walk into a dead end. Always safeguard the continuous flow. Along the same lines, customers browsing also do not like to take the same way twice. So always think in loops.

Irregularities#waiting

A third one is waiting. How often and in how many places do customers have to wait? Probably more than you think: waiting or queuing to pay, waiting to be served, queuing at the fitting rooms or waiting for somebody who is fitting, waiting while being served (gift wrapping, fetching products from the stock,...). At all these moments two things need to be considered: the person that is waiting takes up space (and sometimes stands in the way of others when there is no dedicated space) and waiting is boring. For people waiting at a cash register or an information desk, both apply. Usually they are bored and at the same time they take up space. So you have to think about how people will queue. (Which direction? How many tills? One line for each till or each till a line?) Leave enough space so that when many people are queuing the flow in the store for other people is not disrupted. When the waiting is made interesting or entertaining, time will go much faster for those waiting. Indeed, it is a good place to communicate with the customer, like the mission for example, or information about additional services, or other channels, etc. Digital screens offer a nice opportunity to do this in an entertaining way. Do not make the mistake of communicating specific product discounts on a screen behind the counter. At that point people have already chosen their products and they will unlikely step out of the line, leaving them frustrated because they would have liked to have received that information earlier, while still shopping.

When the waiting is made interesting or entertaining, time will go much faster for those waiting. Indeed, it is a good place to communicate with the customer.

THE BIG BOOK OF RETAIL DESIGN

The same applies to the fitting rooms. How do you deal with crowds there? What do you expect accompanying shoppers to do when they have to wait? Do you offer them seating? Speaking of seating, with an aging population there is an increasing need for resting areas in all kinds of stores. Provide these in quiet places, places that do not disrupt the flow of the other shoppers.

Then you have those people waiting while being served. Served to collect their products which could be at a click and collect desk, but often this is still happening at the cash desk. Think of how to manage that; there is nothing more irritating then having to wait in line to pick up your ordered and pre-paid products with customers who are just waiting in line to pay. So much for time saving! Indeed, it is better to have a dedicated space for click and collect services. I see a lot of large stores that mean well and add service desks throughout the store, but often people are just waiting there to be served, and no one turns up. It is a hard thing to do because it requires more personnel. And on quiet days, usually not enough personnel are present to staff those desks, leaving the customer frustrated again. Think carefully about how the store will operate on quiet and on very busy days. At neither time do we want frustrated customers.

2. Playing pinball

Pinball#focus-points

While it may not sound very polite to play pinball with customers in the shop, that is the best way to think about it. Just like a ball being played back and forth from one point to another, we try to do the same figuratively with the customer by deploying focus points. Focus points should be visually stimulating, having the intention to catch the eye. Indeed, that is why they are called eye-catchers. They are there to excite and make customers curious (yes, research shows that they enhance enjoyment as well). Every time they see such an eye-catcher, they should be stimulated to explore the shop further. It is important that they are placed on sight-lines, from the entrance to the very back of the shop, as my sketch shows. The content can range from art installations to very concrete product combinations for inspiration. But also large screens with moving images are an option. These eye-catchers belong to what I call category-1 eye-catchers.

When placing such eye-catchers, we need to take how far people 'see' in a store into account. Usually, between 8m and 20m is where our eye looks for a focus, depending on the size of the store. Indeed, in smaller, more cramped spaces, we tend to look for focus points nearby. When you enter larger spaces, with higher ceilings, people's eyes will overlook the space, trying to find something to help them orient themselves, usually not seeing what is right in front of them but a bit further away. So when deciding where to place eye-catchers in order to direct people further down the store, you need to take the space and its dimensions into account, as the following sketch illustrates.

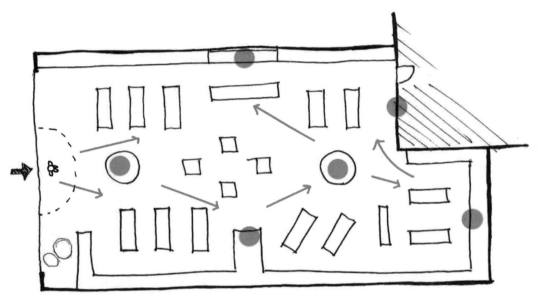

Pinball#personas

What you need to take into account when designing eye-catchers is who they are for. It is possible that each persona or each shopping motivation calls for a different route in the store, so specific eye-catchers are needed to guide these people. Put on the glasses of each persona/motivation and imagine how this person will shop and what they expect. Empathize.

THE BIG BOOK OF RETAIL DESIGN

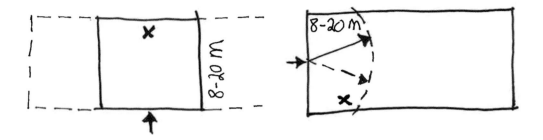

Let's have a look at Daniel, our guy with the smartwatch, again. Daniel is fairly frustrated when he arrives to exchange the watch because it was defective at the time of purchase. To help Daniel in the best possible way, this must be able to happen in a smooth manner, and preferably in a dedicated space. Indeed, a retailer does not want all customers to see and hear about Daniel's problem; not a good advertisement. It is therefore not a good idea to have Daniel traverse the entire store in search of the service desk. That would only make him more frustrated. I have seen retailers experiment with this. Some have tried to make a separate service area with a separate entrance, next to the entry of the store. One had a busy service point, and everyone could see it. Again, not exactly good advertising if you know what I mean. There are others, deliberately placing the service and returning goods area in the back of the top floor. I think I can guess why this is. The store I am referring to is a fashion discounter.

They probably want to discourage customers from returning products. Some people are effectively considering whether they want to go to the trouble of returning the product. They are making up the balance if the money spent is worth the trip. I'm sure many people are thinking 'never mind'. Anyway, just like with the cash and service desk, it is a consideration of where the best place for this is. But my point actually is that Daniel needs help in navigating to this point. Do this with eye-catching signage or have it visible from the entrance. When Daniel has relieved his pain, he might change his mood and is open to impulses and stimuli. So on his way out of the store, some inspiring product presentations might trigger him to slow down and have a look.

Now, picture Maria, a mother of two young teenagers who loves shopping with her children. They are looking to buy a new television and a new laptop so they will enter the same store as Daniel with very different expectations indeed. How do you let her enter and discover the shop? What kind of eye-catchers will help her find her way? Consider that she might want help immediately or that she only needs help after discovering the shop. Either way, she needs visual guidance (by means of eye-catchers) to help her navigate. This empathy exercise and setting out the customer journey needs to be done for each persona.

Let's take a design of a traditional lingerie boutique as an example to showcase different flows and eye-catchers (see floor-plan). Imagine this boutique has three target groups: men (shopping for themselves or men shopping for their partner), women shopping, and women who need special lingerie (nursing bra or prosthetic bra). For the purpose of this exercise, I am not discussing the different personas within each group, but I will stick to the three main groups. Each group should find what they are looking for sooner rather than later. You do not want men shopping for women lingering in the store waiting for somebody to help them out. Also when they are shopping just for themselves, you want that to happen in a dedicated space (for privacy reasons), preferably in their own zone (at the front of the store on the left side in this case). So, show them the way in the beginning of the store with a dedicated eye-catcher (yellow dot). Women who need special care need more privacy so show them the way to where that is (in this case upstairs) (blue dot). The other women wanting to shop and browse the store are led to the right side of the store (pink dot). All three dedicated to a target group eye-catchers also belong to the category-1 eye-catchers. So are the other pink dots further down the store (referring to the #focus-points). They are located on key sight-lines, attracting people further down the store.

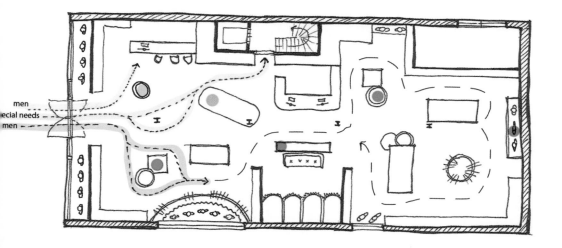

men
ecial needs
men

So, for each of the target groups, we literally draw the 'ideal' customer journey. Each persona/motivation gets its own dotted line on the strategic floor plan. From entering (sometimes already from the parking) to leaving again. Indeed, not every customer will follow that same line on the floor plan, but if it is the ideal way to go for that type of customer, as a designer you need to design the store in such a way that you trigger the customer to follow that route. Never forget to make a loop when possible so the way to the cash desk or the front of the store is not a repeat. Indeed, make this route attractive so that the back of the store does not feel like the end of the journey.

Pinball#communication

Besides these main (category-1) eye-catchers, there is also a second category of eye-catchers. They serve to communicate something instead. They are therefore less conspicuous. Typically, they are placed at the head of a gondola or just at the end, where there is a view of a wall, as the green dots in the sketch show. The content can range from communicating a product category by means of a nice product display created with the products themselves, to creating an atmosphere with visuals. Note that I opt for using products to direct people, instead of signage. Why? People browse through a space by mainly looking around at eye level. We rarely look up. Exceptions are product oriented stores where efficiency needs to be high. Here, signage can be helpful to guide people between the shelves.

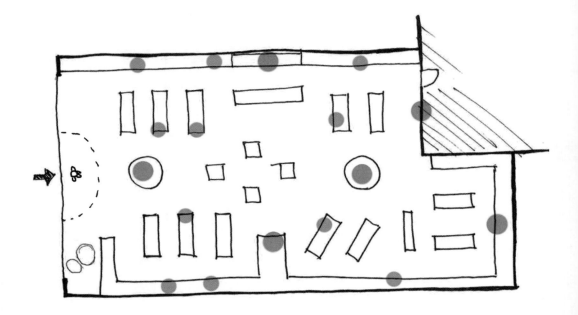

An important note here is that eye-catchers only function as such if they are properly lit. With poor lighting, they will go unnoticed by most people. Did you know that research has shown that by putting additional light to a product display, you will encourage consumers to spend more time there, touch more products and actually take them in their hands? A higher level of light on display (and thus the variation between general lighting and accent lights) induces feelings of enthusiasm and pleasure, and has a positive effect on perceived coziness and the dynamics of the store.

Just as there is no rule for determining how large the landing zone should be, there is also no formula for determining the number of eye-catchers, as mentioned earlier. Depending on the dimensions of the space, the density of the products and the products themselves, a well-considered choice must be made here. Again, putting yourself in the shoes of the target audience but certainly walking through the space or walking through the design is essential to be able to perform this step well.

After the completion of previous steps, with the interaction between them of course, it is time to do a final check on whether the chosen flow strategy is executed well and that the accompanying design elements are in place. This means that there might already be some differences in height in places. In my example it is simple. I choose all wall-facing shelves to be high and the ones in the middle are table height or 1.2m maximum in case of shelving. Now the strategic ground plan should be ready, the engine should be able to run. So it is clear how we divide the space, what dynamics it contains, the density of the products, the density (and height) of the furniture, what route each persona/shop motivation should take and how we encourage that route through the use of eye-catchers.

Creating an optimal experience

...is one that starts outside

We may not forget that the experience starts outside. If a store is not noticed, or it cannot be found, nobody will go in. There are different reasons why somebody might walk into a store. From purpose-driven motivations to an accidental discovery. Either way, the truth is that a store needs to look open. Stores with poor lighting or window stickers blocking the view inside are doing the exact opposite. Thus, making it hard for people to see whether they are open and not making them feel welcome. But there is more to say about the facade. The facade is the first thing people see when visiting a physical store. A facade can have so much appeal when done well, but they are too often neglected. We do need to take a moment to distinguish between a facade in the city and one along an arterial or collector road.

City store

Facades in shopping streets or village streets are often existing facades and here the properties are also often rented. This obviously brings with it restrictions. But I still think it's worth discussing briefly. Even though the facade is something that a retailer in this case has little say in, the communication needs to be in place. When a brand owns a building more can be designed.

From communication...

Make sure the store's name is visibly indicated along all sides. You may take this quite literally, even if you are visible from the air like the example in the sketch.

When people are on top of the nearby museum, this is the view down. Pretty clever thinking if you ask me. So do the test and approach from all sides. In addition to a logo or name right on the facade, there is also a need for a transverse sign.

When appropriate and feasible, it is always good to be the eye-catcher of the street. It is worth investing in this because people will always see you and probably remember you. Again, make choices in line with the DNA. I show two examples. One is the facade of the Citroën store on the Champs-Élysées in Paris. This facade has been around for as long as I can remember, but it is timeless and attracts the eye in a subtle way. The other example is the store of fashion designer Ann Demeulemeester in Seoul. Picture a busy city with a lot of concrete buildings. Then, you walk down a street where you see the building as in my sketch. Not only does the architecture and formal language stand out, but also, of course, the green facade. A very welcome change from all the concrete. Mission accomplished, the store stands out and also shows potential. Indeed, increasing greenery in a concrete city can also be done horizontally, not just vertically.
Finally, also consider what the façade should look like at night time. A facade can be so much more than just a lit up logo.

THE BIG BOOK OF RETAIL DESIGN

...to stopping power...

Use a shop window to create stopping power. The days of overloaded shop windows full of products are over. Use the shop window to make a statement. We often see wonderful examples appear around Christmas. Certainly department stores take the crown here. But you also just see these big players trying to create a celebration in their window displays all year round. They often collaborate with artists for example. So a window display may be a year-round celebration. Especially where people pass by on foot. Window displays are still a very big part of getting people to come in. And know that one or two strong presentations (let's take mannequins for a moment) with eye-catching attractive outfits stand out more than a whole window full of stuff. So go for that eye-catcher here, too. When creating eye-catchers, take into account that bright colors are more effective in attracting our eye because they reflect light. Dark colors are hard to work with in shop windows simply because they absorb all the light and in case of a sunny day, the reflection of the daylight in the windows is simply too powerful. Or, design the whole facade around a product. Look at what Volvo has been doing the last couple of years. They closed their façades but left openings for one or two cars. The result is a luminous glass box-shaped building where all the glass is frosted except for a limited number of square peepholes with the size of a car where the glass is clear, putting that car in the spotlight. I really think this is a bold move by Volvo. This goes against everything we have already seen from car showrooms.

Are having shopping displays not in line with the DNA? Then just create an open window with a clear view inside the store. People attract people, so when we see people shopping, we might get triggered to enter that store as well. The same goes for restaurants. When you have to choose a place to eat when you are on holiday and you are not familiar with the place,.you pick the one that is the busiest because you trust your peers.

...to lowering the threshold

Unless you are a fancy brand with security at the door, you should try to lower the threshold as much as possible. This means blurring boundaries. This can be done by simple interventions such as making the entrance and the shop window a little deeper so people 'enter' the store before they actually realize it, as the sketch illustrates. Or by literally running elements from outside to inside like the tree in the sketch. This provides both stopping power and the blurring of boundaries. Also remember rule #4 about the first impression.

Big box stores

When it comes to detached store fronts, of course, different rules apply. In this case, the casual passerby is not a walking person but a moving car, public transport or bicycle. We are then also talking about very different speeds at which a store is passed. It goes without saying that everything you do on the facade(s) must also be adapted to that speed. All communication and stopping power in this case must come primarily from the building itself. It is only when people slow down or get out of the car that we work back to the scale of a city store. So, make sure you play with large elements on the facade or in the window, if that is large enough, that appeal from afar.

Make sure you stand out and are the eye-catcher of the neighborhood.

Explaining all possible façade and building typologies and options would take me too far, but again the rule applies: make sure you stand out and are the eye-catcher of the neighborhood. Preferably do this in a way that appeals to the target audience. So we don't need to plant massive blue-and-yellow buildings along the highway, think at MPreis that I showed in Part I, and let's take that as our reference.

...is one of doing and undergoing...

Before I dig into how to design an optimal experience inside the store, we may not forget that all of the above is part of the experience. It is impossible to create an optimal experience if the engine is not running.

I talked briefly about what constitutes a valuable experience in the previous part. Experience is a catch-all term and there is no consensus in practice about what it is right, or how best to design it. There have been attempts from theory to define the concept, but how to then put it into practice also remains open to interpretation. There are, however, a few preconditions, or characteristics that we can do something with.

I refer again to Pine and Gilmore's book on the experience economy indicating that an experience is a process of doing and undergoing, with some degree of immersion (mental or physical) in the experience as well. Since exactly what an experience in a store should be is subject to context, the person and zeitgeist, we clearly see the change of the latter. Twenty years ago, the balance was more towards 'undergoing', while in recent years we see that the balance has tipped towards 'doing'. You can also see this change in how flagship stores have changed. Where twenty years ago they were mainly focused on impressing (e.g. M&M store, Toys 'R' Us), today they focus much more on participating, community building, and even education (e.g. Nike, Apple).

...with a beginning and an end...

We also know that an experience has a beginning and an end. I teach marketing students how to shape that beginning even before the physical shopping experience, focussing on anticipation, and how to extend the end far beyond the effective shopping visit. Now this is not the place to go into this in great depth because we as designers often have no control over this, but I would still like to give one example that we can still learn something from, namely Tomorrowland. After all, we can learn a lot from the entertainment industry. Tomorrowland manages to stretch out the experience process completely so that it starts much earlier and ends much later than with the visit to the festival itself. It already starts with the unique packaging and design of the entrance ticket each year (such as, for example, a band with a compass pointing to Boom – the venue). The clever thing about this is that this also already serves as an immediate reminder after the festival, ensuring that the hangover is not what is remembered. Having received the ticket/compass, the anticipation process starts, and every time they see the compass, that is triggered again. Did you know that the anticipation of an event is sometimes better than the actual thing? 'Going to buy or do' something and considering it, making well thought out choices (in case of a high involvement products such as a camera or car, or booking a holiday) could be more exciting for people than actually buying/doing it. This is something to consider. Should we do something to make the search process during the anticipation more attractive? Or should we make the actual buying more attractive? I would say, do both.

We can apply such techniques in the actual store too; make sure that paying is not the hangover that lingers. Take care of the customers and also think of them after they walk out of the store. Give them a reminder, a small gift, or send a message afterwards. Especially when it comes to more expensive purchases like a piece of furniture or a car, a message saying that you hope they are happy with their purchase and that you are always available for questions is a great idea. As a designer, though, you can shape the visit to the physical store from start to finish. This starts outside at the facade or sometimes already in the car park, until the end, back outside. It is up to the designer to shape and elaborate that entire journey as a scenario. Devise the story the customer will experience, from arrival to departure, with a climax somewhere in between.

..with simple delights

Our own research has shown that 'some delight' is needed, such as something going beyond what the customer expects. Something surprising can also be something wondrous. Research demonstrates a link between wonder and increased focus. Which therefore means that by introducing wonder into the customer journey, you make the customer pay more attention to the experience. It goes without saying that a pleasurable experience positively affects our mood and when we become happy(er) about something, we are going to be stimulated to continue with what made us happy(er). Happiness or pleasure is a powerful driving force in humans. When we take pleasure in something, we are more likely to want to repeat it again. That is why it is so important to design a store that offers a pleasurable experience, so people want to come back. Indeed, when they come back a next time they need to be 'delighted' again. Nobody likes a one-trick pony. I mentioned it earlier, experiential retail is hard work. It is a continuous process. Here are some simple 'delighters' that lighten the mood.

Humor

There are some tools to positively affect one's mood. Communication being one of them. As mentioned earlier, this layer is often neglected although it can have a strong added value. For instance, communication is useful to inform people so that when all the shop assistants are busy, a customer can still find his way around, gather information and shop independently in a self-explanatory store. But perhaps an even more important task for communication is to delight people. And the best way to do that is with humor. Think of statements like 'people who say shopping doesn't make you happy clearly don't know where to shop'. Or, 'a smile is a woman's most beautiful curve'. But also graphics could help in this, as the doughnut eating Homer illustrates. Such delights could be placed throughout the store. Choose again in relation to the brand's DNA.

Just as humorous communication can change a person's mood, negative communication can do so too. So avoid negative communication at all times. Always try to formulate messages in a positive way to avoid disgust. I once saw a beautiful example hanging outsides a boutique door: push, if that doesn't work, pull, if that doesn't work, we are closed. That's a so much nicer way of saying a store is closed. A message no one likes to read if they had planned to visit the store. But with some humor, this message will arrive much more gently. Another example shows exactly the opposite. It was a jewelry store in the city center that clearly suffered from theft and bikes in front of the store and shop window. The owner had thought of nothing better than putting some stickers with a prohibition sign (a bicycle on a road sign with a red line through it) on the window and door. With, in addition, prints from the security camera footage of the people who had stolen earlier, again with a red line through. I can't think of anything crazier myself. But who still feels welcome when it is mostly prohibition signs that stand out?

Complexity

I've talked before about a certain legibility of a design. Such as the recognition of certain architecture and structures that help us navigate a store (direction of beams on the ceiling, ceiling height). I also touched on shaping flow (continuity versus tension). But there is a third dimension in design that goes beyond recognition and legibility, which can thus lead to delight: a certain degree of complexity, or maybe even mystery. Complexity can lie in discovering zones, for example, that were not visible initially, or playful visual effects. The Zhongshu bookstores in China are an exquisite example. These stores are designed to surprise the customer, to invite them to stay and enjoy the retail space. Architecture and books are one, certainly in Dujiangyan Zhongshuge, located in Chengdu. As the sketch shows, the two-storey space appears cathedral-like, thanks to the mirrored ceilings and black tiled floors that reflect the bookcases.

Nature

There is no denying that nature affects us, as evidenced by many studies in hospitals and work environments. In hospitals it has been proven that when a patient has a view of nature they heal faster. In work environments, people are said to be more productive and experience less stress. Now, it is not always possible to have a view of nature, but fortunately we see the same result when plants are added to the space. To see if this could also work in stores, a couple of master's students tested this a few years ago in our lab, set up like a supermarket at the time. Two conditions were tested. One with some large plants added and one without. In my opinion, the results were quite impressive taking into account that the time in a store is so much shorter than the time spent in an office. The students found that the stress level of the participants did not increase in the condition with plants, while without plants the stress level while shopping did increase. So that means plants do have an impact on stress levels. Other studies confirm this finding and go even further. Integrating elements of greenery, but also daylight as well as natural materials such as timber in a store reduces stress and creates a stronger feeling of contentment. This has also clearly spilled over into practice. Just notice how many stores are playing with green today. Even fake green, but that's ok. The positive impact of that too has been proven. Daylight is also completely welcome again in stores. That was different twenty years ago. Many stores next to roads were closed boxes. Now we see skylights, large glass facades and patios appearing.

Fitting room

The fitting room in a store is an important part of the shopping experience; this is where the decision to buy is usually made. And yet, they often are not the key priority of a brand. But they should be a delight. It should be an experience to try on clothing. Why is it too often seen as a necessity? There are many people on this planet who do not like trying on clothes. But maybe if the fitting room offered a great experience, maybe some of these people could be turned. How often do people have to wait in line at the fitting rooms? Only to be awarded with a dull stuffy cubicle that still smells of the previous user? How much of a delight is that? Remember this is the place where people decide what to buy and what not to buy.

So spoil them, make them feel at ease and delight them; you will see, they will return the favor and buy more. Just to be clear, mirrors, enough coat racks, seating elements and offering enough privacy by providing a solid curtain, without gaps or openings, or a door that puts the customer at ease, are simple basics. Delight the customer with a shelf for putting glasses on, a scarf to protect the clothing from make-up, a nice smell or air freshener, fun communication, nice detailing and proper lighting. By the way, proper lighting is lighting coming from behind or along the mirror, which lights up the person's face as it were. And it is not a spotlight on someone's head that highlights all the unflattering details!

Atmosphere

The use of senses can be a delight, for sure. Senses excite us in a different way, a way that can lead directly to enjoyment. Because the importance of the senses is so great I like to expand on this in the following part. And although it might seem simple to play around with the senses, it is not.

...and playing with senses

Before I discuss all the senses, it is good to know that much research has been done into the impact of different stimuli such as color, music, light and smell on customers. Each of these elements does have an impact on time spent in the shop, evaluation of the shop, feelings triggered by these stimuli, and shop image. In most studies, these stimuli are examined in isolation, which means that it is the only element that changes in the store during the study. Some studies examine such stimuli together (such as scent and music, scent and light) with a similar result in each case: these stimuli, or the combination of them, have an impact on how people feel and behave, with the main message being that the chosen stimuli must be in accordance with the rest of the store design and products. A good designer knows this and can combine these elements to form a fit. The biggest challenge is to link these elements to the DNA of a brand. Here, too, a match is important. Again, as a designer, most of those connections come from experience and education, however, I do notice that not all connections are as obvious as they seem. Selecting materials that convey 'familial' is less obvious than a material that should convey 'sustainability'. However, if you start combining things like materials, the design and the detailing, then it does become easier to exude a message of 'familial'.

To help to constitute a whole that is linked to the DNA of a brand, we have drawn up a Sense Matrix, shown below. This is the last and final tool to be used in the actual design process. It is important to start from the DNA of the brand, and more concretely from the brand personality traits. As the matrix indicates, you first need to fill these in at the top because they are the backdrop of the decision on whether the stimuli fit the brand or not. There is a lot of knowledge available on each sense so I will explain the matrix via discussing each of them in detail.

	BP1	BP2	BP3	BP4
Scent				
Artificial				
Scent of products, materials,…				
Sound				
Music (radio, playlist, live music,…)				
Acoustics (talking people, footsteps,…)				
Touch				
Touch (material cash desk, seating,,…)				
Climate (temperature, cleanliness,…)				
Taste				
Service (free) (coffee/water, samples,…)				
Products (sell) (coffeebar, snacks,…)				
Sight				
Design language (materials, proportions, colors,…)				
Visual stimuli (lighting, visuals,…)				

To scent or not to scent

In stores generally two types of odors are to be found, present odors and artificial odors. This is also reflected in the Sense Matrix. For the first group, a store like Lush is a good example. They sell bath, body, skin and haircare products with appealing scents. Those scents emit throughout the store and are part of the store experience. The same applies to flower shops, bakeries, and the like. When these scents are experienced as positive or attractive they sometimes are enhanced by spreading them through the ventilation system throughout the store, or into the street to attract people. Think of the scent of freshly baked bread, or coffee. Sometimes a store can even have a scent of the materials applied. A store entirely constructed out of wood will have a different smell than a store constructed out of concrete.

The second group of odors are the artificial ones. This can be a synthetic scent or a natural scent. We have to be very careful with adding scents. From research we see that scents only offer an added value when the scent fits the products and/or the interior of the store. When a scent does not fit, the store is less appreciated by the visitor than when there is no scent present. So better no scent than a non-fitting scent! It needs no further explanation that a bad scent drives people away. So yes, in such cases neutralizing scents should be used. Now, what fitting and non-fitting means is less easy to describe in rules. In science we call this congruence or incongruence. Whether a scent is congruent with a room can certainly be measured, but this requires a lot of time and energy. One of our PhD students laid the foundations for this by setting up an entire experiment in which a scent was used to design a store. A few groups of students and a professional design team were set to work designing our lab on our campus as a cookery store based on this scent. The design teams were presented with a scent sample during the design process. However, they were not allowed to know which scent it was (unless they recognized it, but that is often very difficult with scents). The key question of this research was whether a store designed based on a scent (thus congruent with it) was more appreciated than the same store with a non-congruent scent or no scent. Of the two scents used in this research, in a pre-test one was experienced as fitting the store design, and one was experienced as not fitting the store design (but both were of course pleasant scents). The study then continued by having people shop in the lab under the different scent conditions. What emerged? People who shopped in the lab with the congruent scent on which the design was created evaluated the store more positively than the people who shopped in the condition with the non-congruent, but pleasant, scent.

There is so much to say about the impact of scents on how people feel and behave, and it is a much researched part of store design, too much even to go into detail here. There is one study, though, that I would still like to mention and that is the research of a fellow professor in marketing who did an experiment during her PhD about the impact of certain scents in a bookstore. Without going into details, the result was interesting. When the scent of chocolate was distributed in the shop, there was an increase in sales of cookery books and romantic literature, but a decrease in crime and history books. So, this research shows that when a scent is congruent with certain products, more of these products can be sold. However, it also says that this only causes a shift within the shop, not an increase in sales in general. It could potentially be useful, for example, to be able to get rid of certain products in stock by deploying a scent that is congruent with these products. However, bear in mind that women derive more pleasure from scent in stores than men.

What are we hearing (or not)

Sound also includes two categories, the most obvious being music. Just as with scent, by stimulating the visitor in the store with music that supports the image of the brand (and thus the idea a visitor has of this brand), the relationship between the customer and the brand is reinforced. We know from research that the type of music and the loudness have an impact on our mood and even, if the music has a beat, it can influence how quickly we move around a store. Movements are clearly slower when a low tempo is played and faster when music with a higher tempo is played. So, music with a slow tempo will increase the time spent in the store. Supermarkets play around with this a lot. When the supermarket is crowded, high tempo music is played so customers move around more quickly. In quiet times more relaxed music is played so customers take their time to shop. Indeed, the more time a customer spends in store, the more likely he will buy more. It goes without saying that we can't do this by setting up a radio station; ideally streaming services are used. Why? Because then, as a retailer, you have complete control over the atmosphere of the music. Besides, nobody is served by hearing the news (again) during shopping, certainly not in recent years with the pandemic and crises dominating it. And, it has happened to me more than once that I am shopping in store X while advertising from store Y passes through the speakers.

The second category, acoustics, may not be the first one to come to mind when you think of store design, but it does play a part. The rolling of iron wheels of shopping trolleys on an (uneven) tiled floor is not desirable. Nor is it desirable for other shoppers to be able to hear sensitive information, for example when buying an expensive product or a product one prefers to be discreet about. More surrounding sounds also play a role. Think of the passing cars on a busy road or the sound of ventilation or air heating. On the other hand, hearing the creaking of an old wooden floor in a boutique may be desirable. Indeed, sound must be thought about and it is better to prevent than to cure. If you have to turn up the radio so loud that the hum of the fridges cannot be heard, then you have a design flaw. Also think of sounds like placing keys or a handbag on the glass plate of the counter, the sliding of the rings over the rail of the fitting room curtain, etc. – these are sounds you either want or don't.

Do you feel the DNA?

There is the obvious aspect of tactility, namely touching products and materials, but there is also the less obvious aspect of climate. Both air quality and perceived temperature play a role. Our skin cannot only feel different temperatures, structures and hardnesses through direct contact, it can also feel the temperature of a room. Choosing the right temperature for both staff and customers may not be the biggest challenge, but how you heat/cool is. Air ventilation, for example, involves a lot of air movement, and a collection of dust and dirt in one place is a known problem. In addition, sustainability is playing an increasingly important role and in a lot of cities rules say that doors must remain closed and air curtains are off limits. With the disappearance of an air curtain, draughts naturally get more chance at the opening and closing of (sliding) doors. So pay attention to where the cash register or service point is located so that these people do not have to work in a draught all day. Covid has taught us that air quality and ventilation are important. Badly aired areas and unventilated fitting rooms are not done.

As a retailer, you should have complete control over the entire atmosphere, your branded atmosphere.

When it comes to touching products and materials, this first one should be self-evident. Being able to touch and feel products is an essential difference to online shopping. Making it difficult for the consumer by putting the products behind glass could be a deathblow to the retailer. I am not talking about the products that are in a cabinet that is constantly manned and where service is key (e.g. jeweler). I am talking about the products in glass cabinets 'somewhere' in the store that can only be opened by one or a few members of staff; they are really a thing of the past.

Retail is detail. Every stimulus counts.

In my opinion, coming into contact with materials is an underestimated incentive in the total experience of a store. Through the use of tactile materials a subtle message can be conveyed to the consumer, influencing the feeling of the retailer. Customers come into contact with clothing hangers, counters, seating elements, fitting room curtains or doors, presentation tables, and so on. How these should look visually is often well thought out, but how they feel is not. Once, for example, I tried on some outfits in a boutique that had black steel fitting rooms, entirely in keeping with the old building. Beautiful to look at, but it was not pleasant to change clothes because I bumped against the sides with my bare arms (yes, the fitting rooms were a bit too small), which gave a cold stimulus. Not the most pleasant feeling when trying on clothes. Indeed, research shows that contact with materials that have a relatively low temperature gives us an uncomfortable and unpleasant feeling. Along the same lines, poor quality fitting room curtains in a boutique do not give the right feeling either. Rather go for a luxury fabric or a fabric with a nice leather detail at the height that the customers hold the curtain. Be careful with fitting room doors that often have cold handles and make a chilly sound when closing. Also think about the seating where people wait or have something to consume, how does it feel? Think beyond the appearance here. Link the choice of material back to the DNA of the brand.

Research also shows that bodily experiences of hardness influence the meta-phorical perception of brand personality dimensions of rigor and stability. But the experience of weight, such as gravity and lightness, is also metaphorically linked with feelings such as seriousness and importance. Think of the feeling someone gets when they have to open a very light fitting room curtain or a cur-tain made of a heavy fabric. The second suggests a more serious store.

So, realise that such 'details' have an impact on the brand's image. Just like the difference between cheap plastic clothing hangers and wooden or fabric covered clothing hangers. I don't need to repeat that retail is detail. Every stimulus counts.

I know the next example is not at all 'a detail' nor is it subtle, but just to highlight the power of a material, Balenciaga's pop-up store in faux-fur is appealing, no? They wanted to create a maximalist look to launch its Le Cagole collection by wrapping the interior in bright pink faux fur. It is so furry I could not even sketch it without loosing its visual softness.

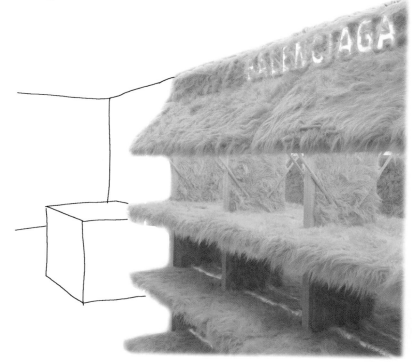

Not something 100% appropriate under touch, but I discuss it here anyway for the sake of the link. I call it 'visual tactility', which is nothing more than the perception of a material in terms of how hot or cold we judge it to be, or how hard or soft we think it is. There are a lot of materials in a store that customers don't touch, but which can be played with or used to visually convey tactile properties. Think of textured wallpaper or a ceramic lampshade. We know these materials and associate them with certain values, even if the material is not real. The lampshade could just as easily be made of polyester with a ceramic look. There have been quite a few studies on this, which show that materials with a structure appear warmer than those without. For example a red concrete wall is perceived to be warmer than a coarse concrete wall. And, a coarse concrete wall is perceived to be warmer than a smooth concrete wall. So be creative.

Adding some flavor

Because people do not like to spend time doing things they do not like to do, retailers are doing everything they can to make shopping as enjoyable as possible, even in supermarkets, where people tend to shop with a functional mindset. Here, too, free coffee is often offered. And we all know about the free tastings offered on weekends. The principle of being offered something to drink while waiting has, of course, long been known from boutiques. But they also go a step further and often expand their offer by adding a bar or bistro. Of course, the food and drinks are no longer free here, but it does ensure that people stay in the store longer and that they are more involved with the retailer. Indeed, it also creates more interaction. These are all ingredients for creating an emotional bond with the customer, a bond that lasts longer than a purely transactional bond.

In the Sense Matrix, a distinction can be made between the free drink that is offered while waiting or the service story where you effectively add a function to the shop, creating a hybrid concept. Anyway, choose tastes and brands that you can associate with the retailer's brand values. And to link to touch again, even think of the type of cups, glasses or plates you use to serve these things in. I do not think filter coffee in a white standard cheap mug is the way to go these days. Neither are plastic cups. Show the customer that you care by offering him quality. If you cannot offer that, it might be better to offer him nothing.

What meets the eye

This is, of course, a very large category. But perhaps the most important because visual stimuli still dominate stimuli from the other senses. Two very important components play a role here: the design language used in the design and the, let's say, slightly more pronounced visual stimuli, the eye-catchers as described earlier. Eye-catchers work best when they are made with care. Attention to the presentation of the products, of course, but also to the communication involved, the choice of materials and, perhaps most importantly, the lighting. Regarding communication, it is very important that it is informative on the one hand. Suppose one creates a display of limited edition handbags that is advertised on different channels, using the same kind of communication and photography in the store so that it is very quickly recognisable. On the other hand, it can also create atmosphere. Enlarge the photo, for example, so that it takes up the entire rack. An eye-catcher stands out when there is a break in the pattern. For example, to create an eye-catcher in a supermarket, header displays are ideal for this. Make a break in the pattern (pattern being the long shelves, in one color) by finishing the header rack with wood, for example. The same goes for any other kind of store. Often shelves and furniture in a store are the same color. By changing a tablet or a shelf here and there, you break the pattern and make it stand out.

When you are dealing with bigger products, like a car for example, it is always good to place a car that stands out. When I was working for a car dealer, studying showrooms, that is one thing that stood out. Car dealers who had a model in a very distinctive bright color, sold more of that specific car model, but in a mainstream color. Even though that specific car will most likely not be sold, it is beneficial to have such a model as an eye-catcher. And make it visible from outside too, to attract people.

To zoom in on lighting for a moment, I discussed the impact of accent lighting on products and eye-catchers. But also flexibility is highly valued in store design. I recommend always working with flexible lighting in a store so that wherever eye-catchers are placed, they can be provided with extra lighting. Bear in mind that lighting has an impact on the perception of the room at the level that a beautiful space can look bad because of badly selected lighting. So invest sufficient time and money when choosing lighting. And never forget that dark colors absorb much more light than bright colors. So be aware when designing a store or when changing the colors of the walls that this has a direct impact on the efficiency of the lighting. A store with black walls consumes twice the amount of light than a store with white walls. I have seen that mistake made several times. It is always a bad idea to remodel a store without (re) considering the lighting. This also counts for shopping windows, by the way. If you change the colors in the display (like the back wall for example) the lighting should be adjusted accordingly.

With regard to design language, our second visual component in the Sense Matrix, I would like to refer to a very interesting study that actually shows the basis of what design language can do. It concerns the Kiki and Bouba story. Kiki and Bouba are two spots. You can see them below. Who do you think Kiki is and who is Bouba?

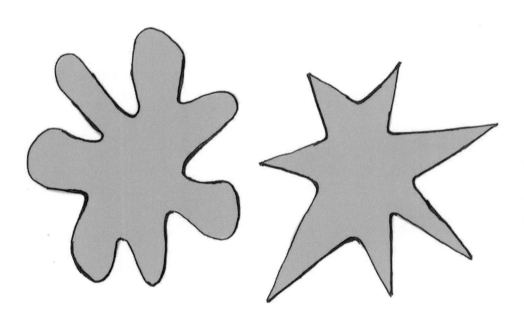

Most of society refers to the spot with the sharp points as Kiki and to the more rounded spot as Bouba. Although this study has been done scientifically, I cannot resist repeating this exercise during a lesson or a lecture. And time after time, whether it is a class of 20 students or a room of 1,000 people, about 98% name the sharp spot Kiki. Amazing, isn't it? It is only a stain and yet we manage to find consensus in naming it. We could, of course, post-rationalize it and make links between the sharp angles of the stain and the sharp sounds of the word Kiki, but the point is that with shapes you can send a message that almost everyone understands. We can take this one step further and associate Kiki sounds and Kiki shapes with speed, directness, edgy and sharp. While Bouba sounds and shapes are more linked to softness, gentle, easy-going and cosiness. So a brand's DNA consisting of speed and power would do better to go for a Kiki interior (sketch). Whereas a brand's DNA that wants to radiate cosiness and friendliness is better served with a Bouba interior (sketch). The possibilities are of course much broader than Kiki and Bouba, but it shows the power of shapes and how they are perceived.

How things are perceived, things like colors, materials and shapes, and more so, the interplay of these is something we call semiotics. It is a scientific approach that focuses on the study of signs, their interrelationship and the processes that occur in the use of signs. In the past, I set up some studies with students to apply this theory of meaning to design as well. And it does work. You can completely dissect a design using semiotics. So it also works the other way around. With a smart choice of design elements, the chosen story can be correctly conveyed to customers. Indeed, interior design students are, or should be, trained in this.

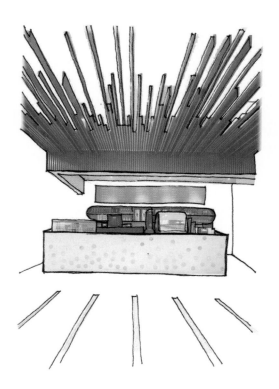

Just look at the following examples. This goes further than Kiki and Bouba shapes; this is about design language. Imagine standing at the entrance to the cathedral in the sketch. It is a huge imposing building with doors twice the size of yourself. You automatically feel small, perhaps a little intimidated. You will automatically adjust your behavior accordingly, silent and impressed. When you walk up and you see the entrance to the luna park in the next sketch, you may be more enraptured and you also know that you are certainly allowed to behave as exuberantly as the facade indicates. Indeed, architecture and design impacts how we behave. We can therefore use architecture and design in such a way that, as designers, we help people elicit or encourage the desired behavior. Of course, this requires some knowledge. Knowledge that a designer should require.

THE BIG BOOK OF RETAIL DESIGN

Something called cross-modal congruency

The congruence principle, as already mentioned with smell, is of course not limited to smell. All sensory stimuli interact and influence each other. Research shows that when all stimuli (or as many as possible) are congruent, the best results can be achieved. This means a better evaluation of the store and its products. So ideally we try to make the stimuli cross-modally congruent. For example, there is the study that showed that when one drinks coffee from an orange cup, it tastes sweeter than in any other color of cup. This illustrates that orange and coffee are cross-modal congruent and that orange seems to have an impact on coffee which other colors do not. There is even research that goes a step further. In a study, researchers created three different rooms entirely in their own specific style. There was a green room with artificial grass on the floor, where the smell of freshly cut grass was diffused and sounds of a summer meadow were played. The second room was a red room where a sweet smell was diffused and high notes such as ringing bells were played. The last room was completely finished in wood. The smell of cedar and tonka beans was diffused and the sound of a crackling fire was played. All applied stimuli in the room were congruent with each other. The participants in the study were asked to taste a certain whiskey while sitting in one of the rooms. The same whiskey was served in each room. The aim of the study was to see if the environment had an impact on the taste experience of the whiskey. And, as expected, it did. The aftertaste of the whiskey was labelled as 'grassy' in the green room, 'sweet' in the red room and 'woody' in the last room.

It is not that all cross-modal correspondences have already been fully mapped out. But we can see how important the senses are and what role colors, smells, sounds, etc. play, although we do not yet fully understand their cross-modal impact. To effectively design by cross-modal correspondences, it is clear one should overcome personal associations and search for the common denominator.

Do not overdo it

The more senses are stimulated, the more intense the experience. But we have to be careful here that this is not a rule every brand has to live by. On the contrary, as mentioned many times before, it has to fit within a brand's DNA. But a greater danger is over-stimulation. Too much stimulation also keeps people away, and I'm not just talking about highly sensitive people. There can also just be too much going on in a store. In one of our eye-tracking studies at a fashion retailer, this came out very clearly. The retailer was engaging all the senses in a proper, congruent way but still half of the study participants turned around after a few minutes and discontinued the search we had given them. The reason? Visually, far too much was happening. As a result, the music also became distracting after a few minutes. We can explain this happening by how our brains work. We receive thousands of stimuli every day, but we do not experience them all equally consciously. That is what our 'filter' in our brain takes care of. In highly sensitive people, this filter fills up much faster than in the average person, and when the filter is 'full', enough is enough and we go or need to go in search of rest. Perhaps everyone has experienced that 'overflowing' feeling, being over-excited. That a growing group of people suffer from this is evidenced, for example, by the low-stimulation day offered by many fairs in big cities. This is a day/half day when the sound is turned off and lighting is minimized. This attracts a relatively large group of people consisting of more than just highly sensitive people. Selfridges in London also committed to this a decade ago. Selfridges is a, say mega, department store where a lot is happening and where experience is central. To see the whole store you need several hours. Of course, hardly anyone can keep this up without a decent break.

Selfridges has therefore resurrected the silent room as part of their No Noise campaign in 2013. London studio Alex Cochrane Architects created their interpretation of a silent room. A literally soft (cream felt covering the walls, floor and seats) soundproof room with only indirect ambient lighting. After removing their shoes, visitors are channeled into a dark corridor to guide them around the back of the rectangular box and through a gap in the wall.The space is not intended to be completely silent but rather to encourage visitors to lower their voices and take time to unwind and empty their filter. Although it might seem a new idea, Mr. Selfridge himself had created a first version in 1909. His silent room was meant for men waiting for their wives while they shopped. Today Selfridges offers a weekly quiet hour in which turning off the music and, where possible, switching off the screens offer a calmer environment. Recently also other stores like Carrefour have adopted this 'quiet hour'.

To learn to work with the Sense Matrix we first use it with our students as an evaluation tool. Together with the students, we visit some shops. Before we do, of course, the brand personality traits must be known. In the store itself, the students fill in the matrix in small groups. The matrix helps the students analyze and look at the space in a different way that involves every sense. Back in class, the matrices are discussed per store so that, on the one hand, we can check whether the matrix is well understood and, on the other hand, the moment also serves to define opportunities for the store. Thus, the students themselves have to think about how the store can respond well to all the senses. It is in a next stage that students will use the matrix as a design tool. See the next chapter for an example.

We receive thousands of stimuli every day, but we do not experience them all equally consciously.

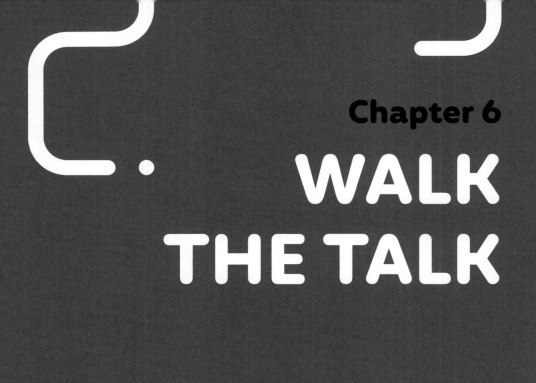

Chapter 6

WALK THE TALK

Walk the talk

I can explain the models as much as I want. Still, it's always better to illustrate them with a real example. For the purpose of this book, I am going to use a fictional example with the aim of illustrating all the tools and models cited above. To include as many sectors and different products as possible, I will discuss a concept store that offers a mixture of products to a very diverse audience. As throughout the book, retail design principles are applicable to any sector. So again, try to see through the products here. By the way, this is always true when one wants to learn about retail and retail design. Sector-specific knowledge is necessary, but inspiration usually comes from other sectors. However, learning to see is not easy. I notice this every time I go out with students or entrepreneurs. You really have to learn how to look. But once you know how best to look, a world opens up. Open your gaze again and again.

NOOK

Who they are....

My fictitious brand NOOK promises coziness and feel-good at home. NOOK offers everything you need to make your home even 'homier' and to relax completely. The brand wants to be a trendsetting lifestyle brand with an eye for quality and locality. Acting responsibly is in their DNA; it is natural for them. Every interaction (online and offline) with NOOK should be surprising and inspiring. Inspiration lies in the presentation of the products, fun ideas to make it cozy and also offering complete sets. These can include, for example, a blanket with matching pillows, a scented candle, a plant in a pot, a house suit and hand cream, all in the same matching look. They aim to also invest in an equally inspiring store design. It is a very approachable brand because it communicates in a very relaxed and open way. NOOK will offer several services. For example, there will be a buy online pick up in-store (BOPIS) point, they offer home delivery and home styling. With the latter, a stylist will visit your home with fabrics, patterns, and colors. Based on that visit, an appointment will be made in the store where an assortment will be shown tailored to the customer.

Furthermore, they are already communicating with the target group through various social media channels. They will also immediately set up a webshop and also sell through a platform (such as Amazon).

What they offer....

NOOK is a one-stop shop for coziness. The two main product groups are home decor products and clothing (cozy home wear and night wear). Both categories mainly include products for the living room and bedroom. They also offer a line of vegan personal care products for healthy skin and hair, a collection of books that includes both interior books and stationery, some plants, and lastly products that fall more under 'gadgets', such as beautiful portable music boxes, cozy headphones, etc. The collections are a mixture of trendy products and timeless items. By cleverly choosing who they work with, they can regularly add new pieces to the store so there is always something new to discover. They work with mostly local producers. All products fall in the middle to slightly more expensive range in terms of price.

To be able to offer even more 'cozy products', they will collaborate with a local wine merchant (who now has a small premises nearby) who will occupy part of the premises and who does want to be connected to the rest of the store as much as possible so that it appears to be one store (with the exception of a separate cash register). The customers the wine merchant already has, are a perfect fit with what NOOK envisions. The wines are also 'local' (French).

People who like to stay at home and want to make this a cozy place. Every moment at home counts; it is a moment to enjoy, whether it is alone or with two, or the whole family. Based on an exploratory market study, three target groups emerged. The first group are **cocooners**. People who enjoy being at home and do their best to make it cozy and invest in this. It is expected that these people will be regular customers and will regularly pop in to buy something small such as a candle, a vase, a plant or a bottle of wine in between larger purchases. A second group are **indulgers**. They like to indulge themselves as well as others. They are especially drawn to personal care products, clothing, stationery and wine. As for the rest, they do come for inspiration and sometimes buy bigger things for the home. Finally, there should be a large group of interested people who are attracted to the store and/or something they have seen on social media. These customers will only return occasionally but they will become loyal followers on Instagram.

Phase 1: Designing the brief for NOOK

I use the questions of the Design Brief to elaborate on NOOK to initiate the next steps. For the company culture, inspiration is also central, with that wanting to be just a bit different. Acting responsibly is a no-brainer. To the outside world, they don't necessarily want to exude that sustainable side just because it's a no-brainer. Last but not least, conviviality seems an appropriate description of how they see themselves.

Next, I start by imagining NOOK as a person. To me, he or she is charismatic, engaged but certainly also playful and relaxed. Someone you kind of look up to and who likes to be seen by everyone.

I now have to choose wine from the wine bottles presented in the Design Brief. I choose the one that is a bit different yet playful and charismatic with a relaxed vibe. Note that I will not necessarily look for a French wine because the wine bottle should be chosen primarily on the basis of appearance, not content.

Another interesting section in the Design Brief which I haven't addressed yet is the part with questions about the competition. In NOOK's case competition actually comes from everywhere. Especially chains that specialize in one particular product group such as decoration products, or bedding and nightwear, cosmetics... Online platforms are also disrupting the market. Although affiliated with a platform themselves, online competition is very tough. Still, NOOK wants to be different by offering a limited assortment with a very distinct individuality. One of the questions in the design Brief is which brand inspirers NOOK. In terms of store design that is definitely Aesop. Their products are usually made of circular materials fitting the brand story. All stores are different yet radiate the same spirit, the Aesop spirit. Also IKEA is a source of inspiration on how they sell coziness. Lastly Rituals succeeds very well in selling mystery. The aura around their products is what NOOK wants for their products.

Always look at what the competition is doing and learn from it.

Phase 2: NOOK's Brand pyramid

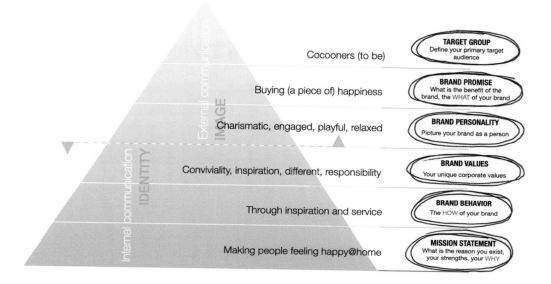

Starting at the bottom of the pyramid with the identity of NOOK which will only be communicated within the company, as far as the mission goes, it seems safe to say that making people happy at home is NOOK's mission. It is the reason for their existence, their WHY. If we start thinking about HOW they want to establish that, it is clear that 'inspiration' is what they want to offer. They will do that in many different ways. On the one hand by offering a wide range of products, which are well curated to distinguish themselves; on the other hand they offer services for those who need help (like a stylist). They also want to stand out on social media. This can be done by being playful but also by communicating in a very accessible and open way. Also the physical store should communicate this. For the brand values I can copy those selected in the Design Brief.

Next, regarding the external communication that eventually determines the image of the brand, I can again copy the personality traits from the Design Brief. NOOK promises its customers the ability to buy a piece of happiness. That happiness can come from the beauty of the product, or the fact that it is local and sustainable, or the fine experience you feel in the store. Indeed, it can be different for everyone. By selling a piece of happiness, NOOK assumes that that is precisely their added value. Customers who experience this are naturally going to want to feel it again and again and that the cocooners (shown by a market study), will become loyal customers.

Phase 2: Understanding NOOK's target group

Personas

Based on the three target groups, I will now create a number of personas. The cocooners will form the largest group. Therefore, it is wise to make two personas for them. The indulgers are already quite clear and for this, one persona will suffice. Being a start-up brand, it is important to get a grip on the potential new-comers. How can we give these people a face so we can better empathize with their emotions and motivations. Therefore, I define one persona for this purpose.

As a first step, we need to define the dimensions. As mentioned, this normally requires delving deeper into the target audience, but for the purpose of the exercise I define them myself. A good starting point is to start from the DNA of NOOK; are there values here that could also be significant as dimensions? Given that NOOK wants to offer inspiration, a dimension could be, for example, 'degree of creativity' because that indicates to what extent customers can or cannot decorate their homes themselves. Another logical dimension is responsibility toward our planet. There will be customers who will come for that very reason and others who will see it as a nice benefit. A link to the services they offer is also a logical one to make. For example, I link the amount of free time people have to enjoy their homes but also to do the search for products and the purchase themselves to the online service and the stylist. Linking to the defined target group is the next option. Thinking about cocooners, I immediately think of people who prefer cocooning alone or in group. Those who prefer to be alone might be more introverted while the others are extroverts. Do they share their piece of happiness or do they keep it for themselves? Also the level of the need of me-time might be relevant to understand what their drivers are. Certainly the 'indulgers' probably like me-time. So it's not too bad to come up with dimensions when looking for connections. Of course, it would be better to be able to extract them from consumer data.

The cocooners

I start with the cocooners and devise a scenario for a 'typical' cocooner, some-one who really likes to spend a lot of time at home and can genuinely enjoy this, sometimes alone, sometimes with others. The market study indicated that these will be regular visitors. I took the liberty of making this a buying lady who loves to embellish her home, where she lives with her boyfriend. She is the best at turning places into cozy spaces. She has a webshop of her own where she sells sustain-able handbags. As an entrepreneur, she is rather extroverted and loves company (in the home, hence the chosen quote). Indeed, she sees her friends as family. I call her **Aisha**. For me, this is also when I start looking for a photo that fits this description. I always use the website of a photographer (Jason Travis) who had the fantastic idea of photographing people with the contents of their bags. That helps tremendously to create a picture of these people and is also very useful for picking personas. So the nice thing is that you can make a link between the products in their bag and NOOK. That's why I chose the lady I named Aisha and that is shown in my sketch. She loves notebooks, pens and fun patterns. So the description of the persona arises along with selecting the photos. Another nice asset of the con-tents of the bag is that you can also create links to the personas' lovebrands. So pay attention to this also when analyzing the contents of the bag.

Regarding the dimensions, the link with responsible behavior towards our climate is quickly made. She is an extrovert and likes to hang out with friends at home, that is how she energizes herself. We already know she is very creative. To get her needs in focus, we imagine what her link to NOOK might be. Why would she go to NOOK? You can also focus the frustrations by thinking about what problem NOOK could solve for her. In Aisha's case, that is a one-stop shop. She will enjoy exploring the store and wants to explore all the products. Having them in one store really saves her time, time she does not have too much of.

Aisha Neven

"

My place at eight!

36 years old
Webshop owner (vegan handbags)
Lives with her boyfriend
She

Bio/scenario

If you say cocooning, you think of Aisha. She is the best in turning places into cozy spaces. Friends love to hang out at their place. She will always change something so she, and her friends, enjoy slightly different settings each time. She sees her friends as family. She has known them, as well as her boyfriend, since they were kids.

Personality dimensions

Caring about our planet

Subordinate ————————————●— Priority

Creativity

Not at all ————————————●— Very

Free time (to shop)

Few —●———————————— A lot

Personality

Introvert ——————————●—— Extravert

Me time

No need ———————————— High need

Needs

She always feels an urge to make it cosy at home. Every year she buys a couple of new items to complete her 'nest'. Older items she would tuck away for some time to use it again in a different setting. If only there was a place where she could get inspiration.

Frustrations

She used to love strolling around in different shops to find catchy items but her business has become so successful that she has no time to do that.

Lovebrands

Aisha's lovebrands are Mud Jeans and Rains, both being sustainable brands. She loves Marvel, as do her friends, so sometimes when they come over they will watch Marvel series and movies together all night long.

A second cocooner may be a little less typical and is more interested in the other product groups. Given the offerings in wine, books and products that would do well as gifts, men are also an important target group. More specifically, I was thinking of someone active and with plenty of time to enjoy himself. He and his wife have worked hard throughout their lives and now enjoy plenty of leisure time, now that they are both retired. I found such a profile in the man I call **Cyrille**. The contents of his bag completely match what this persona needed. As the sketch shows, he is clearly a cyclist and he obviously loves wine and a good book. Especially during the evening hours he enjoys this immensely. He and his wife love being at home and they regularly buy small things like candles and plants to dress the house up. Cyrille is happy that NOOK offers inspiration on how to do that.

So for Cyrille, wine plays a big role. He loves French wines but doesn't really know enough about them. He likes to explore different flavors from different regions and indulge himself in this. Yet, he also favors another part of the store, the part with all the things he can buy for his wife. Yes, he likes to spoil her. She blossoms when he brings her something nice. Indeed Cyrille is more on the cutting edge between cocooner and indulger. Either way he and his wife are both fans of the brand. Every year they update a room in the house and for the living room and bedroom they are turning to NOOK for advise.

Cyrille Bilous
"Life is too short

62 years old
Retired
Married
He

Bio/scenario
Cyrille is a romantic at heart. Now he is retired he enjoys biking and walking while his wife enjoys pottery. But every evening they dine together. Usually they end up on the sofa reading a book with a glass of wine. They both love cooking and having friends over. They love going on holiday in France to explore nature.

Personality dimensions

Caring about our planet
Subordinate — Priority

Creativity
Not at all — Very

Free time (to shop)
Few — A lot

Personality
Introvert — Extravert

Me time
No need — High need

Needs
He loves to spoil his wife and surprise her every week. He misses a place where he can find nice presents for her, which he knows she will love (because she is fond of the brand). A bottle of wine from France being one of them.

Frustrations
Because they both love France, and thus French wines it would be nice to have a place nearby to buy wine. He loves discovering new flavors and supermarkets are not fulfilling that need.

Lovebrands

Cyrille loves nature, but he is not that into sustainable brands, quality prevails. This will just be a nice benefit for him. Cyrille used to be a physicist. So not exactly creative but he is quite extroverted. He does enjoy time at home with his French wine and a book (and wife).

The indulger

As the market study indicated, there is a group of people who like to pamper themselves (as well as others). For me, that immediately links to someone who likes to have me-time but in her job also likes to help or pamper others. So I ended up with a nurse who I can sum up in one quote, i.e. I care... (for herself, for others, for the planet and for her apartment). From that profile I set the dimensions. From caring for the planet, she prefers to invest in quality products that last and are preferably sustainable. She chooses NOOK for that reason. For the same reason she also does not own a car which can be an immediate frustration when making larger purchases. When looking for an image, I looked for someone who had products in her bag to take care of herself such as lip balm, hand cream. I found that with **Amea,** whom I have sketched below.

THE BIG BOOK OF RETAIL DESIGN

Amea is not so creative and when she has the time she loves to spend it on shopping. Her job requires her to be an extrovert, but actually she is a bit more introverted. She is great with patients but is does ask a lot of energy of her leading to a high need of me-time when she is not working. To indulge herself she loves to use the beauty products from NOOK and also the cozy home ware and night wear are a big hit. She has a grooming ritual she performs every evening.entering.

Amea Shilongo

"

I care…

27 years old
Nurse
Single
she

Bio/scenario

She lives in the city and adores her apartment. She has a cat she loves to take care of. Cuddling is their thing. Amea likes to take care of everything, people, animals, the planet and herself. After busy workdays at the hospital the enjoys quietness. She performs a grooming ritual every evening.

Personality dimensions

Caring about our planet

Subordinate ————————————— Priority

Creativity

Not at all ————————————— Very

Free time (to shop)

Few ————————————— A lot

Personality

Introvert ————————————— Extravert

Me time

No need ————————————— High need

Needs

Amea does not like to over consume so she saves until she can afford to buy decent quality products. Preferably locally produced. She is looking for a treat.

Frustrations

She only has a bike and uses public transport to travel. Indeed, going to a store takes too much time. She would like to order more online but few stores selling beauty products offer that.

Lovebrands

The lovemarks are not explicitly present in her handbag but based on her bio we can link to brands that have a sustainable edge. She loves Vinted where she can buy secondhand clothing of high quality designer brands.

The newcomers

Someone who passes by the store or who comes to NOOK through an online search will not see corporate responsibility as the most important thing but rather as a fine added value. It is someone who has a sudden need, such as upgrading her home, and is looking for products specifically for this purpose. To put variety into the personas I chose a lady with a family this time, I call her **Frauke**. You can tell she is a mom by the toy she is still carrying around from the last time they went hiking. As you can see from the contents of her bag in the sketch, she is prepared for everything: rain, waiting, taking notes, etc. Having been disappointed by online purchases, she is looking for a store she can visit.

Frauke teaches arts to undergraduates. So she is quite creative. But teaching and preparing classes takes up a lot of time not giving her the chance to visit many stores. She does spend her time looking for products online, that is how

THE BIG BOOK OF RETAIL DESIGN

she found NOOK. She is an introvert but she does not require much me-time. Time with her family is what keeps her going. Because of some bad experiences with buying online, Frauke will definitely visit the store first to see the quality of the products. Afterwards, she will make her choice of what she wants at home. That way, she can make a good estimate from her couch of what will go with the existing furniture. When visiting the store she is surprised by the shop's nice and varied selection and can't resist taking some small items. She is also an instant fan of the gadgets and is already anticipating the gifts she will soon have to buy for her children's birthdays (nine and ten years old). As her Lovebrands indicate, she likes quality products. And, she is fond of Zara because they offer so many different styles she can really be creative with.

Frauke Gibbon
"
Supercalifragilistic -expialidocious

41 years old teacher married with 2 children she

Bio/scenario
Teaching and having two kids (9 and 10) takes up quite some time. But now that the kids are becoming more independent she enjoys the extra free time that she has for herself and with her husband. She has always loved spending time at home but she feels it is time for a small update.

Personality dimensions

Caring about our planet
Subordinate — Priority

Creativity
Not at all — Very

Free time (to shop)
Few — A lot

Personality
Introvert — Extravert

Me time
No need — High need

Needs
She feels she has a good taste but she fails to find the products. She spends a lot of time browsing on the internet looking for products on (too) many webshops. She would love to have a one stop shop with everything to upgrade the living room.

Frustrations
What you see online is fake. Photos of products are clearly manipulated. She has ordered stuff before but it did not meet the expectations.

Lovebrands

And just as variety in personas is advisable, so is variety in dimensions. It is good to plot all personas together on the dimensions to see if there is enough difference between the axes. If not, you can further tune the personas so that they do. The the following chart shows this.

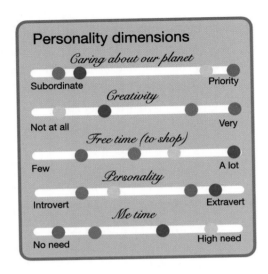

Shopping motivation model

From all of the above, it does seem that personas can cover the load. So I'm just going to test which shopping motivations NOOK incorporates. 'Just browsing' is one of the most prevalent motivations. NOOK mainly wants to offer inspiration and thus will commit to letting people explore the entire store. This is the ideal customer journey for Amea. Frauke and Aisha are more likely to explore the home deco department more often and ignore the rest. They lean a little closer to purpose-driven shopping, but it is still more than that since only the product category is known, but within that it can be 'anything' they choose. In doing so, NOOK does not want to miss the opportunity to entice these women to explore the rest of the products as well. Cyrille on occasion needs advice so NOOK needs a service point. Not knowing which wine to buy, Cyrille will also need information so also the winery needs a place where advice and tasting could take place. Frauke will also sometimes use the click & collect so she can double check everything again for quality.

As mentioned earlier, every store will include all four buying motivations to a greater or lesser extent. It is important to assess the design impact of these. NOOK will primarily focus on browsing behavior but with a clear product layout. NOOK will also put an info point visible from the entrance where it should not take too much time to pick up ordered items. The place where advice can be given may be set up a little more to the back (more privacy) but still visible because that is a service not everyone is familiar with. Also, the wine store needs to be able to make a respectable turnover so it is important that it is visible (and if possible accessible) from the street and very approachable to walk in whether or not via NOOK.

You notice that when you choose which shopping motivations are most important, you automatically start making choices about the layout of the store. It is therefore tempting to start working on the bubble plan, but that would lead to a very product oriented store (which sometimes is asked for). But I would advise taking the creative process a bit further to not only move away from thinking in products but to tell a story. A story that will help the customers to enjoy the store, to understand the brand and to build a relationship with the brand and the store itself.

Phase 3: Cocooning

Although at this point in the creative process many small ideas probably arise, it is best to focus on the bigger picture. What will the concept, or the big idea of the store be? You might think that the big idea is the homely feeling, but of course that is not distinctive enough; it is almost something the customer expects today in stores such as these. The cocoon of a caterpillar, hanging free in nature, may not be the most innovative idea, but for the purpose of this exercise it seemed like a good starting point to me. Beginning with the target group and the concept of a cocoon, I went looking for inspiring images and sketched my own version, as shown in my sketch. The design, round shapes and drop shapes are something I will keep in mind from now on for the next steps. Indeed, definitely having a large portion of 'Bouba flavor'.

Phase 4: Making it work

Organizing
Bubble diagram

We know that NOOK has found a property in a B location in a provincial town where many people pass by, by bike or on foot. The property is about 370m² and has an irregular shape considering it grew out of two adjacent buildings. This is enough information for now to get started on the bubble plan.

We start from a blank sheet; the only goal we have is to establish an ideal layout where the link between the functions becomes clear and how big each function is. Normally when you work for a brand you get a list of the running meters of shelf space needed for each product group needs. Given our self-devised brand, I can now determine that myself. It is clear that home deco will be the largest group and also the wine store will need some room given that the building they are in now is too small. Anyway, it is always wise to make a list of requirements first; see it as an inventory.

So yes, while you will often get a list of running meters for each product group, the first reflex should always be how they get these running meters. How much space do the products get? What price perception do they want to project? This partly determines how close the products will be to each other and whether there should be a lot of stock. A product on a nice pedestal looks much more expensive than that same product stacked together ten on a rack. Is there also enough space left for testing the product, for example? Or to make mock-ups? Depending on the brand message, choices will have to be made here.

It is always wise to make a list of requirements first; see it as an inventory.

Inventory product groups:

- Home decor: pillows, plaids, vases, pots, candles, small furniture, accessories, mugs, lighting, wallpaper, plants, fragrances
- Clothing: home suits and nightwear
- Natural care products (from different brands): creams, shampoos, conditioners, lip balm, soaps, bath products, bath accessories,...
- Books & stationery: limited collection of books, notebooks, pens, greeting cards
- Gadgets: headphones, small music boxes, scent dispensers,...
- Wine: French wines

The challenge with these products is that NOOK should not look like a junk store. They are carefully selected products that are slightly different (and also slightly pricier). So I choose to give space to the products. NOOK will also present sets across all product groups together to inspire people. So enough attention may go to inspiration islands.

Inventory other functions (without already deciding whether they could be merged or not):

- Place for giving advice
- Checkout point
- Click and collect
- Small stock/unpacking area (preferably at the entrance where deliveries can also be made)
- Desk
- Demo area
- Workshop space
- Staff area
- Toilet for customers
- Acclimatization zone

Making bubble diagrams is a creative process best done sketchily on paper. By sketching and making connections, drawing arrows, adding colors, it becomes increasingly clear how the store can be laid out. For example, you soon find that some of the spaces where services are offered are best grouped together. So you have the advice area, the demo area and the workshop area that can happen in the same place. Nothing is more annoying than an empty space in a store that is only filled when something is actually organized. You don't want to put these spaces behind closed doors because you want to make a statement. Possibly the office could also be here, but that is a decision best taken with the staff/manager. Why? Because if an office is visible to customers it can also have disadvantages. Think clutter. Keeping an office tidy where work is done daily is a task that should be feasible for those who work there. Another disadvantage, but what is an advantage for some, is that customers always see you sitting there. I have already worked with retailers who absolutely do not want this as they never have a moment's rest. Especially local retailers who are close to their customers are 'bothered' by this. Of course, it is an advantage if you are alone in the store. Note that this is a process that is very difficult to perform on a computer. You can't 'scribble' on a computer. Well, if you have a trackpad of course you then mimic the drawing process. Naturally, ten possible solutions for the layout of the store arise. But by scribbling down some ideas, keeping the buying motivations in mind, putting on the glasses of Aisha, Cyrille, Amea and Frauke where possible, I finally arrived at two concepts. One starts from one of NOOK's brand values: inspiration. If they really want to exude that, that might also be the best way to start the journey. The second concept departs more from the product, and given the main product is home-deco,

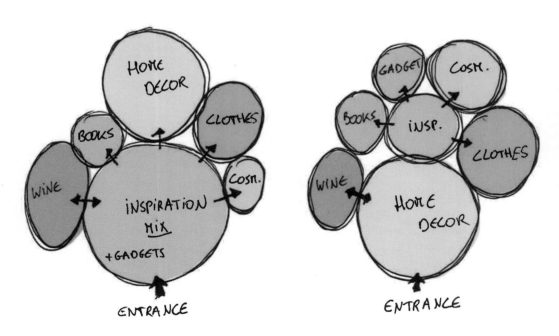

THE BIG BOOK OF RETAIL DESIGN

that will be the first thing a customer encounters. The sketches below show both. Perhaps wonderful designs could be made from both bubble diagrams. And in reality, you will explore both further as well. But for the sake of the process, I'm going to continue with the idea of putting home decor at the heart of the store and using the inspiration zones to get customers in (i.e. at the window) on the one hand, and on the other to connect the different product groups. My main argument is that a large central inspiration zone where many products come together may annoy the customer as it may become too much, especially in the case of NOOK where a range of small items also needs to be displayed. Home decor is also the department where you can create the most atmosphere. So it seems ideal to start at the entrance and ideal to connect all the product groups.

Refinement first idea

Now that the idea is clear, I can start refining the bubbles a bit, as my sketch illustrates. I chose based on the buying motivations in the bubble plan to place both the wine and some of the inspiration at the window if possible so that it is clear what all NOOK offers. If the premises allow it, the ideal place for the wine is on the left side so that when entering it is not at the start of the journey (we are going to stimulate the customer's intuitive behavior by having them interact along the right) but at the end. The intention is to create a soft boundary between NOOK and the wine store (by e.g. a different ceiling or atmosphere).

Also important to NOOK is the BOPIS business. It is not the first thing customers need to see, but perhaps the second. Therefore, this may be on the right side, a little deeper in the store. Further, it only makes sense that clothing, cosmetics and books & stationery should be accessible from home decor. And again, since inspiration is an important pillar for NOOK, these zones will be connected by inspiration islands that go across all product groups. Given that the advisory service needs to be visible I link these to the home-decor department on the one hand, but with more back of house functions on the other. I also group other items that require staffing around here so you don't end up with unnecessary staffing on calm days. It could be that on a quiet Monday, one person should be able to handle the store (outside of the winery). So it stands to reason that these staffed functions are not scattered around the store.

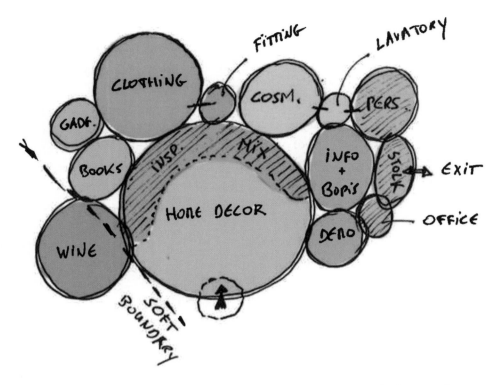

Thinking about it this way also clearly reveals zones in the bubble diagram. Logically, the largest zone is the product-oriented zone. Then there is a zone where service is needed. This is BOPIS and cash register but also the stylist (although he or she won't be there full time in the beginning) and a demo area that can also be used as a workshop area. But grooming products also often don't sell themselves and advice is needed here. So it makes sense that it should be close to the other services that require staff. You also don't want the fitting rooms too far away from this so that advice can be sought here as well. And we must also admit that some social control is also necessary so as not to encourage theft. Lastly, I grouped the non-customer accessible areas but with the office and the advice area linked to each other. Providing a restroom for customers is not a luxury today. The most logical thing to do is to link them with the other functions that require water. That would be the staff area but also at cosmetics where a demo sink is appropriate.

THE BIG BOOK OF RETAIL DESIGN

Cut & paste

Now that we've organized our thoughts, let's add the plan. I start first by analyzing the existing location. The property is located on a side street of the main shopping street. It consists of two adjacent properties that are already connected by the previous owner. He has also provided a staff room at the back of the smallest building, which is the one on the left. There are also two toilets for the staff. This was a logical decision since daylight could be brought in through skylights. There is also a water connection and sewage system. Above the retail space there are apartments which of course have an entrance from the front. Apartments on the higher floors go up to 12.5m deep. The rear section (from the toilets) has a flat roof. The smallest property is a little older and has a lower ceiling. It immediately offers the possibility of putting the wine store there since it has a different atmosphere and a lower ceiling. Under the stairs, on the right hand side of the property, which leads to the apartments there is also a staircase to the basement that can be used for the store. So it makes sense to make a link with the stock there.

Given the concept of cocooning it is important to immediately investigate whether we can bring in daylight. In addition, daylight and greenery in a store have an impact on the mood of customers, as mentioned earlier. Fortunately, the back part of the building allows for a patio. This is perfect for my concept and fits perfectly with the product range as it also makes the link to a garden, courtyard or terrace at home. The patio also gives the opportunity to possibly present products outside in the summer and thus adjust the offering accordingly. I will have to be creative with space though, as it seems that I need the square meters to get all the products in. But including a patio is really what would make the space NOOK. Worst case scenario is that I can only make a huge skylight when the patio is not feasible.

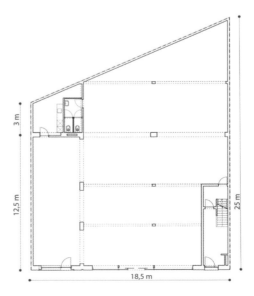

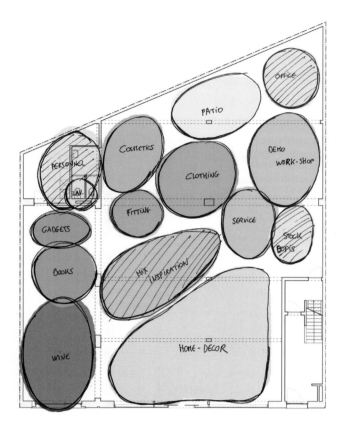

Since a number of things are already fixed given the existing situation of the property, the next challenge becomes to give the remaining bubbles a place and preferably as well as possible in line with our initial layout. It works pretty well to stick the spheres into the floor plan. Only, due to the connection of the water that was already there, I have to switch the care products with the clothing line. Also, the staff area and the office and stock are no longer connected, but that in itself is not a very big problem. We just need to make sure that there are not too many doors disrupting the shopping experience. By drawing in the bubbles, the shape and size of the patio is also starting to become clear.

THE BIG BOOK OF RETAIL DESIGN

Choose a flow strategy

Since exploring and inspiration are the main pillars within the store concept, choosing an appropriate flow is relatively easy. We are also not dealing with a very large building so the concepts that call for separate zones would not be appropriate here, nor would the loop plan – it would defeat the purpose of browsing. I don't want a functional arrangement with shelves left and right but the placement of the furniture should encourage browsing. From that point of view, the concept of the free-flow plan and the open plan remain. For the free-flow plan with real visual partitions, the building might be too small, but we could apply the strategy of curvilinear, amorphous forms to encourage people in a certain flow. Since discovery is important to NOOK, playing with vistas and hidden nooks is recommended. So we are going to apply the free-flow plan on a small scale in combination with the the open plan.

To get this flow-strategy right, once the design is finished, I will have to check whether the right architectural features are in place.

Optimizing

Now that we know how functions and product groups relate to each other and have also determined the strategy we will use to send people about, it is time to further develop the current bubble diagram into a strategic floor plan. Remember, a strategic floor plan shows the customer journey of each persona, the associated eye-catchers, and a first conceptual design of the floor plan. The first step we normally do is calculating. But as we are working with a fictive brand, which is also new, I will work with estimations. So for the purpose of this exercise I now show the plan that I came up with.

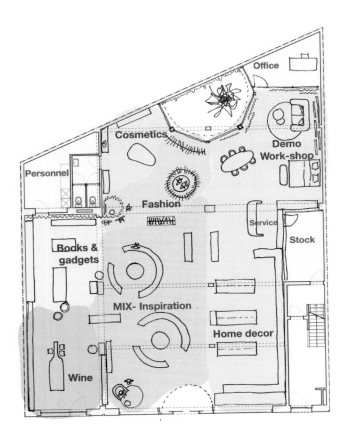

Designing a flow

I start with making sure that the free-flow plan in combination with the open plan works. In order to do that I have to make sure that I create smallers zone with the help of higher elements that mean something in height and thus not only visually on the floor plan separates zones, but really visually horizontally. These are the darker grey colored elements.

Knowing that experience and inspiration is as important as presenting the products I decided to invest space in some bigger architectural elements that could also serve to catch people's eye and make them explore the store. First and foremost the idea of cocooning needed to take shape. To this end I chose to place to large 'cocoons' in the middle of the store. These should serve as inspiration, showing surpassing product combinations. Just as important was my link to the outside, the patio. To make the design in line with NOOK and Bouba, also the patio will have a round shape with a tree in the middle. The patio and the cocoons are category-1 eye-catchers on key sight lines. To draw attention to the wine shop an impressive wine bar will be designed. And as a final category-1 eye-catcher I choose the service/BOPIS/cash desk to stand out. This for the simple reason that these services are of incremental value for NOOK so need to be visible immediately upon entering the store. Note that services such as interior styling and placing orders will take place at the large table or in the office in the back of the store. The four large pink dots are the category-1 eye-catchers. These eye-catcher function independently from the personas. Since we are working here with larger shapes that will make a visual statement spatially we need fewer of them than in a store that is primarily product-oriented, like the example I gave at pinball#communication.

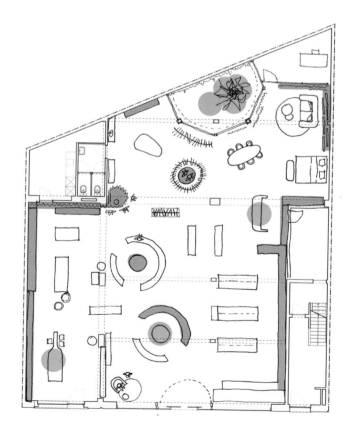

Apart from the shelving indicated in dark grey and the eye-catchers, all furniture is flexible. Meaning that it can be moved around to change the store slightly from time to time and to and optimize it according to the needs or seasonal updates.

In this case I chose not to do anything different with the flooring in the different zones. It is a better option to work with carpets. Indeed, the shop window, the fitting room and the demo zone are ideal places to do this. Of course customers can buy or order these carpets. Now, to give some direction to the space and to highlight certain areas, I do advise working with differences in ceiling and lighting. Remember, the wine and books corner has already a lower ceiling. Without making an actual design in this phase I would suggest to continue playing with the circles the cocoons now make on the floor, onto the ceiling (with lighting, plants, or whatever), throughout the store. This will make the space more dynamics without restricting its flexibility.

Remember, a good flow is created when people shop intuitively and are able to do what they set out to do. So for Aisha, Cyrille, Amea and Frauke I need to draw up their ideal journey and choose the eye-catchers wisely.

Aisha

Aisha's ideal customer journey is exploring the entire store but especially with the home deco products she looks for inspiration. She leans very much towards "just browsing" in terms of the different shopping motivations. So it is essential to show her around the entire store. As mentioned, not everybody will take the same route, but I will do as much as I can to make people see the entire store. In the plan I drew the 'ideal' customer journey for Aisha. She will be immediately attracted to the first cocoon upon entering.

After exploring it, she continues into the home deco area and explores it completely. Just before she gets to the service zone/checkout I try to steer her to the other side of the store by shielding the checkout area with a higher rack (see dark gray corner in previous sketch). Now the second cocoon will attract her attention and thus send Aisha to the area with wine, gadgets and books. The three mannequins standing in front of the fitting room curtain will lead her into the cosmetics and clothing zone. Finally, she gets triggered by the demo corner where she can play with curtains and different wallpapers. These are mounted on panels on rails so you can play with the different layers. Aisha ends up at the cash register to checkout.

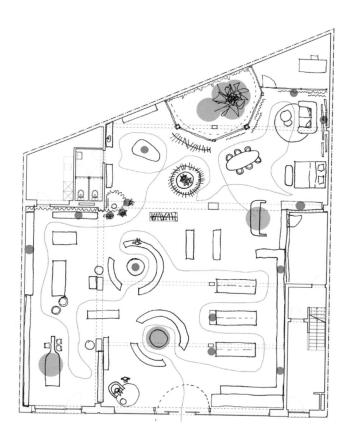

Cyrille

Cyrille's favorite place in the store is the wine bar. He will always pass through here first to taste a wine before looking for a book or candles. It is important to Cyrille that he can quickly ask where he can find the latest goods to surprise his wife once again. He is pointed towards the middle gondola in the Home decor corner where he immediately finds what he needs. While his gift is being wrapped he is entertained by the content that is appearing on the screen behind the counter.

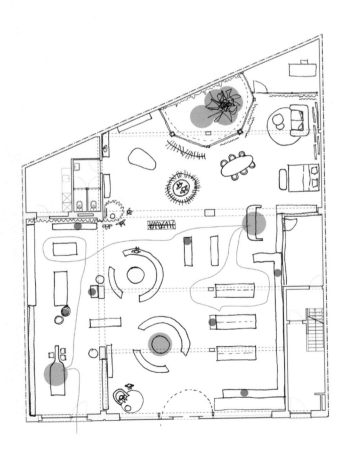

THE BIG BOOK OF RETAIL DESIGN

Amea

Remember, Amea is fond of the smaller stuff of NOOK: stationary and cosmetics. It is important to show her these small products as soon as she enters the store. This is why the first cocoon is so important. It should show products from across the store as well as the most recent. This cocoon thus serves to show both novelties and offerings in surprising combinations. The second cocoon serves the same purpose. Amea is drawn from there to the intimate corner with books, stationary and gadgets. She too is then stimulated to explore the clothing at the sight of the three mannequins. The large amorphous island near the cosmetics draws her attention by its design. This whole corner is very atmospheric and makes her feel good so she takes her time to browse and try on. Because the cosmetic area has a visual connection with the service counter, the staff can see immediately when she requires help. The sun shines in through the patio making Amea enjoy it even more. She ends her journey by paying for the products.

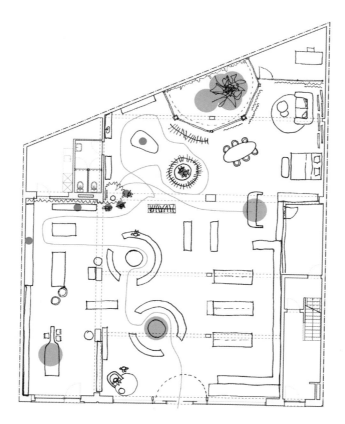

Frauke

Frauke coming to the store for the first time will walk in and take a split second to orient herself. Turning right would be the most logical route to take for two reasons. On the left is the large cocoon that visually screens the rest of the store and on the right she has a clear view of the low shelves. As a result, this side is more inviting to her. In addition, she is right-oriented so intuitively she chooses right. Then Frauke purposefully follows the route to the products she came for: home decor. She looks at the curtains and wallpaper and checks them for quality. She also thoroughly analyzes the pillows. After she is reassured, she is drawn to the surprising product combinations she sees both in the Cocoon and in the middle of the store in front of the checkout counter. She gets stimulated by the fun gadgets and passes by that corner as well. Frauke rounds off her visit by asking the cashier if she can also request samples of the wallpaper through NOOK's website (which she of course can).

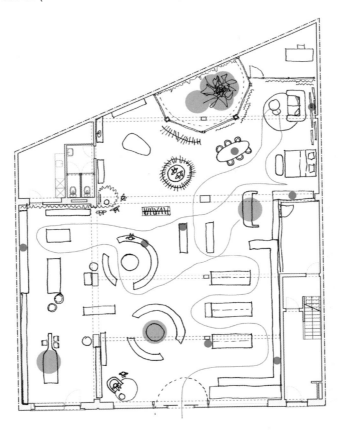

THE BIG BOOK OF RETAIL DESIGN

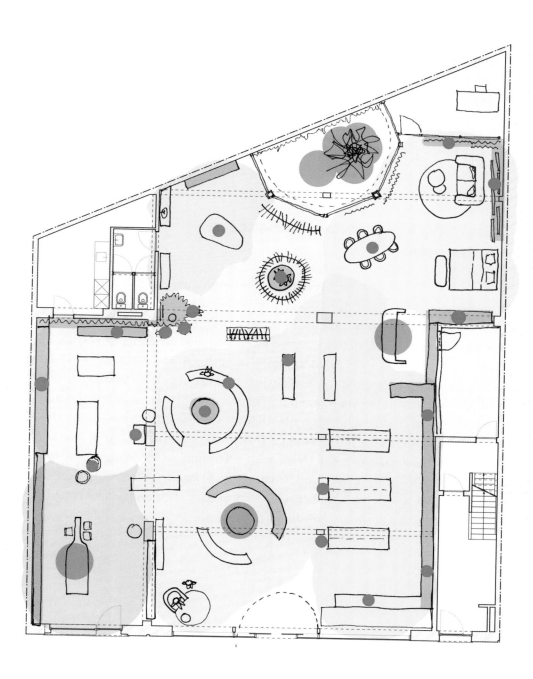

As a final step, I add all the eye-catchers together to make sure there is not too much overlap. Some eye-catchers will serve for two different personas, which in itself is not a problem but is a point of attention. So, our final strategic floorpan looks as our the following sketch, indicating the eye-catchers (category-1 and -2), the higher elements that are part of the flow and the indication of the zones (bubbles).

Basically, as a designer, you've also been busy creating a mood board at this stage. But as mentioned earlier, the purpose of this book and this exercise is to illustrate our tools. One tool remains that I have not yet applied, the Sense Matrix.

Creating an optimal experience
Sense matrix

It may feel a little premature to engage the senses so early in the process. Still, it is already a good exercise to do because it briefly opens all the doors and to see opportunities. Even if you work in a team the ideas can start to come together in this way. As you can see in the matrix, I started by placing the four personality traits at the top. Remember, this is what the brand wants to radiate and show to its customers. Thus, what we will also apply in the store. I start by thinking about scent. NOOK will definitely have scented products in the store (such as candles and personal care products), which is why I don't want to bet too heavily on an artificial scent. Still, I think it makes sense that when customers come in, they are welcomed by a relaxing scent. Not that I need to commit to this right now, but I am already thinking about lavender or vanilla. Always have fragrance experts assist you when this choice effectively needs to be made, as we aim for congruency between the scent and the design of the store.

Also for the music, I choose to go for a relaxing style. Yet not too sleepy or slow, hence my choice of something more funky. The product NOOK offers is itself fairly acoustically absorbent. Think of the furniture, fabrics and clothing. But since it really should feel like home, it is best to invest in additional acoustically absorbent materials. I am thinking of acoustic plaster against the ceiling and applying fabrics in the space. This can be done when upholstering furniture or hanging curtains to separate areas. Tactility offers the opportunity to definitely exude playful charisma. Using fractions of high-quality offcut timber, sourced locally from building sites or sawmills for example, bound with a unique water based formulation binder creating the aesthetics of traditional terrazzo might do the trick. It also seems like an eco-friendly charismatic material. Recycled felt is also best eco-friendly and gives a soft and relaxing feel. I want to use transparent curtains to get a playful effect. Especially on the patio, this can create a nice effect if I work with different layers, for example. The wooden details I would like to use should stand out and are used creatively so that they surprise. This is the link to engagement for me. Wine tasting speaks for itself. This, too, is showing engagement for me.

Finally, I would like to share some ideas regarding design language and eye-catchers. With the cocooning story, NOOK definitely comes in the design language of Bouba.

This can radiate both playfulness and relaxation. To make it even more playful, I want to add nice color accents that can be popping to also radiate charisma. As a sign of engagement, there will be a digital screen behind the service desk and cash register that will show inspirational images while people are waiting or queuing.

	Charismatic	Engaged	Playful	Relaxed
Scent				
Artificial				Lavender
Scent of products, materials,...				
Sound				
Music (radio, playlist, live music,...)				funky lounge music
Acoustics (talking people, footsteps,...)		acoustic plaster	using different fabrics	
Touch				
Touch (material cash desk, seating,....)	Terazzo look wood waste	wooden details (e.g. bamboo)	sheer curtains	desk covered with recycled felt
Climate (temperature, cleanliness,...)				already floor heating in place
Taste				
Service (free) (coffee/water, samples,...)		tasting wine		
Products (sell) (coffeebar, snacks,...)				
Sight				
Design language (materials, proportions, colors,...)	robust gondolas		furniture with curves	bouba design language
Visual stimuli (lighting, visuals,...)	popping use of color	digital screen behind service desk	Cocoons	lighting dominated by spot lighting

This last tool completes the strategic exercise. One could already show the design to this point to the client to align the strategy. Also, discussing how the brand personality can be translated into the interior at this phase can already generate interesting discussions. The strength of the sensory matrix is that it immediately defines the playing field, namely all stimuli to be chosen must be a translation of the personality traits.

With the basis of the design we now have, one can go on to elaborate on the design. Here a good dose of creativity is still needed to make the embodiment of the design real. With the lab this is where our consultancy stops. To make sure all aspects of the store design will be covered in the following steps we do highlight again what the different parts and their impact on store perception are. Just showing our 6-bubble REXS graph again suffices.

PART

3

An educated guess about the future

Let me start questioning what role shopping today plays in our daily lives. Some would argue that it is (becoming) the principal source of public activity. And I am sure that in some cases this is probably true. A fellow researcher based in Hong Kong told me that in Asia, shopping is a popular leisure activity and whole families and groups of friends see this as a day out. Brands are responding to this by opening huge experiential palaces to entertain the customers. In her opinion, retail in Western Europe has become quite boring. But, in Western Europe people do not see shopping as the leisure activity it was before anymore. Covid did play a part in this. So, the pandemic definitely has pushed the pause button in the further development of experiential stores. People are, however, returning to the shopping streets. Indeed, people like shopping and retailers are investing again in experience. Even now, with the current energy crisis. But we do not know the long-term effect of it yet. Anyway, I do have to say that the reason for why and when we shop has changed somewhat. We look for contact, we like to be among people, and yes, we also like to buy things. But that will no longer be the main reason for coming out. Retail has much more significance than strictly economic. The corona pandemic has made visible to many people that they value lively centers with their own local stores. Though I see numbers passing indicating this is decreasing again and that people find their way to bigger cities again. But there is more. Retail, together with the hospitality industry and culture, among others, contributes to the livability of cities big and small and has an important social added value. It is also a place to meet, to be among people, to experience something and have personal contact. Just look at supermarkets that have integrated a "chat counter" into the store for people who are not in a hurry and want to meet and chat. In this part I will discuss what roles physical stores will take on, and what consequences that has on the profession of retail design and the competences one needs.

People are, however, returning to the shopping streets. Indeed, people like shopping and retailers are investing again in experience.

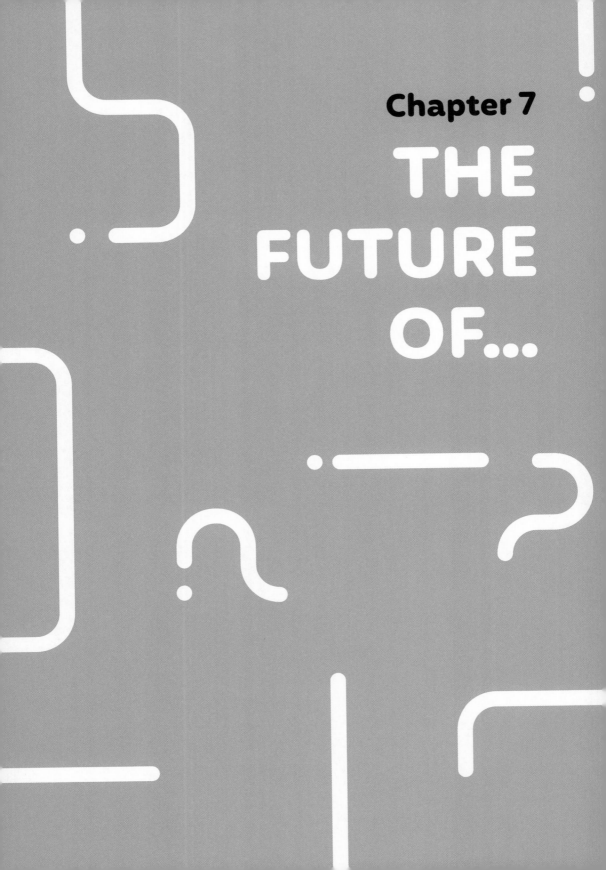

Chapter 7

THE
FUTURE
OF...

A. Physical retail

From fluid experiences…

I have touched on how retail and retail design is evolving now and in the coming years a bit here and there. Things that are happening now such as the digitization of society and therefore of the customer will continue. Experiences will become limitless throughout society. Boundless in the literal sense, boundaries between online and offline will blur more and more. So also in retail. Differences between online and offline will disappear and digital will become an integral part of our lives. This fluidity will continue not only in the experience of something, but also in buying something. Or renting, as the sharing economy will also increase and hopefully soon make us a little less dependent on our possessions. But back to shopping, shopping can already be done almost anywhere. There are so many possible channels and also these will continue to expand or keep changing to the most popular channels. And the physical channel will always be one of them. I don't believe that real shopping, or shopping in real life, will ever disappear.

Stores take on so many different roles, and selling is just one of them. Just as the physical store is also just one channel in the whole. In and of itself, it doesn't matter where a customer makes their purchases, in-store or on Instagram, as long as it stays within the brand's world of buying opportunities. Thus, the value of a brick-and-mortar is no longer tied to sales, but in part as a marketing and branding tool for transactions occurring elsewhere within a brand community.

... taking up different roles...

The question then arises as to what other roles a physical store will play in the future. If it is no longer always the main purchase channel, what will it be? At Shoptalk Europe (Spring '22), I heard someone from Sephora talk about the role they envisioned for their brand in the coming years. They spoke of curation, community, celebration and culture. To me, this was a reflection of what the role of physical stores could be. Let me explain.

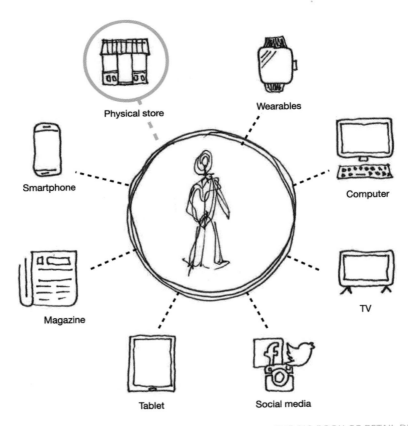

Curation and community

Curation and community are not really novel. I've talked about curation before. Every retailer should see itself as a curator. A curator of products but certainly also of experiences, and the latter is perhaps the most new. If we look back for a moment we see that retailers, brands, society, technology, designers, etc. have each had an influence on where we are today in the retail landscape, but rarely simultaneously. There is always one dominant. In retail 1.0 the manufacturer was in charge and no designer was needed. Retail 2.0 (say, from the late 1990s to the noughties) was a phase where the retailer was in charge, but hired an architect or interior architect to design the store following the brands' or retailers' ideas. Retail 3.0, from 2010 onwards, is a time where the consumer is more and more in charge. Customer is king is perhaps the most important credo. Retail designers are also trained to put the customer with his needs and requirements first. We are now gradually evolving toward something else, retail 4.0? To me, this is where the brand or retailer regains power and takes control as a curator or perhaps even a conductor. A conductor of experiences, with the co-creation of customers. Remember I mentioned under-designing is this regards. Customers become co-creators by just being customers.

As far as community building goes, big brands have been doing community building for some time, with great success. We only see that the smaller ones will also have to start doing this. A bakery, a local supermarket – they have been doing this on their own for a long time. Although this happens mostly implicitly and out of love for the customer. Making it more explicit and bigger than the physical store itself is the next step. Remember the time, some 15 or 20 years ago, when convenience stores were swallowed up by large chains. Local supermarkets almost completely disappeared from the scene. We started shopping en masse in hypermarkets. But like a pendulum swinging both ways, it didn't take long for the need for a neighborhood supermarket to rise again. Indeed, those same big chains then went on to open convenience stores to fill the gap and to be closer to the customer. Also recently, a discounter such as Aldi even opened a convenience store, and they have access to data, lots of data, making them a true competitor to local supermarkets. As mentioned earlier, Covid has made us appreciate our local retailers again. But there will come another time when the pendulum swings back the other way and we may all start looking back at larger players. So today's small retailer better get ready for what's to come and make sure that whatever train passes, he's on it, with his customers. Today I see that it is the players in between – too big to know all their customers personally but too small to deploy large budgets to expand and explore data – who have the most difficult time with this community building aspect. It is clear however that we will have to rely on data. Data that in the near future hopefully can be managed better and that one can count on 100% to build out a fan base/community.

Celebration

I personally like this one the best on the list. Celebrating the physical, celebrating products and experiences. Looking at how celebrations are already happening today, how brands celebrate themselves, foreshadows the future. Just look at high-end luxury brands like Dior, Prada and Burberry. Their physical manifestations range from flagship stores, to art galleries and exhibitions, hotels and culture clubs. But recently we are seeing more and more immersive art installations. We were used to art installations in shop windows, but now they are actually stepping out of an existing store, in the form of pop-ups. These often striking and brightly colored installations are really there to immerse people in their branded world. Here, then, the experience seems to be momentarily more important than the product. In the summer of 2021, Louis Vuitton, for example, set up shop at a temporary residency (South Florida) with an installation to showcase the house's creative muscle. The installation made use of LV shipping containers, oversized inflatables and an interactive approach using augmented reality via QR codes. It also showcased the latest capsule collection. Whereas with luxury brands we will see this more and more, with smaller brands or SMEs the party will be more about celebrating a product. But also in an immersive way. Just recently Miss Sixty collaborated with Andre Saraiva resulting in the 2023 Angel collection. To promote this collection a pop-up installation was set up in Chengdu (China). As the sketch shows, it is a celebration of the collection, but also of art. Surely this too is a celebration.

Culture

What is 'culture,' this last and fourth item on the list? To understand what culture means, let me take a very familiar example from the 1980s when Pepsi and Coca-Cola were engaged in a real cola war. Pepsi had created a campaign based on an experiment that made it clear that when people tasted both brands blind, the taste of Pepsi was clearly preferred. And yet Pepsi was unable to win this war and make people buy more Pepsi. Why not? People associated Coke more strongly with good times, relaxing, fun in the sun, etc., than they did with Pepsi. Coke continues to dominate the marketplace to this day. That's what culture is about, the idea of 'more than just a product' is at the core of 'cultural brands'. They are creating a world around their brand where communities are formed and the brand becomes part of an everyday social ritual. We no longer live in an era where it's possible for brands to independently define what their culture and values are. In today's hyper-connected world, consumers have an integral role in shaping what brands represent. Physical stores are also increasingly going to be indulgences of this culture. Where previously it was often limited to choices in marketing, it will increasingly manifest itself in the physical world. Stores are more and more part of a marketing strategy, so it makes sense that they will be more aligned.

...to plasticizing formats...

More fluid experiences also call for plasticizing formats, even in the physical world. Look at how the concept of a pop-up shop has been evolved to something very broad, something that has become normal and is fluid in itself. This fluidity will be reflected throughout a brand's store portfolio, which is thus no longer rigidly divided into a flagship store and a bunch of roll-outs, but will thus be much more adapted to location, time and context. Louis Vuitton's pop-up art installation that I just mentioned is another clear manifestation of this.

Now, when we zoom in on smaller retailers, this fluidity will increasingly seep in even within a store. Although this is mostly about building in flexibility. Because the role of stores is changing and will continue to change, there must be room for adjustments. Not necessarily over the entire retail area but over parts. Parts that can also change function so that, for example, events, pop-up spaces and workshops can be organized. This also leaves more room for experimentation, trial and error. Small adjustments can sometimes have big consequences. When a space allows for play, there is also room for improvement. The attitude we now see online, the measuring, the testing, is an attitude that should also return more in the physical store. And of course the circle is complete if I now also bring back the previously mentioned co-creation of the shopping experience with customers. People like to be part of something anyway, to get a sense of belonging. When brands open the door to their customers to participate in their development that feeling will only get stronger. When executed very well then we can also talk about 'cultural brands' again, just because of that participation process.

...and service hubs...

With the example of Coolblue in mind, you do notice that brands are increasingly using retail outlets as service hubs. Apple is also a very good example of this with their Genius bar. But the trend also exists the other way around, of course. Service players like the ING bank are starting to think more commercially, opening cafes in an effort to get closer to the customer. Another great example is Box, the parcel shop of Finnish postal service Posti who, in the heart of Helsinki on a 1,100 square-meter space, opened a self-service collection point with 600 lockers. Next to pick-up and return packages ordered online, customers can open and try on their online shopping in fitting rooms, as you can see in the first sketch. At the same time, they can leave all of the packaging material at Box to be recycled or reused by other customers. There are show areas so that the Instagram generation can take a few photos or unboxing videos in the appropriate surroundings, as you can see in the second sketch. Last but not least, in the front of the shop there is an area called 'spotlight', which can be used by online companies to present their products to the consumers. And all this in a trendy colorful design where a coffee can also be grabbed.

More fluid experiences also call for plasticizing formats, even in the physical world. Look at how the concept of a pop-up shop has been evolved to something very broad.

This is an example of how services and retail are growing closer together to be closer to the customer. To help them in as many aspects of their lives as possible. Because that's what it's all about, relevance. To this end, I recently launched an academic network group where the design disciplines of retail design, interior architecture, fashion design, hospitality and service design come together. This special interest group 'Designing retail and service futures' aims to bring all knowledge together. Indeed, it is clear that we can learn a lot from each other.

...leaving no place for just stores being stores?

Stores will no longer be used as warehouses. Brands and retailers need to look for their added value. If they don't, it will soon be over. A few years ago, I remember giving retailers the message that if they could excel or distinguish themselves in one or two aspects, they would be fine. For example, my list included standing out with staff and/or service, in terms of product or product offering, having a distinctive concept, store design or experience, or excelling in efficiency. But today, this is no longer valid. Rather, it has become an and-and story. And then again... A store that is just a store is not, in my opinion, the winning formula. Again, this is a reflection of society. Look at how cities are designed. The time where functions were separated as much as possible is a thing of the past, but of course cities are still often built that way. Living, working, leisure and shopping have long been considered separately. Cities that were built or renovated in the middle of the last century, such as Rotterdam, for example, still suffer from this. The center of Rotterdam was completely rebuilt after the bombing in the Second World War with the separation of functions as the main idea. Thus, living, shopping, culture and work were each allocated to a different zone. This results in empty shopping streets after six, thus a dead city center. Although Rotterdam has since taken many steps to mix more functions, architecture remains a limitation. To make cities liveable, mixing functions is preciselya city's strength. I can give numerous examples of situations where mixing is better than segregation. But my point is that we also see this in the commercial world. Functions are being mixed into hybrid stores. Banks are combined with cafes, cultural houses with stores, or stores with exhibitions. Anything is possible today (but actually in the past too, i.e. department stores, remember?). Moreover, there is something to buy almost everywhere. Anyone can be a retailer that way. And of course that anyone also constitutes competition from anyone to some extent. So what do you think, that just playing store as we have done for decades will be enough in the future?

Functions are being mixed into hybrid stores. Banks are combined with cafes, cultural houses with stores, or stores with exhibitions. Anything is possible today.

B. The ones designing for it

You see, everything comes together, runs through everything else. Fluid experiences and spaces, mixed with art, stores as social hubs providing services we could never have imagined. So what does this mean for the knowledge and skills a retail designer should possess or develop now and in the near future? It is not getting simpler, that is for sure.

One of my PhD students did thorough research on what skills and competencies a designer needs to be able to design for retail, now and in the future. She interviewed more than 30 experts from Western Europe with questions about qualities needed to be a good retail designer today and what will be needed in the future. These were experts with different disciplinary backgrounds, from architecture, interior design, to product design and graphic design, and different levels of seniority, but all working in design offices specialized in retail. These offices ranged in size from eleven to over a hundred employees. From these interviews, more than 70 competencies emerged, which were then structured according to a holistic retail design competence model (first introduced by two academics: Graham Cheetham and Geoff Chivers). The model was developed in an effort to provide an overview of the desired competencies of future retail designers in the context of ongoing developments in the retail domain. As you can see, the model includes some meta-competencies and eight sub-competencies. Based on the data we gathered from the interviews, which are published in a scientific journal, I sketched the following model. The size of the spheres and the relationship between them are a direct representation of the data.

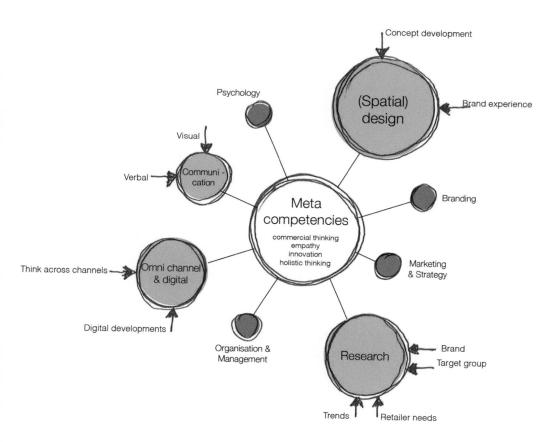

At the core...

As you can see, at the core meta-competencies are situated which are more generic in nature. They are needed to as a designer to be able to develop the competencies in the eight other categories. Four such meta-competencies stood out: **commercial thinking, empathy, innovation, and holistic thinking**.

Commercial thinking is referred to as the commercial objectives and/or the financial aspects of the project in relation to the aesthetics, making sure that the new store concept works. Moreover, commercial thinking also relates to designers ability to think and work from the perspective of the retailer, the brand and the consumer. Indeed, earlier referred as 'empathy'. Retail designers need to be able to place themselves in the position of the retailer or customer. This requires putting personal taste, vision and style aside. Understanding people and consumers is actually a full-time job. I never stop looking, asking questions and analyzing. It even goes as far as not being able to shop normally anymore. I always look at the store first, how people behave, before I turn to the products. That is called professional deformation and it is not something you can reverse. But it also means you are constantly learning. I often enjoy it when I have taught my students to look at shops and they subsequently indicate that this process cannot be reversed. That they themselves now indicate that they can no longer visit a store without taking a critical look at it. I love that, that's when they get the retail design vibe.

As a third important meta-competency, innovation came to the fore, relates to the designer's ability to come up with innovative ideas or concepts, which have impact and are distinctive from existing concepts or brands in the market. Consequently, retail designers are constantly challenged to come up with new, distinctive and innovative solutions. Indeed, as a designer you need to be able to think out of the box, be creative.

The last meta-competency refers to retail designers' ability to think and work in a holistic way. This in terms of considering the total experience of the store, as well as approaching the brand in an integral way to create a fully consistent story or concept across all channels, and thinking and working across disciplines, as I discussed before.

In my opinion, these qualities are indispensable when you are or want to be a retail designer. It is not by chance that I mention these competencies first when our interior architecture students receive their first retail design assignment. It is important for them to realize that, as a retail designer, you are truly at the service of the client. In the commercial world, it's not about egos and big names (outside of the occasional exception here and there, of course). Do you know who designed the supermarket in your neighborhood? Or your favorite clothing store? Even with big brands like Nike or Samsung, the majority of people don't know and don't think about that. So, as a designer, forget about your ego. Also forget that it's always pretty pictures you create as a designer. That's the second thing what I want to instill in students. I show them a picture of a store of a discounter accompanied by the words 'this is retail design' and then leave a moment of silence. You then see the students hesitate and think. Is she serious about this now? Or is it meant as a joke? But no, it is not a joke; this too is effective retail design and, make no mistake, there is a lot of thinking behind this. Maybe a little less creative, but mostly a lot of knowledge. So yes, even the Aldis and Lidls of this world need retail designers.

...it is still about designing...

Not fully unexpected, the group of design skills remains the most important of the eight groups. What was striking, to me at least, is that every expert mentioned or referred to the design abilities of a **trained spatial designer**. So, regarding the fact that a lot of disciplines are intertwined with the discipline of retail design, and that fluidity in experiences and spaces is occurring, the actual act of spatial designing remains key, and thus competencies related to this. Also, the experts not trained as spatial designers highlighted that every designer can be part of the retail design process, but the designer overlooking the whole, or taking the lead needs to have these spatial design skills, either by training or by experience.

Other competencies within this group relate to the different steps within the actual process of designing the commercial environment. Standing out is '**the ability to develop a concept'** which was mentioned by all interviewed experts, also 'the ability to translate the concept into a design' was highly appreciated, including skills like defining the store layout, creating logical customer routing and defining sight-lines and focus-points. Indeed, all aspects I previously discussed in optimizing the design process. Remember that a store is not a sum of several ideas, but the best designed stores are the ones with a clear big idea or concept. Last but not least was the quality of 'creating brand experiences'. In this context, the ability to put personal style preferences aside comes to the fore again. Hence, retail designers need to gain an in-depth understanding of the retailer and the brand identity, requiring some level of research, which already refers to our next topic.

...based on research...

The competencies in the category of research reflect skills relating to the study of different project aspects such as the brand, the target group, consumer behavior and the customer journey, and trends, which are needed in order to frame the project objectives and strategy, or to inform the concept development and design. This includes all competencies related to the activity of analysis, critical reflection, evaluation and drawing conclusions.

Some bigger design offices and big brands have a group of people dedicated to doing research, so the design team can focus more on the actual design.

So, it is not about the research as such, but more about being able to work with it. Some bigger design offices and big brands have a group of people dedicated to doing research, so the design team can focus more on the actual design. But even within the same company designers should always have that research mindset on, being critical, being able to reflect and evaluate.

...and having knowledge of omni-channel & digital...

This category clusters competencies related to omni-channel and digitalisation in retail. Although omni-channel thinking is closely related to marketing, the competencies in this category reflect more the influence of the topic on design and the design process. All experts referred to the '**awareness of digital developments and understanding the functioning and application of digital solutions**' and almost all 'the ability to think across channels'. Apart from being aware of digital developments, experts value the fact that retail designers have a basic understanding of how these digital solutions function and how they can be integrated into the store environment. According to the experts, thinking across channels should take place at the beginning of the process, to ensure that everything is fully integrated into the concept since certain decisions to integrate digital solutions might, for example, influence the layout of the store.

...communication...

This relates to competencies required to effectively exchange information or ideas, either verbally, visually or writing, with others. Those others can be colleagues or clients or even external parties such as suppliers. One competence seems to stand out: 'visual communication skills'. This entails addressing and convincing the client of the new or updated design by means of visual communication abilities, such as being able to produce plans, 3D visualizations, posters, sketches, mood boards, story boards or representations of customer journeys and the use of appropriate reference images. Many of these visual communications skills are part of any design education. Another thing students are well trained in in a design course is verbal communication. Indeed, in practice verbal skills are also required, meaning being able to build up a strong argumentation, as well as personal abilities such as persuasiveness, the ability to sell yourself and your idea, courage to negotiate, engender trust and empathy.

...branding...

Here, the competency 'branding' refers to understanding the process of branding and the theoretical construct of a brand and its underlying concepts. Besides understanding what a brand is, retail designers also need to know how a brand can be developed and how they evoke meaning or gain relevance for consumers. Furthermore, retail designers should also be aware of the competitive value of a brand and how they can communicate or can be translated over a myriad of channels and mediums. Indeed, 'knowledge and understanding of branding' and of 'brand communication' seem quite relevant. The latter includes external communication, referring to brand communication across different communication channels or media, and internal or in-store communication, transmitting different types of messages such as price, values/identity, information, inspiration, etc. Indeed, retail designers should be able to reflect on the brand and the way it communicates across all available media, but the actual design of internal and external brand communication belongs to the field of designers specialised in graphic design.

...marketing & strategy...

Marketing and strategy refers to understanding the retail sector on a macro level as well as the processes and activities that occur within a store environment, such as the functioning of a store but also sensorial marketing. Indeed, 'having the knowledge and understanding of retail marketing and strategy' is key. Note that most agencies have designated in-house specialists who undertake these activities, or agencies can hire professionals with expertise in this matter. However, this ability provides the opportunity for retail designers to step in at the early beginning of the process or to help retailers in translating their initial commercial ideas into viable conceptual stories.

...and socio-cultural sciences...

This category relates to the required competencies in the field of social sciences (e.g. sociology, psychology, philosophy) and cultural sciences (e.g. art history, architectural history). 'Knowledge of psychology' is cited most frequently, also mentioning different sub-disciplines such as environmental psychology, behavioral psychology, perception psychology and the psychology of shopping. Central here is the more general understanding of why people/consumers behave/

think in a certain way and how these findings can inform the development of a commercial concept. The application of this knowledge can contribute to the development of strategies, concepts and designs.

...all this mixed with a good dose of organization & management skills

This category clusters the required competencies for the effective management and organization of people, processes and concepts as well as interpersonal competencies to collaborate with others.
The personal competence of 'being able to work in a multi-disciplinary team and with external partners' was mentioned frequently in our study. Intertwined with this, but clearly separate, is the ability 'to guard a concept'. Indeed, working with people with different backgrounds entails the challenge to maintain focus and guard the concept. Because of the increasing complexity in retail, the multidisciplinary nature of retail design and the size/scope of retail projects, there is a growing need for more knowledge and skills during the process. Consequently, this causes the need for multi-disciplinary teamwork since one designer is not able to develop such concepts on his/her own.

Meaning...

So, based on the opinion of experts in the field, the future retail designer is still expected to have spatial design skills. Although there might be a much stronger convergence of the physical and the digital and an uncertainty of what the future will look like, a 'good' physical retail environment will remain important. As for the future retail designer, this could be summarized as follows.

The future retail designer should have skills such as understanding the consumer, defining and analyzing the retailer's needs, and translating them into a concept, design and brand experience. Besides the necessary design competencies, the retail designer should have a broad understanding of all retail parameters and should be able to integrate knowledge and skills from marketing & strategy, branding, omni-channel and digital. They should be competent in conducting research on a multitude of contextual aspects (e.g. brand, retailer, market, consumer, trends, etc.) to inform the development of commercial strategies, concepts and designs. Apart from developing concepts for the physical store environment, the retail designer needs the ability to think across channels and to generate ideas for seamless retail concepts in which all relevant customer touch points are considered as well. Since the practice of retail design is characterized by highly multi-disciplinary teamwork, a retail designer needs the ability and willingness to collaborate with others. In this context, the retail designer can communicate effectively (visually and verbally) with all stakeholders who are involved in the process, is able to manage people and processes and is able to guard the overall commercial concept.

Just because design is the most important competency it does not mean that it will be the main task of a retail designer.

Note that just because design is the most important competency it does not mean that it will be the main task of a retail designer. It strongly depends on the team and the size of a design office. It is perfectly possible to put together a team that together contains all these competencies. Indeed, the competency diagram mainly indicates the diversity of competencies. While this is of course a snapshot in time, with some reflection on the future, we have clearly seen in the past how unpredictable the future can sometimes be. Regardless, I do not think that in the future there will be additional groups of competencies, but the emphases within these eight groups may shift. For example, I suppose the omni-channel story will continue to grow and so will the importance, and perhaps difficulty, of this competency. Within a group of competencies, change does occur. The best example here is the aspect of sustainable design. This was not mentioned by the experts a few years ago, but we see the evolution in this and its importance increasing. So it will only be a matter of time before it will be an important competency within the group of 'design'.

In the future, and maybe already today, it will be impossible to be a specialist in all possible physical brand manifestations, from art installations, to events, to hotels, restaurants and pop-up stores and this for all sectors ranging from food, to fashion and DIY. It will rather be a choice to be a specialized retail designer in some of these or be a generalist, or strategist, as I also see myself. The act of designing in this case, my case, has become less prominent.

To teach or not to teach

There is only so much training that one can receive in any educational programme. It will be very difficult to teach all of the competencies in equal depth in one course. Choices will have to be made. The most important competencies for me that are inseparable from retail design still remain the meta-competencies of commercial thinking, empathy, innovation, and holistic thinking. With these at the core, the rest can be constantly developed, honed or taught. I would even add multi-disciplinary to this list because working in teams with people with different backgrounds will only increase since the diversity of (physical) brand manifestations also increases. Regarding the other competencies, some are also constantly evolving so it makes sense that they should be honed after study. For example, while communication is certainly addressed to a greater or lesser extent in design courses, this is of course only a starting point. This skill certainly needs further development in practice. And depending on the team you join as a designer, one skill or another will be developed to a greater extent. It might so happen that the office one works for works with teams led by a project manager or an account manager or even a senior strategist who have the role to communicate with the client. Also because of the wide choice of drawing programs, the visual communication skill is further developed within a design agency. The best example here is the sudden attention to and application of AI. On social media I see beautiful text-to-image images of designs that are just mind blowing. One image is generated through a conceptual exploration for a product line inspired by two brands, Bentley and Tiffany Co. The example in the sketch is the interior of a Bentley. The image is generated by Omar Alnemer from McRae Imagining. He mentions that it is a great tool for inspiration and conceptual brain storming. Ten people can use the same software yet produce diverse versions of an idea based on their understanding of the AI tool.

The other two examples show the exploration of a design for the facade of a concept store for Nike in Kyoto. The designs show the combination of Nike's brand and the local architecture of Kyoto. The visuals were generated by Benjamin Benichou from Drop. He believes the possibilities of AI are endless. I have to admit that it does scare me, the vast evolution in AI. It is not clear yet what role AI will play in the future. At our university we already notice that students use AI to write papers, so it won't be long until they discover the benefits of AI for designing as well. Which I guess I am fine with, as long as they keep on thinking, being critical, and never forget who they are designing for.

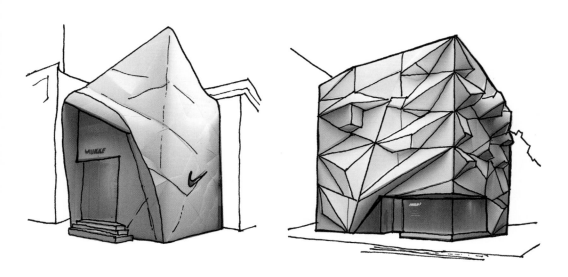

I have just realized that, by explicitly naming the competencies of (future) retail designers, I had quite a progressive retail design education in Rotterdam, back in the day (2005). It is a shame it is no longer offered. It touched upon a lot of competencies of our competence diagram. The book 'Retail & Interior Design', edited by Raphael Van Amerongen and Henri Christiaans, still reflects this. It contains different chapters written by the experts who were teaching in the educational program at that time. At our Faculty of Architecture and Arts at Hasselt University are students interior architecture can choose to be trained in retail design in their master. This is one of the Master choices they are offered. Indeed, our interior architecture program is a master's program. Thanks to the Bologna Declaration in 2004, the Bachelor-Master's structure went into effect for all higher education in Europe. This also meant that research had to be inherently connected to education. And this is where my academic story actually started, with doing a PhD in architecture. Our department (now a faculty), had then made the choice to spearhead retail design within research and teaching. It is also since then that we have been able to develop our research. This evolution has also had the benefit of making our students accustomed to research right from the start of their Bachelor's degree. We teach them to conduct actual research, including setting it up and analysing the results, to understand research and research results, and to critically evaluate it. Indeed, these cover the second most important group of competencies of our model. So, in my opinion, teaching retail design at university level makes total sense because of this link to research.

I envision a program that opens up to multiple disciplines.

But you see, it is still rooted in interior architecture. If I could dream of future retail design education I would envision a program that opens up to multiple disciplines. I imagine a retail design course at a higher level, a conceptual level that teaches you all the ins and outs of retail and designing for retail. After such a course students can choose which design aspect they want to specialize in (e.g. web design, graphic design, store design, packaging design, etc.). But in my opinion, you need that spatial knowledge or awareness to be a good graphic designer in retail, just as designing packaging will also help if you understand spatial retail principles. And if we look at how the market is evolving today, this becomes more and more relevant as I can state that we are moving towards the idea of a *gesamtkunstwerk* once more (as the early boutiques were). Maybe one day, my dream will become true...

C. Responsibilities that come with retail design

While working on that dream, there are some final issues I want to discuss because I feel the responsibilities of retail designers are increasing. And, as a designer we must never forget the impact our designs might have. As we have learned through this book what power good retail design can have, I have to acknowledge its full breadth. So as a retailer or designer, you do have an impact on how the customer behaves. There are positive aspects to this, but we should certainly not forget the ripple effect, leading to the ethical aspects involved. By means of design, you can indeed steer people or stimulate them to perform certain actions, and that is not a bad thing, but it should be done with some caution and with a conscience.

Ethical considerations stand out...

When you are doing research in retail design, discussing results on the impact of lighting, for example, on customers, they will always raise the question of whether I feel that I am manipulating people through design. They are right to think that and challenge me on that, because indeed, we do have an impact to some extent on people's choices. But I would never call it manipulating, it is rather stimulating or seducing. Stimulating impulse buying is a well-known example of this. In supermarkets, for example, by placing sweets and snacks at the checkout, you stimulate/tempt people, especially children, to take an unhealthy snack at the last minute. So, why do they do this and why don't they put healthy(er) snacks here? Or just no snacks at all, but fruit? Well, I have asked myself the same question and it would indeed make a difference since you can encourage people to buy a healthy snack or an unhealthy one simply by the choice of products placed at the checkout. We call this phenomenon nudging. Nudging is a term used to describe the technique of subtly encouraging people to behave in a desired way, and comes from behavioral psychology.

The technique can be seen as giving people a 'nudge' in the 'right' direction. On a larger scale, there is the example of American supermarkets where, at one point, a conscious decision was made to place fruit and vegetables at the very front of the store, where drinks and snacks would normally be. By putting fresh products first, people spend their (limited) disposable budget on these and there is less left over for the unhealthy products that come later in the store. This switch therefore encourages people to eat healthily and is a small step towards bringing down the obesity rate in America. But getting back to the question of why sweets are placed at the checkout, this is because sales usually wins out over ethical issues. To my great surprise, though, while writing this book my local supermarket, partly remodeled their store and what did they do? They placed a beautiful healthy snack display right at the cash desk where before, there used to be a candy display. And it looks great as you can see in the sketch.

The question of how you deal with such ethical considerations as a designer comes up again. Do you just do what the retailer asks you to do or do you try to push the boundaries? I would resolutely go for the second. Often, people just act out of habit, not out of ill will. So give everyone the benefit of the doubt and make people involved in the design process aware of the impact of certain design decisions. Thus even when it comes to what one puts at the checkout, we should rather look at the long-term effect that it might have on both customers and retailers. Fruit at the checkout won't yield an immediate profit – on the contrary – but you are sending a certain message with it, a message that can have a longer-term effect because there is a group of people who value that choice and therefore will faithfully choose that retailer. So back to my question about the lighting being used to manipulate customers. If you would think of it short term and you really distort colors with lighting, making meat look extremely red, this might triggers customers to take that product. But what will happen when they reach home and the meat looks brown? Indeed, they would feel scammed and they will not make that mistake again. So in the long run, a retailer does not benefit from manipulating a customer into anything, it will only costs customers.

Anyway, I do feel responsible to make our students aware of ethical issues, so I ask them if they would, for example, design a really cool and stimulating flag-ship store for a well-known vape store or alcohol brand if the question comes up when they are in practice. Apart from the fact that I am often surprised by their swift choice to agree to such an assignment, I want them to know that this is not a choice that can be taken lightly. I want them to realize what an impact a store and its design can have on product sales. So think about whether you want the store to encourage people to buy vapes or stimulate the use of alcohol. Of course, this discussion is becoming increasingly difficult as more and more products appear on the 'naughty list'. Candy, fatty foods – there is something to be said about everything. Fast fashion has also made this list. Should we, there-fore, no longer design for Primark? That's a choice that everyone should make for themselves, of course, but we should be aware of what the store's design impact on sales can be.

...but design is a key to success...

A store is a means to an end, not an end in itself. Indeed, it is a vehicle to achieve a goal, as is the design of the store. As the creator or designer of a store, you do bear some responsibility in achieving that goal. Whether that is selling, or image building, the design choices that are made affect this. That is why I love to use science. It helps to make informed design decisions. Decisions that lead to a higher chance of design success. But when is a design a success? When it sells more? For the retailer, perhaps it is. The retailer wants to have a return on the investment in the design, and preferably more. Although, I do question this in the very last part of this book, of course we want to facilitate this, but, to me, great success is achieved when the reactions are positive, when customers of the store are happy, when the staff indicate that they like working in the new store and when the retailer also sees that it is good for these people and derives pleasure from this himself. Which brings me seamlessly to my next point, which is well-being.

...considering well-being...

A design influences how people feel in a store. Spaces can make people feel good, but also bad. Colors, materials, smells, sounds, you name it, all contribute to a feeling. This counts for both employees as customers. How design influences customers is expressed throughout the book, but I also want to highlight its impact on employees. Human capital is still the driver in retail today. Good staff is extremely important, so the environment they end up in is also very important. This is about back of the store as well as in the store. If staff don't feel good, it will reflect on the brand. You don't want the staff to feel bad because of the design of the store. You want people to feel good through the design of the store and back office for that matter. Therefore it is best to include staff in the design process of the store. They usually have good insights into what they need to do a good job. And even when it comes to customer behavior, by the way, they are good informants as they are on the shop floor all day and see what is happening.

For the designer, some knowledge of what constitutes a good working environment is required. But sometimes it is about very simple things that can have a big impact. For example, I once travelled to a pharmacy with great expectations to see for myself the design that was so beautifully presented in magazines. The pharmacy consisted of one large curved counter surrounded by transparent pharmacy cabinets in a semi-circle made of green glass, as the sketch shows. The light from the workroom filtered into the pharmacy, where only indirect light was used, apart from the spotlights above the counter. A very nice idea if you ask me, but still, the image was not right. At least, not compared to what I had seen in the photos before. The counter was now full of small (impulse) products (of course they offer great margins), and had lost its slickness due to this. The green color of the pharmacy wall radiated off people, leaving them (and me) looking sick. As you can see in my sketch, that was based on the pictures in magazines, the medicines and other products were perfectly arranged in the drawers of the transparent pharmacy cabinets. They were even ordered from large to small, starting at the bottom (although I think this was mainly done to take nice pictures, at least I hope so, because organising products in a pharmacy according to size is madness). In reality, of course, such transparency does not work. Firstly, a pharmacist does not have time to constantly arrange the products neatly in the drawers, and if he does, it is difficult to maintain as such drawers are constantly opening and closing, with products occasionally tipping over onto their sides. That is exactly what I saw in reality (and what the small sketch illustrates). Insight into messy drawers where products seem to be mixed up. Perhaps neatly alphabetical and easy to find for the pharmacist, but on the consumer side it created a sense of disorder. Not a brand value a pharmacist wants to be associated with, leaving them with a frustrated feeling of not being able to keep up.

Thus, besides knowing the customer as a designer, it is just as important to know the retailer. How does he work and does it fit with the design? In the case of

this example, this was a design failure. Along the same lines, it is not a good idea to 'force' people into specific working habits that are not theirs. Although open kitchens and open ateliers are trendy, if you are designing for a bicycle mechanic who knows his trade very well but who cannot keep order and/or does not have time for this, then it is better not to go along with that trend.

...and sustainability

Although sustainability is a much used term, it remains (too) broad. In the case of retail I prefer to talk about responsibility. Responsibility towards our planet and towards the people living on it. Both are worth a book on their own but here I want to focus on the part as far as the physical store is concerned. Fortunately, I can already see a positive evolution appearing here. Instead of completely remodeling a store every six to seven years, as we did until a few years ago, I see trendsetting retail design agencies taking a different approach. The approach of Brinkworth design mentioned earlier, in which the design process is an ongoing process and the aim of store design is not a total renewal every seven years but a more flexible form, works in favor of more sustainable store design. This also becomes apparent in research. One of my PhD students is currently exploring the principle of 'under-designing'. This literally means that you design at the level of a prototype. The idea is then to optimize and further develop the design after it is in use to achieve the best possible result. This process, with the same prototype, can be repeated every so often to also stay up to date. It is a continuous circle of evolving and updating, constantly changing the design with low impact interferences. Indeed, this is not mainstream yet. But the idea of ever evolving stores, seems more responsible.

Aspects more general to architecture, such as solar panels and heat pumps and even LED-lighting, are not what I want to discuss. The latter is the obvious thing to do and is already established in store design. In my view, there are two main things to consider while designing that lead immediately to lower impacts. One is by selecting the materials we work with more carefully, and one is by changing the way we design furniture. While I already touched upon the latter when discussing 'under-designing', there is more we as designers can do. A couple of years ago we did a study to get a grip on the way stores were designed, how materials were selected, and how furniture was detailed. By understanding this better, we wanted to capitalize on this and see where and how we could intervene in this process to be able to support retailers and designers in making more sustainable choices. One of the many things that came out of it was the Lifecycle Design Strategies (LiDS) wheel. This is a tool I have not discussed before but it is (or should be) part of the design proces. The original LiDS wheel is a specific eco-design tool and is widely used by product designers. It is a form of environmental product benchmarking, showing in what aspects a product design should be improved in terms of eco-friendliness, compared to its alternatives. Together with a few experts in sustainability, we developed the wheel further so that it has become a tool that can guide designers in making or considering more sustainable choices, specifically for the field of retail. Knowledge that designer should acquire better sooner then later.

As the sketch shows, the LiDS wheel addresses six eco-design strategies. Within these strategies, a whole series of eco-design guidelines fit, tapping into the way we should design furniture and which materials we should choose if we want to act more responsibly.

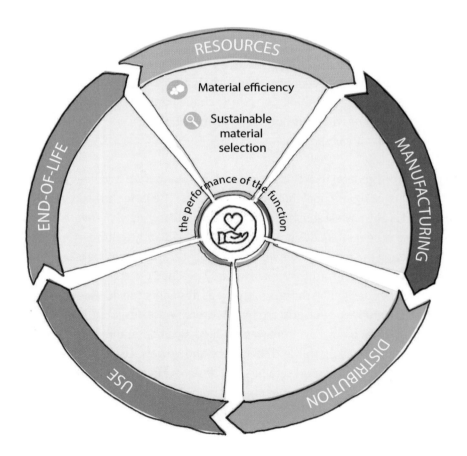

In the heart of the circle we actually start with the most important strategy: the performance of the function. In order to design store furniture that is more sustainable, we have to design it in such a way that it performs this function effectively and optimally. Consider multi-functionality of furniture. Would it make sense, for example, to combine the presentation function of the furniture with a seating function and thus save material/transport volume? Which functions can be replaced by a service (e.g., renting light from a manufacturer, rather than buying it), or which functions need less space? For instance, how large does a counter really need to be? If you need one? Try to reduce the need to use 'physical' resources as much as possible. This immediately taps into the second eco-design strategy: material efficiency.

Although flexibility has been discussed before, on the level of a fixture anticipate a later change of function of store fixtures. By anticipating this at the design stage, the furniture or finish can remain in use longer. I also briefly refer back to the idea of under-designing here.

Material efficiency

Regarding the second eco-design strategy, 'resources', material efficiency plays a large part in this. We have to consider how we can design and build the store concept and layout more smartly, using fewer materials and with fewer types of materials. This is an aspect where a designer has the most impact. So I would like to take a moment to give some design guidelines here.

- First, select materials that reflect the intended life of a store. Something to look out for is the material passport. The passport provides easy traceability of a store furniture's origin or finish, its condition, insight into the used (sheet) materials, raw materials, profiles, fittings and finishes, and this in function of easy disassembly and reuse or recycling. For the materials without a passport, we must either use our logical mind or for the more technically savvy, look to Life Cycle Assessment calculations (LCA). A life cycle assessment is the act of measuring the environmental impact of a product or service throughout its life cycle, from the resources used to create the product or service, across its use by the user, to its final end-of-life destination. This helps us compare between materials. The problem here is that these calculations are based on an average life cycle of 50 years, as regular buildings have. Something not typical for a retail store. I personally do use these figures because they give an indication, but we still need to think further about this. So then back to common farm sense. Materials that are specifically made to last, such as tile and metals get a relatively low, i.e. good, LCA score because they are calculated to last 50 years. But when they leave the cycle after 10 or 20 years, that figure flies sky high. Also, materials from nature like marble are also best used during this life span because otherwise they have too great an impact on our planet as we replace them faster and faster. Bottom line, choose materials where the technical lifespan matches the intended years of use.

- **Second,** limit as much as possible the diversity of materials used in the overall store design. **Aim for as few material types as possible. Among other things, this facilitates material separation during dismantling and waste disposal (reuse or recycling) after the materials are used.**

- **Third,** design the furniture or building solution so that waste during production and processing is minimal. **The less waste during production, the less material has to be produced and the smaller the environmental impact of the production phase (less raw materials needed and less waste disposal). This can be done e.g. by sawing sheet materials optimally (in the factory or on site) and taking the typical standard dimensions of sheets and other materials into account in the design phase. Working with standard dimensions of materials also facilitates repair, makes components interchangeable and extends the life of the furniture or store fittings.**

- **Fourth,** design for ease of assembly and disassembly. **Ensure that the furniture or finish is easy to install and dismantle again after use. This can significantly reduce the assembly and disassembly time, as well as the environmental impact of the construction and disassembly phase. This also facilitates the replacement and recovery of the various components and raw materials at the end of life.**

- **Finally,** work modularly. **Working with partial modules in a piece of furniture or finish allows for easy replacement of parts and reduces the logistical impact. Being able to replace partial modules also extends the life of the entire furniture or finish.**

Sustainable material selection

While considering resources, favor single, pure materials over composite materials when selecting them. Glue is required to produce laminates and composite sheet materials, for example. Glue can result in more complex material separation at end of life. In general, choose single materials. And source materials for global expansion locally. This reduces the impact on the environment and additionally ensures that in the case of any problems or changes the material can be supplied quickly and efficiently. When possible, choose renewable materials. These have a smaller impact than recycled materials.

Manufacturing and distribution

I discuss the following two eco-design strategies together because as a designer or retailer, you have no impact on the production process of materials. But you can choose to limit the number of (post-)processing operations as much as possible. Natural, untreated materials are preferable provided they can fulfill their intended function that way. We also do not have a choice of how materials are transported; however, we can decide where it should come from. All means of transport do not have the same environmental impact. For example, the environmental impact per tonne-km by ship is lower than the environmental impact per tonne-km by train, which is lower than the environmental impact per tonne-km by truck. Basically, the greater the capacity of the means of transport, the lower the impact per quantity of material transported, in general.

Usage

This fifth eco-design strategy is again a difficult one for designers. However, do consider the maintenance, cleaning, or repairs necessary during the use phase of the material because that also requires energy. But also the choice of colors plays a role. Remember, this is because the darkness of the color determines the amount of lighting needed and darker colors need more light because they absorb all of it. Different colors also often require different maintenance.

End of life

When all the previous strategies have been considered, then this sixth strategy is 'easy' to implement. When waste streams become clear and simple through the materials passport, processing in separate waste streams is feasible and thus reuse and recycling can be promoted. When a minimum of different types of materials are used, waste streams are also limited. Modular furniture, demountable furniture – in short, furniture designed for easy assembly and disassembly – ensure that the assembly and disassembly time as well as the environmental impact of the construction and disassembly phase can be significantly reduced. So pay adequate attention to connections when designing. Make use of quickly (de)assembled connections with a minimum number of operations. Also aim for as few different types of connections as possible and try to use standardized connection techniques that are non-permanent and reversible (click, clamp, screw connections, dowels, staples,...). And prefer reuse to recycling. The more the value of retail furniture and floor, wall and ceiling finishes can be retained after a use cycle, the more limited the environmental impact. If you can reuse a piece of furniture in its entirety (with some parts that may need to be replaced), this leads to a lower impact than reusing the parts individually.

Lastly, also consider other business models. There are leasing models on the market where you rent furniture. The manufacturer then takes on the responsibility of supplying the retailer with quality furniture, which is then returned to the manufacturer at the end of the leasing period for reuse or recycling. This creates a closed circuit.

In short, as a designer you can do a lot to design more responsibly. However, we are not yet at the point where it is widely accepted. The willingness of retailers to invest (time and/or money) is still very low. But as Anne Marie Bonneau, the Zero-Waste Chef, said, we don't need a handful of people doing it perfectly, but millions of people who do it imperfectly. So every step that is taken today to deal with materials more consciously is a win.

Back to the future

I have quietly come to the end of my story. A story that seeks to help designers and retailers arrive at better-designed stores. What I have not yet done, and what I had said I would do, is to challenge the role of stores as such. It is clear what role designers can have once they are awarded a commission to design a store. But should stores and designers do nothing but encourage consumption? It may seem a little like that if you've read my whole story. And of course it is true that everyone has to earn a living and therefore it seems an obvious thing to sell stuff and to design stores that facilitate this as much as possible. Nevertheless, I would like to add a critical note. Also clear in my argument, I think, is that I am more in favor of quality rather than quantity. It doesn't have to be more and more and more, but better and better. We need to think about what we offer, what quality and what impact it has on society and our planet. I talked earlier about the responsibilities of the designer and the ethical questions that travel with this. As well as questions around sustainability. But these reflections and considerations are rather at the end of the chain. If there is going to be a store at all, we can try to act ethically and sustainably. But what about the store and the products? I do think we should dare to challenge these. People are already looking very critically at the production of products and how they can be made differently, how to get rid of fast fashion and how to eat less meat. Too little thought is given to what role the retailers or brands play or can play in this. In short, you can promote (increasingly) sustainable clothing, but as long as the Primarks of this world don't change, the consumer won't either.

I am more in favor of quality rather than quantity. It doesn't have to be more and more and more, but better and better.

Also look at shopping days like Black Friday. This day did not start at all as a 'buy as much at a discount as you can' celebration. Black Friday is the first day after Thanksgiving, which is always celebrated on the fourth Thursday of November. On Friday, most workers in the United States have the day off and the season of Christmas shopping begins. Black Friday has multiple explanations as to its origin. In the 1960s, the term was first used by the police to refer to the massive traffic congestion in and around the city of Philadelphia on the day after Thanksgiving. Around 1981, an alternative theory was reported: on that day, retailers first 'go into the black', that is, begin to make a profit for the year. In fact, in the United States, the practice in accounting was to write losses on the books in red ink. It illustrates how important the Christmas period is to the annual revenue. My point is that in Europe, it does not have this significance and only the discounts are adopted from the US and then spread out over an entire week. So it has become a mega-discount week that no longer has anything to do with Thanksgiving or Christmas. It is simply an incentive to buy even more. To my regret, the success of Black Friday in Western Europe seems to grow every year. But for the first time this year, I saw brands go against this and stand up against consumerism. There were stores that were effectively closed on Black Friday. I hope it doesn't stop with those few pioneers.

I do realize that living in Western Europe it is almost a privilege to be able to think of how to deal with sustainability because we are in a luxury position socially and economically. But I also need to say that we are the cause of the problem. So who else should intervene?

I know it sounds cynical, but we all know the expression 'never let a good crisis go to waste', by Winston Churchill. In times of crisis, we tend to be inventive and think more about our daily routine as well as our role or contribution to society. Just look at what happened during Covid's two toughest years. The world was completely shut down for a while. And in some places a little more than others, but suddenly our world was reduced to a few square meters and the only link to the outside was our screen. Family gatherings, meetings, classes – everything suddenly had to go online, and it worked. We flew less, drove around less in the car, walked more and made peace with silence for a while. Many people were happy with the forced silence, and I myself hoped we would learn from this. Why do we have to fly to the other side of the world for a meeting? Why must we be in the office every day now that we have found that telecommuting is quite productive? But the truth is, and perhaps against all odds, as soon as everything is allowed again, we apparently fall back into our old habits very quickly. And this when it could have been a momentum toward more responsible behavior. However, today, once more, an opportunity presents itself; we are facing another crisis, an energy and economic crisis.

Again there are positive ripple effects; more and more people are taking bikes and the train to work because fuel prices are skyrocketing. People are more likely to get products repaired instead of throwing them away, which they did for years. Platforms such as Vinted and eBay are also celebrating highly under this economic situation. There is even a major player that slapped you in the face with discounts at Black Friday that has now discovered that there are also big profits to be made from services such as repairs and subscriptions. A bit contradictory, isn't it? But it does support my contention that if there is profit to be made from it, everyone is on board. But without the profit? Who then remains a truly responsible brand?

So how do I see the role of the retailers and brands in this debate? Just as in the past, retailers and brands can take on a leading role and set an example, like Patagonia, for example. But of course, consumers also play a vital role in this. And as we all make the extra effort together, we can enjoy shopping, visit wonderful stores AND be responsible at the same time.

Retailers and brands can set an example but of course, consumers also play a vital role in this.

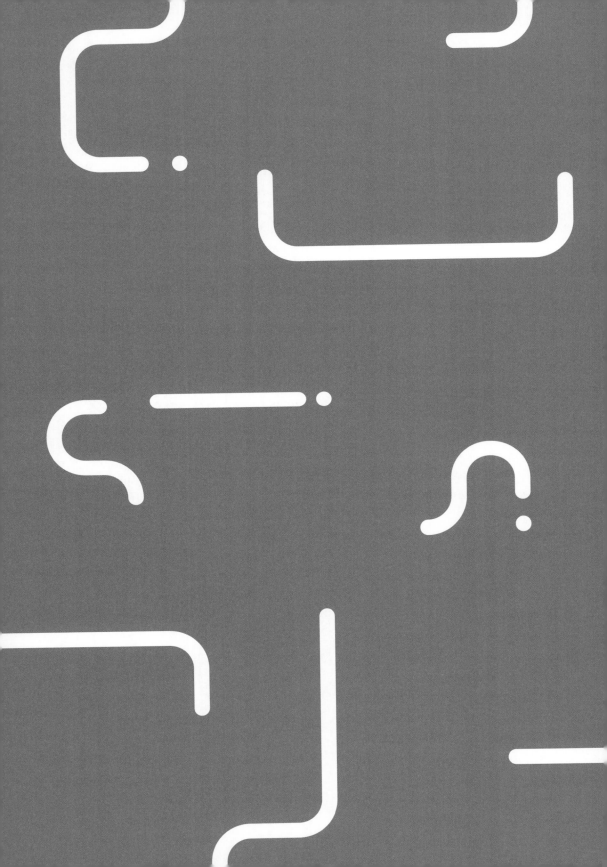

Bibliography

- Alnemer, A., n.d.. Home [LinkedIn page]. LinkedIn. Retrieved from https://www.linkedin.com/in/amar-a-2560352/
- Anderson, S., and Mesher, L., 2019 (and first one 2010). Retail design. Bloomsbury Publishing: London.
- Antunes, N., n.d.. Home [LinkedIn page]. LinkedIn. Retrieved from https://www.linkedin.com/in/nunoalexandreantunes/
- Boswijk, A., Peelen, E., Olthof, S., 2015. Economie van experiences. Pearson: London.
- Brinkworth, A., 2018. A new design model for apparel retail environments. Doctoral thesis submitted to Middlesex University.
- Cheetham, G., and Chivers, G. 1996. Towards a holistic model of professional competence. Journal of European Industrial Training, 20(5), 20-30.
- Dennis, S., 2020. Remarkable retail. Wonderwell: LA.
- Din, R., 2000. New retail. Conran: London.
- Dudson, G., n.d.. Home [LinkedIn page]. LinkedIn. Retrieved from https://www.linkedin.com/in/grantdudson/
- Fitch, R., 2001. Fitch on Retail Design. Phaidon Press: New York.
- Kapferer, J-N., 2008 (fourth edition). The new strategic brand management. Kogan Page: Philadelphia.
- Keller, K., 2002. Branding and brand equity. Marketing Science Institute.
- Kindleysides, J., 2007. An Introduction to Retail Design. Available at

http://www.designcouncil.org.uk
- Klein, N., 1999. No logo. Knopf: Canada.
- Kooijman, D. 1999. Machine en theater. Rotterdam: Uitgeverij 010.
- Koolhaas, R., 2001. The Harvard Guide to Shopping. Taschen: Köln.
- Münster, M., 2018. Intention vs. Perception of Designed Atmospheres in Fashion Stores. Doctoral thesis submitted to Copenhagen Business School.
- Murialdo, F., 2013. practice of consumption and spaces for goods, e-book, Francesca Murialdo, ISBN-13: 978-8890866104.
- Pegler, M.M., 2015. Designing the Brand Identity in Retail Spaces. Bloomsbury Publishing: London.
- Petermans, A., and Kent, T., 2016. Retail Design, Theoretical Perspectives. Routledge: London.
- Pine, J., and Gilmore, J.H., 1999 & 2019. Experience economy. Harvard Business Review Press: Massachusetts.
- Powershop series. Frame Publishers.
- Retail Design International series. Avedition.
- Retail Design Lab, n.d.. Home [website]. www.retaildesiglab.be
- Quartier, K., Claes, S., & Vanrie, J., 2020. A holistic competence framework for (future) retail design and retail design education. Journal of Retailing and Consumer Services, 55, 101914.
- Quartier, K., Petermans, A., Melewar, T.C., and Dennis, C., 2012. The Value of Design in Retail and Branding. Emerald Group Publishing: Bingley.
- Underhill, P., 2007. Why we buy: The science of shopping. NY: Simon & Schuster.
- Underhill, P. 2011. What Women Want: The Science of Female Shopping. Simon & Schuster: NY.
- Servais, E., 2023. The value of experiential retail environments and in-store experience. Doctoral thesis submitted to Hasselt University.
- Scamell-Katz, S., 2102. The Art of Shopping: How We Shop and Why We Buy. Lid Publishing.
- Shoptalk Europe, 2022. [Conference]. London, UK.
- Sinek, S., 2009. Start with Why: How Great Leaders Inspire Everyone to Take Action. Penguin Group: NY.
- Stephens, D. 2013. The retail revival. John Wiley & Sons Inc: NY.
- Snoeck, J., and Neerman, P., 2017. The Future of Shopping. Lannoo: Leuven.

- Stephens, D., 2017. Reengineering Retail. Figure 1 Publishing: Vancouver.
- Teufel, P., and Zimmerman, R., 2015. Holistic Retail Design. Frame Publishers: Amsterdam.
- Van Amerongen, R., and Christiaans, H., 2004. Retail & Interior Design. Episode Publishers: Rotterdam.
- Van Belleghem, S., n.d.. Steven Van Belleghem [YouTube channel] Retrieved from https://www.youtube.com/user/StevenVanBelleghem/videos
- Van Ossel, 2018. De digitale hysterie voorbij. Lannoo Campus: Leuven.
- van Tongeren, M., 2013. 1 to 1 The essence of Retail Branding and Design. BIS publishers: Amsterdam.
- Zola, E., 2001. Au Bonheur Des Dames. Pearson: Lond

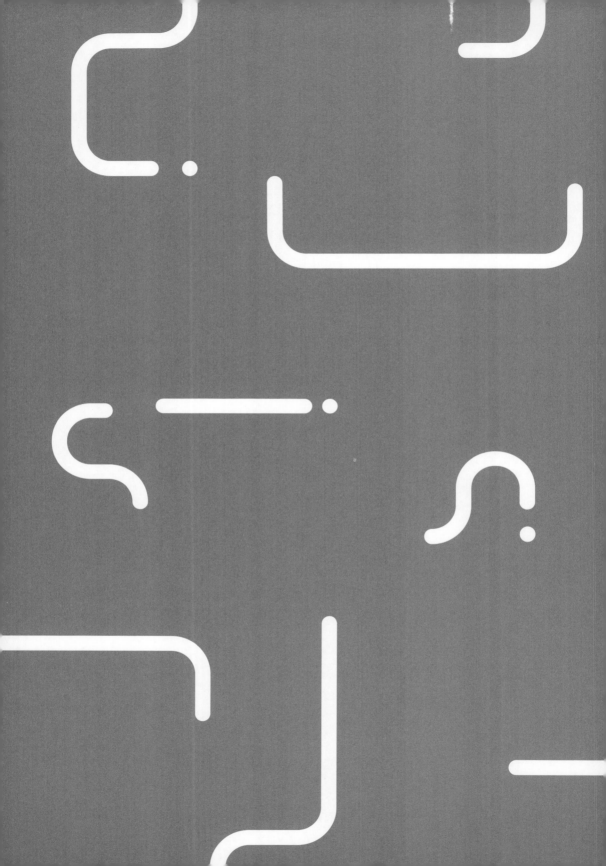